MW01224745

Edited by
Nino Pagliccia

Foreword by
John M. Kirk

To Saul
in friendship & Solidarity
Nino Pagliccia
March 2015

Cuba
Solidarity
in Canada

Five Decades of People-to-People
Foreign Relations

FriesenPress

Suite 300 – 852 Fort Street
Victoria, BC, Canada V8W 1H8
www.friesenpress.com

Copyright © 2014 by Nino Pagliccia
First Edition — 2014

Edited by Nino Pagliccia
Foreword by John M Kirk
Cover design by Tamara Hansen and Ali Yerevani

Canadian Network on Cuba

www.canadiannetworkoncuba.ca
This book has been published under the auspices of the Canadian
Network on Cuba who granted permission to use their logo.

All rights reserved.

No part of this publication may be reproduced in any form, or by any means, electronic
or mechanical, including photocopying, recording, or any information browsing,
storage, or retrieval system, without permission in writing from the publisher.

ISBN
978-1-4602-4380-0 (Hardcover)
978-1-4602-4381-7 (Paperback)
978-1-4602-4382-4 (eBook)

1. Social Science, Anthropology, Cultural

Distributed to the trade by The Ingram Book Company

Cuba Solidarity in Canada: Five Decades of People-to-People Foreign Relations / Edited by Nino Pagliccia / Foreword by John M Kirk.

Includes bibliographical references and index.

1.

Solidarity—Canada-Cuba – 1960-.

2.

People-to-people relations--Canada-Cuba.

3.

Foreign relations.

4.

International relations.

5.

Activism.

I Pagliccia, Nino

II Title

CONTENTS

Endorsements

⸺⸺⸺⸺⸺⸺⸺⸺⸺⸺⸺⸺⸺⸺⸺⸺⸺⸺⸺⸺⸺⸺

"An insightful and valuable examination of the continuous relationship Canadian organizations have maintained in support of the Cuban socialist experiment, founded on unselfish, people to people experiences. Told through an impressive assembly of many of the most important organizers involved in the solidarity movement, this collection is an important contribution to understand the unbroken respect these nation-wide groups have for Cuban self-determination and its attempts to forge a new society."

—Keith Bolender, author of Cuba Under Siege and Voices From the Other Side: An Oral History of Terrorism Against Cuba.

"Through a lively blend of personal accounts and scholarly analyses, different voices and experiences concur in telling the multifaceted story of Canadian solidarity toward revolutionary Cuba. This book is evidence of the ways people can connect despite their belonging to two contrasting systems."

—Claude Morin, professor (retired) of Latin American history, Université de Montréal.

Endorsements

"This excellent work exposes the heart of solidarity. Pagliccia and the other authors clearly show that the relations Canadians have with Cubans go far beyond the beach. We are bound in the most intimate realms of friendship, solidarity, and, dare I say, 'love' of the belief that a better world free of hegemony is possible. This book provides a compelling example of alternatives to traditional diplomacy. The authors show that solidarity involves engagement and commitment that values friendship and love above pressure and force. In times of apparent hopelessness the importance of solidarity between people demonstrates a political force of hope and love that overcomes fear and despair."

—Robert Huish, Dalhousie University.

"My recollections of Cuba and the Cuban people started as a young girl growing up in Grenada. In 1993 I chose to join the Canada-Cuba Parliamentary Group visiting Cuba for conversations with Cuban Parliamentarians and officials. This book is a reminder of why annually I show up at functions and activities of the Canadian-Cuban Friendship Association to show respect and love for the people of Cuba. The Essayists' range of experiences, long-standing commitment and engagement with Cuba then and now deserves the attention of all Canadians."

—The Hon. Jean Augustine, Privy Council and Member of the Order of Canada.

Foreword

This book illustrates ties of solidarity among Canadians and the Cuban revolutionary process over several decades, and in a variety of formats. As will be discussed, since 1961 groups of Canadians have provided a collective response to both the aggression stemming from Washington and the indifference from Ottawa, at all times supporting Cuba's right to self-determination. This commitment is something to be proud of, since it reveals an independence of thought, an awareness of social justice, and a determination to fight for what is right. Ultimately it boils down to respecting Cuba for what it is—and not how the media paint it.

Full disclosure is necessary here. While I have been teaching about Cuba here at Dalhousie University for 35 years and see myself as a fairly traditional academic, I am also proud to have participated in various solidarity initiatives over the years. For me this process started in 1976 when - while a doctoral student at the University of British Columbia - I joined the Canadian-Cuban Friendship Association (CCFA) in Vancouver and went to Cuba for the first time as a delegate of the Association. I have also participated in activities of the groups in Toronto and Kingston, while here in Halifax I was one of the founders of NSCUBA in 1989. Since that first visit to Cuba I have never stopped supporting Cuba's right to self-determination, its program of social justice, and its acts of international solidarity. In addition I am proud to maintain ties with ICAP and Cubans from all walks of life, and count myself as fortunate for having travelled to the island on numerous occasions. These thoughts, then, come from an academic activist, and are based upon respect for the people and the initiatives featured in this book.

The term "solidarity" has a multitude of meanings, but in essence it boils down to the concept of cooperation arising from common interests, and often it implies responsibilities to act. Shared objectives and aspirations, accompanied by mutual support and respect, form the basis for any meaningful solidarity. Talking about Cuba's role in Africa, Nelson

Mandela summed up well the extraordinary solidarity shown there: "Cuban internationalists have made a contribution to African independence, freedom, and justice unparalleled for its principled and selfless character." The Cuban approach was based upon this amalgam of solidarity and the qualities noted above. In many ways our own respect for Cuba stems from this "principled and selfless character" that many of us have observed on the island and in its foreign policy. Like Mandela, we are pleased to support Cuba's initiatives in this regard.

These qualities of solidarity, based upon principles and respect, pervade each and every one of the chapters in this collection, as the contributors draw upon their own experiences with Cuba to illustrate this phenomenon of solidarity. From worker-to-worker support to farmers' cooperatives, from humanitarian campaigns to the 20-year old *Che* Guevara Volunteer Work Brigades, all of these activities are based upon respect for Cuba, and Cubans - and a desire to show solidarity with both the people and the country.

The CCFA statement of its objectives puts it well, since the organization seeks to "promote friendship, respect, cooperation and solidarity between the peoples of Canada and Cuba." While we in Canada come nowhere close to the massive solidarity shown by Cuba to the peoples of the developing world, all of the initiatives mentioned in this book contribute to these objectives. In the Canadian context, members of solidarity groups do make a significant difference in supporting the need to tell the truth about Cuba and urging respect for Cuba's distinctive development model.

From 1961, when the Vancouver-based CCFA was formed, until the present, all of the people, whose work features here, have "walked the talk," in some cases for decades. From demanding justice for the Cuban Five to explaining the essence of Cuban democracy, from supporting Cuban humanitarianism to weeding vegetable plots in Cuba, Canadians whose work appears here have consistently participated in constructive initiatives. Perhaps the aspect of this story that needs to be emphasized most is just how long some of the people featured here have been fighting the good fight, since we often forget the struggles of the past too easily. Fortunately several of the essays here do help us to remember those early days when promoting respect for Cuba was a tough row to hoe. The Cold War cast a dark shadow on Canadians seeking to develop ties with Cuba, as veterans of those days will remember.

This book is an eloquent testimony of how the people featured here and the organizations to which they belong have consistently provided support for Cuba, often in difficult times. In some cases this took the form of material support (such as the remarkably successful financial support for Haiti after natural disasters), but it is also expressed in the necessary educational work undertaken by the solidarity organizations. Together these initiatives have kept alive a strong interest in Cuba, promoting various projects to strengthen ties with people on the island.

In particular telling people the truth about Cuba is essential. There is a tremendous need for balanced analysis of contemporary Cuba, warts and all, since in general our media do us remarkably few favours. On the few occasions when we receive news about Cuba we are usually fed information taken from U.S. media feeds. Our principal newspaper (The Globe and Mail) has just one reporter based in Brazil who covers all of Latin America, while in Mexico the CBC has another journalist who covers stories (for both radio and television) for the entire region. In sum, there is remarkably little coverage of Cuba in the media (I was once asked if the Cuban Five were a salsa group!), and most of that is negative. Providing alternative views is therefore extremely important, and in general solidarity organizations do this well.

If anybody has any doubts about this distorted picture of Cuba provided by the media, all you need to do is to analyze the scant coverage of Cuba's enormous and sustained support for the people of Haiti. While U.S. and Canadian navy ships spent just under two months there after the 2010 earthquake, hundreds of Cuban doctors had been in the country since Hurricane Georges in 1998. They remain there to this day, as do the

600 Haitian doctors trained by Cuba (at no charge). Sadly, mainstream media ignored all of this - and one CNN report even represented a Cuban doctor (wearing a *Che* Guevara t-shirt) as a "Spanish" physician.

It is significant that there are so many solidarity groups with Cuba in Canada: all told just over 50, including a dozen in Québec. We come in all sizes, ages, interests, and political persuasions. Some have always identified with the Cuban Revolution for ideological reasons, while others have become interested after a vacation in Cuba and meeting Cubans. What matters, and what unites us all in our work, is the need to respect Cuba—and to let Cuba be. In addition one of the underlying issues for which we work is a rejection of any attempt by any government to coerce Cuba, as well as insisting upon respect for the many positive aspects of life in Cuba about which our media sadly say little.

Despite scant positive media coverage, and despite a federal government that has a lack of understanding of the importance of Cuba in Latin America (and for that matter lacks a decent foreign policy for the region), we Canadians are fortunate to have tremendous potential for developing ties with the people of Cuba. We are the major source of tourists to the island (1.1 million in 2013, about 40 percent of tourist arrivals), while a Canadian company (Sherritt International) is the largest foreign investor in Cuba. In addition there are two important historical facts to bear in mind. In 1962 when Washington pressured allies to break relations with Cuba, only two countries refused to do so: Canada and Mexico. And finally there was the deep personal friendship between Pierre Trudeau and Fidel Castro, both lawyers, trained by the Jesuits, with vast international experience and an understanding of the development process.

Perhaps no better symbol of this wellspring of potential for Canada in Cuba is the annual Terry Fox run (now in its 15th year), in which over 2 million Cubans (out of a population of 11.1 million) participate. After Canada, no other country in the world has as great a participation in the Marathon of Hope as Cuba does. Based upon conversations with people throughout the island it appears that everyone in Cuba is aware of Terry

Fox, whose life is studied in Cuban schools. Fortunately, due to events like this and the large number of Canadian tourists to the island, people-to-people contact is alive and well.

Yet sadly, in recent years our governments have not been able to understand the enormous potential that these unique ties offer us. Despite being a small country, Cuba has an enormously significant role throughout Latin America and the region, and Ottawa ignores this to the detriment of Canadian foreign policy as a whole. The Harper government in particular has ignored the sweeping changes throughout Latin America in the past 15 years, and has preferred to have as little as possible to do with the dozen left-of-centre governments there. Instead it prefers to promote "free trade" deals with right-wing governments, several of which have atrocious human rights records, and to support investors in the mining industry - many of which are guilty of environmental degradation and destruction of local communities.

Given the massive amount of (largely negative) media coverage on Cuba emanating from the United States, the lack of solid reporting from Canadian media, and a government in Ottawa whose right-wing ideology ignores Cuba and most of the other left-wing governments in the region, solidarity groups therefore have an enormously important mission in promoting an alternative view on Cuba. This is not easy, but in general most groups participate actively in getting the truth out about Cuba. I once remember standing with a group of NSCUBA members at a busy Halifax intersection one rush hour with a sheet that said simply "Google 'Posada Carriles,'" and was amazed by the number of people who later informed me that they had been astonished to learn about him - since media reports had ignored his terrorist activities. Canadian solidarity groups have to maintain, and indeed increase, this role.

Fortunately, most Canadians, unlike their American cousins, are indeed prepared to listen, providing they can obtain balanced information. With over a million people going to Cuba every year (and with a high return rate of tourists), Canadians easily develop ties of friendship with Cubans. In addition we do not have the colonial baggage that the United States does (Canada has never invaded any country in the region, unlike the United States). Our basic characteristics as polite, self-effacing, easy-going, and patient people are a better fit than those of our neighbours to the south. As a result we become friends with Cubans very easily. Undoubtedly these people-to-people contacts are far, far ahead of any bilateral government ties, which means that Ottawa has to bear in mind the potential displeasure of over a million people that any negative turn in the official bilateral relationship would have.

Solidarity ties between Canada and Cuba have resulted from these diverse experiences, with Canadians from all walks of life, and over a period of five decades. But our ties of solidarity can take inspiration from what Cubans do every day, in a host of countries. Mandela was quoted earlier, speaking about Cuba's solidarity with the people of Africa. Today Cuban solidarity encircles the globe. In the early 1960s, for example, when one-half of Cuba's 6,000 doctors had left the island for Florida, Cuba sent medical missions to Chile (1960) and Algeria (1963)— doctors that it could ill afford to spare. Yet they went because the need there was greater than in Cuba. That is true solidarity, a model to emulate.

In more recent years Cuba has provided medical care on the island for 25,000 children following the 1986 nuclear meltdown at the Chernobyl reactor, and this just as the Soviet Union was imploding (taking away 85 percent of Cuba's trade and 90 percent of its fuel). It has trained at ELAM, the largest medical school in the world, 15,000 doctors from poor backgrounds and continues to take in 1,500 new students every year; together with Venezuelan officials it has made a commitment to train 60,000 doctors in Venezuela. Cuba has sent its Henry Reeve Contingent to the site of natural disasters in various countries, and even offered 1,500 medical personnel to the United States after Hurricane Katrina devastated New Orleans. (Sadly George W. Bush refused the offer, preferring to play politics instead of saving lives). Its "Operation Miracle" ophthalmology program has restored the sight of some 3 million people throughout Latin America and the Caribbean. And all of this, at no charge to the people who have benefited from these acts of humanitarianism. This is amazing solidarity indeed, summed up well by José Martí who once noted that "Patria es humanidad" (All of humanity is our motherland). What an example of global solidarity, and from such a small country.

In Canada we have no official government strategy to pursue such noble goals, and indeed the Harper foreign policy continues to be driven in pursuit of a narrow, right-wing ideological agenda. The efforts of the solidarity groups in Canada are therefore to be commended, and indeed are more needed than ever. The end result is that, over fifty years after the Vancouver group was formed, the initiative shown there has spread throughout the country, with solidarity groups based from coast to coast. Back in October 1961 I doubt very much if the brave souls who formed the CCFA could ever have imagined the concept of over a million Canadians travelling to Cuba every year, or two million Cubans running to raise money for cancer research in honour of a Canadian hero—or even there being over some fifty solidarity groups established in Canada alone.

In this collection there are some excellent insights into the varied work undertaken by people from a variety of backgrounds, but all with the single goal of showing respect for, and working in solidarity with, Cuba. We have come a long way in those decades and, while much remains to be done, we should also take pride in the tremendous amount of solidarity that has been shown in these past five decades. Now the challenge is how to continue and build upon that illustrious history…

John M. Kirk
Halifax, Nova Scotia

Preamble

Kenia Serrano Puig,
Cuban Institute of Friendship with the Peoples.

Relations between Cuba and Canada date back to our wars of independence when several Canadian-born individuals were linked to these struggles. William Ryan, a native of Toronto, attained the rank of Brigadier General in 1871, and figures like Jacques Chapleau and Georges Charette played significant roles in the War of 1895.

In 1903 a Cuban consular office was opened in the city of Halifax, and in 1909 the Department of Commerce of Canada established an office in Havana that was the first permanent representation of that country in Cuban territory.

However, deep friendly and solidarity relations were built gradually between the two peoples ever since the beginning of the Cuban Revolution, which captivated more than a few Canadian friends who felt the influence of a new social project at the doorway to the Caribbean Sea.

And that is precisely the central theme of this book, the heartwarming story of the solidarity movement with Cuba in this vast northern neighbour. There, where it is reported that the first friendship association in a capitalist country was founded, and where close friends got involved since 1960 in sponsoring the inspiring education at the special school for the blind and visually impaired children, "Abel Santamaría". Braille's machines, school supplies, medicines and even financial aid were sent to Cuba since those years when the United States persisted in isolating our Revolution.

Great bravery and wills joined together in the hundreds of Canadian friends who decided not only to defend the society that we were building, but to remain faithful to our people: from that young woman who visited Cuba in the 1960s and first contacted our Cuban Institute of

Friendship with the Peoples (ICAP); and that other young member of the Canadian Communist Youth who traveled with a delegation and fell in love with the Cuban Revolution; and that brilliant intellectual who translates Martí's verses into English like few can; and that affable and sincere university professor who defends Cuba from simply supporting a Cuban sailor to showing his firm attitude at an international conference or in a prestigious journal; and that valued friend who directed the *Che Guevara Brigade* for over 12 years; and other organizers of projects that have brought hundreds of Quebecers teens to share with their Cuban counterparts; and that other friend who received our Commander Fidel during a flight stop over in Vancouver, the city where laborious young people today also work hard in solidarity actions.

Such efforts were brought together into two solidarity organizations of great importance: the Canadian Network on Cuba (CNC) throughout the Anglophone Canada and *La Table de concertation de solidarité Québec-Cuba.* Their actions and campaigns have been varied and valuable such as the support to the U.S.-Cuba Friendship Caravan and the *Venceremos* Brigade in their crossing through various cities, the raising of funds for Cuban hurricane victims and for the Cuban medical brigade in Haiti, and the support to visiting Cuban athletes, artists and officials to Canada.

But where the sincere friendship of our Canadian friends has shone the most has been in the tireless struggle against the blockade that the U.S. government has imposed on our people, and the campaign for the liberation of our Five compatriots imprisoned in U.S. jails. And precisely by reading these pages we will be able to appreciate the full extent of that support and involvement. May this simple preamble be recognition of so much effort and dedication; because with you the endeavour of our revolution has strengthened and fortified.

Kenia Serrano Puig
President of the Cuban Institute of Friendship
with the Peoples Havana, Cuba

June 2014
Translation: Nino Pagliccia

Original in Spanish

Las relaciones entre Cuba y Canadá datan desde nuestras guerras de independencia cuando varios individuos de origen canadiense estuvieron ligados a estas contiendas. William Ryan, oriundo de Toronto, alcanzó los grados de Brigadier General en 1871, y figuras como Jacques Chapleau y Georges Charette desempeñaron roles significativos en la Guerra de 1895.

En 1903 se estableció una oficina consular cubana en la ciudad de Halifax, y en 1909 el Departamento de Comercio de Canadá creó una oficina en La Habana siendo la primera representación permanente de ese país en territorio cubano.

Sin embargo, relaciones profundamente amistosas y solidarias se edificaron paulatinamente entre ambos pueblos desde los inicios de la Revolución cubana, la cual cautivó a no pocos amigos canadienses que sintieron el influjo de un nuevo proyecto social a la entrada del Mar Caribe.

Y ese es precisamente el tema esencial de este libro, la reconfortante historia del movimiento de solidaridad con Cuba en ese inmenso vecino del norte. Allí donde dicen se fundó la primera asociación de amistad en un país capitalista y donde entrañables amigos se enfrascaron desde 1960 en apadrinar la sublime educación en la escuela especial para niños ciegos y débiles visuales "Abel Santamaría". Máquinas brailles, materiales escolares, medicinas y hasta ayuda financiera se envió a Cuba desde aquellos años cuando Estados Unidos se empeñaba en aislar nuestra Revolución.

Ingentes arrojos y voluntades se aunaron en cientos de amigos canadienses que decidieron no solo defender la sociedad que construíamos, sino permanecer fieles a nuestro pueblo: desde aquella joven que visitó Cuba en los años 60 y contactó por primera vez nuestro Instituto Cubano de Amistad con los Pueblos (ICAP), aquella otra joven militante de la Juventud Comunista canadiense que viajó en una delegación y quedó prendada de la Revolución cubana, aquel intelectual brillante que como pocos traduce los versos de Martí al inglés, aquel profesor universitario, afable y sincero que defiende a Cuba desde el simple apoyo a un marinero cubano hasta la actitud firme en una Conferencia Internacional o en una prestigiosa revista, o aquel valioso amigo que dirigió la Brigada Che Guevara por más de 12 años, aquellos proyectos que han traído a cientos de adolescentes quebequenses a intercambiar con sus pares cubanos y hasta aquel otro amigo que recibió a nuestro Comandante Fidel en una visita relámpago a Vancouver, ciudad donde hoy laboriosos jóvenes también trabajan con denuedo en acciones de solidaridad.

Tales empeños quedaron agrupados en dos organizaciones de gran transcendencia: la Red Canadiense de Solidaridad con Cuba (CNC) en toda la parte anglófona y la Mesa de Concertación Québec-Cuba. Disímiles y valederas han sido las tareas y campañas que han desarrollado como el apoyo al cruce por diversas ciudades de la Caravana de la Amistad EE UU-Cuba y la Brigada Venceremos, la recogida de fondos para damnificados cubanos por los huracanes y para la brigada médica cubana en Haití y el apoyo a la visita de deportistas, artistas y funcionarios cubanos a Canadá.

Pero donde más ha brillado la amistad sincera de nuestros amigos canadienses ha sido en la lucha sin descanso contra el bloqueo que el gobierno de EE UU ha impuesto a nuestro pueblo y en la campaña por la liberación de nuestros Cinco compatriotas presos en cárceles estadounidenses. Y justo a través de la lectura de estas páginas podremos apreciar en toda su magnitud el alcance de ese apoyo y contribución. Sirva este sencillo prólogo para reverenciar tanto esfuerzo y dedicación; porque con ustedes la obra de nuestra Revolución se ha fortalecido y consolidado.

Kenia Serrano Puig
Presidenta del Instituto Cubano de Amistad con los Pueblos
La Habana, Cuba
Junio 2014

Preface

It is somewhat of a wonder to pinpoint exactly from where and how the idea of a book comes. I believe that ultimately it comes from a place of interest or passion that matures over time, and eventually compels us to want to tell a story or pass on a message we believe is worth sharing.

I have always been fascinated by the concept of solidarity so beautifully made universal by the phrase "*La solidaridad es la ternura de los pueblos*" (Solidarity is the expression of care of the peoples). Beyond a mere feeling, solidarity for me is the real binding fabric between peoples as well as an essential tool for democracy. It is common among activists and particularly within the labour movement to speak of solidarity or to act *in solidarity with* someone or a cause. When I say, I am in solidarity with you, I mean to say, I am at your side. Not that I blindly accept everything you claim or represent, but that I place myself close to you so that I can better hear your plea, and support you with my respect, my dialogue, my voice and my actions.

In the last twenty years I have visited Cuba more than twenty times organizing work brigades or doing collaborative academic work as a university researcher in global health. I have also had the pleasure of meeting many peers within the Cuba solidarity movement in Canada and elsewhere. During that time I have strived to understand the true meaning of solidarity. I have read, studied and written about it all the while I was looking at Cuba as a case study of a nation steeped in solidarity. I cannot claim I have the ultimate word on solidarity, however, I do feel that we have not given it too much credit outside the world of activism. I believe we should.

I have discovered that the word *solidarity* is not necessarily in the vocabulary of certain sectors of society. In fact, I suspect that there is even some reluctance to its use. Perhaps reflecting this reluctance, sociologists have chosen, instead, a more neutral-sounding and conceited expression, *social cohesion*, which in the end they define as the extent of connectedness and *solidarity* among groups in society. I, myself, prefer to speak of solidarity as the extent of connectedness and social cohesion among groups in society and between peoples. Many appear to value a great deal social cohesion, rightly, but they do not credit the solidarity that would indeed act as the bond.

Some even consider the expression of solidarity as threatening. It does not have to be that way. I have come to understand solidarity as a sentiment of shared vision and integrity that empower us, make us equal, connect us to a collective and propel us into action. Normally, social instinct moves us towards unity. That is why the history of repression is full of examples where the first weapon to be launched is fear: be it of barbarians, witches, revolutionaries, visionaries, unions, radical ideas, communism or terrorism. If fear breaks unity, i.e. solidarity, the sense of vulnerability immediately rises and with it, the ensuing power struggle that creates social breakup, imbalance and domination.

I have not been alone on this journey into discovering and practicing solidarity. Along the way I have met many people on the same journey. They showed me the different ways solidarity could be expressed (and at times misinterpreted). Often I have disagreed on how solidarity should be practiced. But I am a firm believer that if a value has any hope of contributing to social justice and peace it must be given a chance. I believe that human connectedness is the best way to peaceful and respectful relationships.

At some point during this journey, I asked myself: what would it be like to have foreign relations between countries based on solidarity instead of hostility? What would it be like to tap into ongoing people-to-people relations to boost state-to-state relations with a more human face and diversity?

A follow up question I asked myself has been: how could I put a spotlight on this enhanced type of foreign relations? Then I realized that many of us in Canada have been doing precisely that in our solidarity work with Cuba independently from the formal Ottawa-Havana relations. Why not begin by joining our experiences to recount the kind of work we have been doing collectively for over five decades and take stock of how we might have contributed to establishing those relations? Let our collective empiricism over five decades guide our understanding and potential for a paradigm shift in international relations.

Based on this realization, my task has been based on formulating a proposition, gathering a group of willing authors, collecting their ideas and searching for common themes of solidarity on the backdrop of current foreign relations with Cuba. This book is in essence the result of that work plan.

So this volume represents the collective memory of stories over more than fifty years as told by many voices with a single message of sincere human connection. The reader may find a certain degree of repetition of events and facts about Cuba and our work in various stories. But repetition cannot be avoided in a book with several authors, who have often worked together, writing about a common friend, Cuba. In the end, the consistency of the stories also lends more authority to them.

This book is definitely the product of collective work and I am very grateful to all the authors that have accepted my invitation to contribute their time, knowledge and experience to this exploration in solidarity with Cuba. Their words are their own with only minimal direction about the aim of the book. I personally know and have worked with all the authors at some point or another. It has been gratifying for me to read their essays as well as about the tremendous amount of volunteer work performed and achievements over a long time doing Cuba solidarity. It has been thrilling to discover the relevance of their insights to the fundamental issue of people-to-people relations.

I also want to thank all those who have not been able to contribute to this volume but who have remarkably contributed to the people-to-people connections we speak about. I greatly regret and take responsibility for being unable to ask many others to be part of this endeavour.

Preface

I am referring to the hundreds of people who have tirelessly been part of a strong solidarity movement in Canada. Their contributions would have definitely enhanced this work, but their work has without doubt enhanced Cuba solidarity in Canada.

I feel particularly honoured that John Kirk, whom I deeply respect, has offered to write the foreword to this volume. His reputation as a practitioner of solidarity and a respected scholar well versed in the topics of Cuba and Canada-Cuba relations validates the stories in the book, many of which he has been part of.

Solidarity is a two-way street. So it is in order for me to thank the many Cubans, in government, within civil society and among ordinary people, who constantly have facilitated the Cuban side of the people-to-people relations. They have contributed patiently Cuban explanations to the endless Canadian drilling questions about the Cuban way of doing things. Cuba's invaluable solidarity has raised our level of awareness about the possibilities of a more humane world. *Muchas gracias a Cuba por su solidaridad*!

The preamble to this volume by the *Instituto Cubano de Amistad con los Pueblos* (ICAP), through the words of Kenia Serrano Puig, its current president, generously gives the Cuba solidarity movement in Canada a recognition for our work, and we appreciate it and are humbled by it. However, I know I have the support of many in the movement when I say that our work would have not been possible without the assistance and the backing of the ICAP team.

I am personally grateful to the friends of ICAP who have tirelessly organized the most welcoming and informative programs for the Canadian work brigades and all the group visitors to Cuba. ICAP has facilitated the access to all sectors of Cuban society in all Cuban Provinces, from Havana to the smallest rural community, so the people-to-people links could be established. I have particularly benefitted from the many meetings around Cuban foreign policy from where I have learned a great deal about Cuba's international solidarity and have derived my own enthusiasm about the topic. I hope I have conveyed some of my learning in my own contributions to this book.

It was not until 2002 that various organizations in the Cuba solidarity movement in Canada came together establishing the Canadian Network on Cuba (CNC), of which I have had the privilege of being the co-founder and the first co-chair, and *La Table de concertation de solidarité Québec-Cuba*. The CNC and *La Table* today, together lead the way towards coordinating solidarity with Cuba, and monitoring and influencing Canadian foreign policy on Cuba. I am thankful to the CNC for their continued commitment and for endorsing the development of this volume. *Je remercie La Table et les amis québécois pour leur solidarité, non seulement pour Cuba mais pour le reste du Canada. Nous devons travailler ensemble.*

I would like to give a special recognition to those in the solidarity movement who have passed on in the last fifty year, three of them recently: Marvin Glass, with whom I shared the first co-chair in the CNC, Elspeth Gardner, with whom I worked in the Canadian-Cuban Friendship Association in Vancouver, and Lee Lorch, whose love for social justice and Cuba has been exemplary to many of us.

On a more personal note, I give a heartfelt thank-you to my wife. I was fortunate that we met when she joined one of the work brigades to Cuba that I organized. Cuba has been the cradle of our friendship that eventually developed into a deeper relationship. Thank you, Mridula, for your solidarity with my cause!

To the reader: thanks for picking up this book and for your interest. If you like what you read, get involved and join us on this journey to solidarity. If you don't like what you read, get involved and make our journey better. This is work in progress.

As for my expectations, I look forward to constructive comments and reviews of this book, but most of all, I look forward to the continuation of this examination of people-to-people links. May this be the initial seed of a campaign demanding for solidarity in our foreign policy!

In solidarity.

Nino Pagliccia
Vancouver, British Columbia
June 2014

Introduction

Solidarity-Based People-to-People Foreign Relations

NINO PAGLICCIA

"I find nothing contemptible in the search for solidarity, however fraught that quest may be."

—Gosse (1993: 9)

◇◇◇

The Cuban Revolution of the 1950s represented an unparalleled departure from the United States-supported dictatorial governments and military coups taking place in Latin America over the same period. This was a revolution inspired by ideals of social justice and equality, which replaced the authoritarian and repressive government of Fulgencio Batista, and represented a paradigm shift in the political trend of the region at the time. This inspiration has persisted over time and likely has contributed to sustaining the social and political achievements of the island, in spite of the unrelenting interference from the United States to subvert a government legitimately chosen by Cubans and ratified by subsequent generations.

The sincerity and authenticity of the Cuban Revolution transcended Cuban borders and sparked the imagination of many social justice activists around the world, particularly in the Americas. Leaders of the Cuban

Nino Pagliccia

Revolution such as Fidel Castro, Ernesto *Che* Guevara, and Camilo Cienfuegos became legendary figures of a people-inspired uprising and of resistance to injustice and oppression. Indeed, while the United States government viewed the Cuban Revolution as a dangerous example to the region because of its clear socialist imprint within its claimed area of influence, many - including large sectors of the population in the U.S. - symbolically and politically embraced it.

Groups supporting the Cuban Revolution sprouted up across Latin America, the United States, and Canada almost immediately and they have grown to form a social movement based on a spirit of friendship and solidarity with Cuba, and its political and social aims. Author Cynthia Wright gives a detailed account of the Canada-Cuba solidarity beginnings following the Cuban Revolution in the early 1960s (2009). Like other movements, it started spontaneously and vigorously by the initiative of a few and grew into dynamic organizations and networks whose mandate was shaped over time by events perceived to be unfairly hostile towards Cuba.

Mapping the Journey of Solidarity

Many books and essays have been dedicated to analyzing and critiquing Cuba and its revolution, society, and politics. The country has been the subject of research by many scholars, self-proclaimed experts, and journalists in order to provide the latest interpretation of the latest Cuban policies and events. Many of these reports suffer from researcher bias and at times introduce misinformation into public discourse.

This book takes a different approach by turning the spotlight away from Cuba while retaining it as a backdrop. Cuba is not a case study for this book. Rather, a group of Canadians is, who have had a long-standing direct and pragmatic knowledge of Cuba and are united by a common interest that has created a movement over half a century: a Cuba solidarity movement in Canada. The book maps this journey of solidarity by trying to answer some basic questions: what did they see in the Cuban Revolution that motivated them to become and remain activists for Cuba? How have they been involved in supporting Cuba? How does the movement fit within Canadian society and what can we learn from it?

In short, the main goal of this book is to give highlights of the evolution and growth of the Cuba solidarity movement in Canada by some of its protagonists in the last fifty years. These accounts will bring to light the early beginnings, the motivations, the ideals, the events and the actions of the movement, as well as its current role in Canadian society and possible impact on the Canada-Cuba relationship. These accounts, far from being isolated stories, are part of a larger framework that I call "solidarity-based people-to-people foreign relations."

I first take a look at how Canada, the United States, and Cuba view and practice foreign relations. Then I advance the argument that the practice of solidarity involves establishing people-to-people relations that run parallel and are indeed akin to state-to-state foreign relations. This type of solidarity-based people-to-people international relations is grounded in respect, genuine co-operation, and shared aspirations within diverse objectives; it embraces causes rather than self-interests, and is capable of producing long-lasting connections that are stronger and more meaningful than diplomatic ties. It is a relation where people, rather than ideology, are at the centre of policies.

In the concluding chapter of the book I will capture and follow the common threads across the writings of contributors who have witnessed, coordinated, contributed to, and participated in Canada-Cuba solidarity activities over the last fifty years. I expect to see the extent to which the Canadian solidarity movement towards Cuba reflects and fits in the proposed framework. Readers will gain a better understanding of why such a small island nation in the Caribbean is so significant to many people in

Nino Pagliccia

Canada, and will also learn how Canadian society has contributed to the enduring and epic journey that is the Cuban Revolution.

State-to-State Foreign Relations and American Outlook

Governments internally develop policies that are applied in bilateral, state-to-state relationships. Most have dedicated governmental organizations that administer and manage those foreign policies.

The field of foreign relations can be simply viewed as a blend of diplomacy, economics, trade, and power politics where *realpolitik* and ideology are the main components in the state-to-state relationship. The U.S. may exemplify the true meaning of power politics: U.S. foreign relation are backed by about $16 trillion economy (GDP), almost double that of China and nine times that of Canada (World Market Index n.d.), and by military spending of about $800 billion (4.35 percent of GDP in 2012) (CIA World Factbook n.d.). While it is not the scope of this chapter to present an in-depth analysis of U.S. foreign policy, it is important to bring up its principal ideological characteristic. In fact, given its influence and predominance on the world stage, many governments adopt a certain international posture based on the relationship they have with the U.S. Canada is no exception.

U.S. foreign policy has a distinguishing feature that is entrenched in the commonly recognized "doctrine of American exceptionalism" (McEvoy-Levy 2001). This doctrine is based on the theory, generally accepted by both U.S. parties but not necessarily by the American people, that the U.S. is culturally and politically unique and is endowed with moral powers to assert itself in the world. Therefore, "exceptions" should be admissible when U.S. policies break international legal and moral standards. The American historian Howard Zinn has stated that

"[George W.] Bush's national security strategy and its bold statement that the United States is uniquely responsible for peace and democracy in the world has been shocking to many Americans." However, "it seems that the idea of American exceptionalism is pervasive across the political spectrum" (Zinn 2005 n.p.). In a recent address to the nation, President Barack Obama tried to make a case for a military intervention in Syria by concluding, "That's what makes America different. That's what makes us *exceptional*" (Obama 2013; emphasis added).

The phrase "American exceptionalism"[1] came to replace the older and somewhat less defined notion of "manifest destiny" that was used by American presidents in the 19th century to justify their expansionist drive. The U.S. manifest destiny implied that it was considered "natural" to conquer territory in the Americas as a God-given providence based on the "virtues" of the American settlers (Hofstadter 1996, Weeks 1996).

Canadian author and former leader of the opposition for the Liberal Party of Canada Michael Ignatieff offers a very sharp analysis of American exceptionalism that identifies three of its variations in the area of human rights. The first type is the one by which the U.S. grants itself exemption to abide to multilateral agreements. According to the second type, the U.S. adopts double standard positions in relation to positions expected to be taken by other countries. The third type of American exceptionalism is a legal isolationism, that is, the rejection of legal precedents on human rights established by other countries as not applicable within the U.S. judicial system (Ignatieff 2005). These features are certainly not flattering for a self-appointed leading country in the world, instead giving the U.S. a prerogative for nefarious foreign policies that threaten international

---

1   Ironically the term American exceptionalism was first used by Soviet leader Joseph Stalin in 1929 and formalized at the American Communist party convention in 1930. A 2012 news article on the topic can be found here: http://www.theatlantic.com/politics/archive/2012/03/how-joseph-stalin-invented-american-exceptionalism/254534/

peace and stability and whose consequences can be devastating and long ranging.

American exceptionalism came into the public discourse as an identifiable doctrine in the 1980s, at a time when U.S. foreign policy in its hegemonic form touched virtually every country in the world, often using intimidation as it continues to do to this day. Mark Weisbrot, the co-director of the Center for Economic and Policy Research in Washington, D.C., and president of Just Foreign Policy, suggests that the U.S. media may use self-censorship in order to avoid reporting the most severe cases of interventions. In a recent article for The Guardian, Weisbrot (2013) brings to light an account of the "horrendous slaughter of almost the entire village of Dos Erres, more than 200 people", in Guatemala in 1982. He states, "The UN specifically noted Washington's role and President Clinton publicly apologized for it." It is this type of disregard for outrageous crimes that entrenches exceptionalism in the psyche of American foreign policy. As Weisbrot poses, "What would U.S. foreign, military and so-called 'national security' policy look like if the media reported the most important facts about it?"

A closer example in connection with Cuba is illustrative of the dangerous intrigue that may be involved in the implementation of U.S. foreign policy, putting lives at risk and going beyond diplomatic intervention. Released top secret documents reveal that in 1962 the Joint Chiefs of Staff of the U.S. Armed Forces drafted and approved a plan in order to fabricate a tragic or even aggressive event that could be blamed on Cuba. The plan included suggestions such as "blow up a U.S. ship in Guantanamo Bay and blame Cuba," and "Create an incident that will demonstrate convincingly that a Cuban aircraft has attacked and shot down a chartered civil airliner...The passengers could be a group of college students off on a holiday." (National Security Archive pp. 8, 9). Then-president Kennedy did not approve the plan but even if the alleged casualties were only meant to be simulated, the callously deceitful nature of the plan testifies to the types of interventions that U.S. foreign policymakers would entertain. Further, there are innumerable examples of hostile U.S. foreign policy towards Cuba. Interventions in Cuba's internal affairs (including attempts against Fidel Castro's life) by the U.S. government have been well documented by Jane Franklin in her chronological history of U.S.-Cuba relations until 1995 (Franklin 1997). It is precisely in the presence of this persistent "siege" that author Keith Bolender, expert on the U.S. blockade of Cuba, provides a compelling validation of Cuba's defiance in his book *Cuba under Siege: American Policy, the Revolution and Its People* (Bolender 2012).

Within this backdrop of U.S. attitude towards international relations I turn the attention to the position that Canada takes in its foreign policy. How is it implemented? What is Canada's vision of its own foreign relations in the international arena and with Cuba in particular?

Canadian Foreign Relations Outlook

The Canadian government maintains relations with most nations in the world. Canada has a Department of Foreign Affairs, Trade, and Development (DFATD) whose mandate is "to manage Canada's diplomatic and consular relations, to encourage the country's international trade and to lead Canada's international development and humanitarian assistance" (Government of Canada, DFATD 2014). Among other things, this mandate includes "ensuring that Canada's foreign policy reflects true Canadian values and advances Canada's national interests" (Government of Canada, DFATD 2014). Canada's mission is further detailed in the stated priorities for 2013-2014 where references are made to economic prosperity, democracy and human rights, trade and commercial relations, food security, and poverty reduction in developing countries. The economic agenda of Canada's foreign policy is enhanced by the promise of concrete propositions such as the Global Commerce

Strategy, the Canada-EU Comprehensive Economic and Trade Agreement, the Comprehensive Economic Partnership Agreement with India, and the Canada-U.S. Shared Vision for Perimeter Security and Economic Competitiveness. Not counting programs for research and development, the only concrete proposition to enhance food security is the offer to work with other countries to implement the U.N. Food Assistance Convention ratified by Canada in November 2012.

On the democracy and human rights side of Canadian foreign policy priorities, an incongruent item stands out: "Defend Israel's right to exist." The only other instance where the word "defence" is used is in the context of the Canada-U.S. continental defence cooperation. Although Canada is not a stranger to military interventions it is still odd, though not unfathomable for the reasons given below, that Israel is singled out in such a strong, committal language. At least one analysis offers plausible reasons for such a Canadian position towards Israel that include: (1) the growing interdependence of both countries with the U.S.-economy since the 1980s; (2) the construction of a "War on Terror" by neoconservative currents in North America and the related growth of a booming continental 'homeland security' market; (3) the Israeli desire for 'normalization' and the role of market-oriented strategies in achieving this policy objective; and (4) Canada's special relationship with the U.S. and the multiple pressures (including the introduction of U.S.-style foreign-policy lobbying models) that are pushing for a greater harmonization of Canadian positions in international forums with those of the U.S. (Kilibarda 2008: 3).

By and large, based on trade, Canada's most important relationship is with the U.S. and has given rise to questions about political dependency leading to a deterioration of Canadian sovereignty. The debate about whether or not Canada follows a foreign policy independent from that of the U.S. was first initiated by several scholars in a book edited by Stephen Clarkson in 1968 with a telling question as title, "An Independent Foreign Policy for Canada?" More than forty years later, in the era of globalization, obsession over free trade agreements, and fear of terrorism post-9/11 has seen Canada boxed into the North American Free Trade Agreement, a more active armed forces involvement in foreign lands, as well as domestic border security and immigration reforms, all of which have created an inextricable Canadian interdependence with the U.S. with doubtful economic benefits and a clear loss of autonomy as a sovereign country. It is commonly accepted that the image of Canada as a peacemaker has deteriorated over the years as a result.

Authors Brian Bow and Patrick Lennox re-open the debate about Canadian independent foreign policy and state that "the time is right to revisit the question of Canada's foreign policy independence, not simply because forty years have passed since the publication of Clarkson's original volume, but because looking back from our own time to the late 1960s stirs up a profound sense of *déjà vu*." Later they also challenge us to raise "profound questions about the nature and quality of America's global leadership" (Bow and Lennox 2008: 6). Indeed, while the Canadian government asserts territorial Arctic sovereignty (Parliament of Canada 2006), some would argue that threats to Canadian sovereignty might well be thrust on us from the south through more subtle political means. We take the broader notion of a state sovereignty not only as territorial control of the state, but also as a legitimate right and accountable obligation of the state to protect its own nationals from any form of coercion (economic or political) coming from another state that threatens their integrity as individuals or as citizens and community members of the state. Succinctly put, "sovereignty is a declaration of political responsibility for governing, defending and promoting the welfare of a human community" (Fowler and Bunck 1995: 12).

Given what we know about Canadian foreign policy, where can we situate the Canadian outlook on its relations with Cuba? Canada diverges from the U.S. on this point. The U.S. broke diplomatic relations with Cuba in 1961, and it was not until 1977 that, under the Carter administration, the two countries exchanged Interests Sections in their respective capitals: far from full diplomatic relations. The U.S. has maintained

Nino Pagliccia

an increasingly tight economic blockade[2] of Cuba since February 1962 while Canada and Cuba exchange full diplomatic relations, uninterrupted even after the triumph of the Cuban Revolution in 1959. Is this a sign of independent Canadian foreign relations with Cuba?

The greatest divergence between U.S. and Canadian policies toward Cuba was displayed around the U.S. Helms-Burton Law[3] of 1996. The government of Canadian Prime Minister Jean Chrétien unyieldingly opposed the extra-territorial nature of that law and immediately introduced legislation to counter it, seemingly in the spirit of Fowler and Bunck's notion of sovereignty. The legislation aimed to protect Canadians doing business in Cuba by allowing them to initiate counter-suits in Canadian courts for monetary loss caused by the U.S. law.

Authors Peter McKenna and John Kirk have noted that "relations between Canada and revolutionary Cuba have been intriguing, complicated, and, at times, unusually fluid" during the terms of various Canadian Prime Ministers from Pierre Trudeau to Stephen Harper (McKenna and Kirk 2009: 163). The most turbulent years between Ottawa and Havana occurred during the Chrétien period varying from an initially very pro-active "constructive engagement" with Canada advocating for Cuba to re-join the Organization of American States in 1994, to the "northern ice" approach toward Cuba that culminated with the official Canadian statement that Cuba was not invited to the April 2001 Summit of the Americas in Québec City. Other Prime Ministers after Chrétien have been strategically quiet about Cuba (McKenna and Kirk 2009: 165-172).

---

2   We use the term "blockade", preferred by Cubans, instead of the widely used term "embargo" to refer to the stringent nature of the U.S. government measures that prevent any type of financial and commercial transactions with Cuba and retaliates against other countries that do.

3   The Helms-Burton law expands the economic blockade and penalizes, through legal suits, foreign companies doing business involving properties formerly owned by U.S. citizens in Cuba. The bill was introduced and passed in Congress as a result of the downing of civilians private planes operated by the anti-Castro group Brothers to the Rescue while making provocative incursions around Cuban airspace.

In their book *Canada-Cuba Relations: The Other Good Neighbor Policy*, Kirk and McKenna provide a chronological review of the ever-changing Canada-Cuba relations under different prime ministers until the early Chrétien years. They concluded that Canada "seeks to recognize some self-evident truths: that Cuba does not represent a threat to any nation in the Americas...[and] that Havana has shown every desire to leave behind its policies of exporting revolution and now is struggling to maintain the core of its social policies in the face of harsh, post-Soviet realities" (Kirk and McKenna 1997: 176-7). We are today still in pursuit of those truths.

Except for the usual snubbing about human rights and democracy in Cuba, the Harper's government has not been very active on the Cuba portfolio. This policy of non-engagement was unexpectedly broken in February 2013 when Foreign Affairs Minister John Baird met with Bruno Rodríguez Parrilla, Cuba's Foreign Affairs Minister, in what was the first visit to Cuba by a high-ranking Canadian government official since Prime Minister Chrétien's visit in 1998 and previously Lloyd Axworthy's in 1997.

The DFATD media release on Baird's official visits to Latin America indicated distinct goals for each of the six different countries about to be visited on the trip. In relation to Cuba, "Baird will focus especially on democracy, human rights and economic liberalization... Baird will conduct visits to Cuba and Venezuela to engage with government representatives." (Government of Canada, DFATD 2013, February 14).

The National Post newspaper reported the item with some editorial additions in regards to the timing of Baird's visit: "Baird...is pushing for deeper economic and commercial engagement for Canada in both countries [Cuba and Venezuela] because that can promote change at what is looking like a pivotal moment in history" (National Post February 17, 2013)[4]. The "pivotal moment in history" is a clear reference to the current

---

4   In the same article the National Post felt obliged to forego the assumed journalistic lack of prejudice by referring to Cuba as "the hemisphere's most repressive anti-democratic country."

process of the Cuban government to update their economic model that is viewed as an opportunity to promote a free-market system to reflect Canadian *values*.

It is still too early to assess the impact of Baird's visit to Cuba. Peter McKenna presented a well-reasoned argument why "Canada should engage Cuba" (McKenna 2013), however, given the current Canadian government right-wing ideology we do not expect any major changes in the short term. As author Robert Wright explains in reference to Axworthy's and Chrétien's politically failed visits, "Cubans do not accept – any more than Canadians or Americans would – the intrusion of foreigners into their domestic affairs, whether this intrusion takes the form of the [U.S.-style] iron fist or the [Canadian-style] velvet glove" (Wright 2009: 196). Most certainly, the trade relationship between Ottawa and Havana will continue[5] to the benefit of the two countries in what has been called a "win-win situation," at least from a commercial standpoint (McKenna and Kirk 2008: 265). In spite of the continued apparent Canadian "constructive engagement" – seemingly at variance with the U.S.'s relationship with Cuba - we cannot conclude that Canada has an entirely independent foreign policy. At best it appears to be more like a *hesitant and conditional* constructive engagement. How has Cuba, under these conditions, reacted and shaped its own foreign policy not only towards the U.S. and Canada, but also towards other countries?

---

5   "Cuba is Canada's top market in the Caribbean/Central American sub-region and bilateral merchandise trade between the two countries is over one billion dollars annually. Canadian companies have significant investments in mining, power, oil and gas, agri-food and tourism." (Government of Canada February 2013).

Cuban Foreign Relations Outlook

In her engaging and informative book *Cuba: What everyone needs to know*, Julia Sweig identifies three distinct periods of modern Cuban foreign relations: 1) From 1959 until 1991, the period of the Cold War; 2) After the Cold War until 2006, when Fidel Castro's illness forced him to step down from the presidency; and 3) Under the leadership of Raúl Castro (Sweig 2009).

During the period of the Cold War the world was a socially and politically turbulent one where poverty, exploitation and social injustice prevailed, and countries sought much-needed social development by aligning themselves with either of the two world powers: the U.S. or the Soviet Union. At the same time many countries tried hard not to succumb to the persuasive forces of the two poles and pursued independent political paths. Cuba, having emerged successfully from its own struggle against oppression, was reliant on its own experience believing that similar revolutions were possible elsewhere, and that economic and social change could be brought about from within as a popular sovereign choice[6].

With this vision Cuba embarked on a mission of internationalism, supporting people of countries in South and Central America to reclaim their sovereignty, often undermined by the dissent of their own governments. Remarkably, Cuba not only provided troops and weapons, but also doctors and teachers to support local communities in revolt. After all, that is what the Cuban revolutionaries did in Cuba with communities they came in contact with as part of the liberation process. Many oppressed people saw resistance as their only alternative and therefore welcomed Cuba's support.

---

6   So strong was the belief that at times this position was at variance with that of the Soviet Union. While Ernesto *Che* Guevara was a proponent of the armed struggle, the leadership in the Soviet Union adopted a policy of peaceful coexistence among states.

Nino Pagliccia

However, many Latin American governments did not welcome Cuba's internationalism in their territories, albeit under pressure from the U.S. government, and made that clear by eventually supporting a resolution to suspend Cuba from the Organization of American States (OAS) in 1962. The suspension came in spite of the OAS' own charter "to achieve an order of peace and justice, to promote their solidarity, to strengthen their collaboration, and to defend their sovereignty, their territorial integrity, and their independence." (OAS 1993, Article 1).

In his remarkable analysis of Cuba's role during the Cold War period in North America, Van Gosse traces the influence that Fidel Castro and his revolutionaries had in the U.S. even prior to the 1959 triumph of the Revolution "before Castro was seen as a direct threat to U.S. interests." Cuba's struggle was largely viewed as positive for Cubans but it was also one to be emulated by Americans in their own domestic civic aspirations. Gosse also informed us that many authors writing about the sixties largely ignored any admiration for the popular resistance in Cuba and the incipient Fair Play for Cuba Committee in the U.S.[7] (Gosse 1993: 3, 5). Expectedly, this deliberate dismissal changed when the U.S.-endorsed invasion at Playa Girón (Bay of Pigs) in 1961 failed in what was seen as a major defeat for the U.S.

The Playa Girón defeat may well have redoubled the U.S. military role in Latin America during the Cold War period in order to prevent a second Cuba. For instance, in Central America, "No leader came to power or remained in power without the United States' consent" (Nieto 2003: 105). Most countries in Central America were referred to as "Banana Republics" as a reference to the American United Fruit Company semi-colonial exploitation in the region. "Through pressure, threats and bribes it obtained concessions and privileges outside the law...Such 'services'

---

7   The Fair Play for Cuba Committee (FPCC) was formed by a group of activists in New York in April 1960. Its purpose was to provide grassroots support for the Cuban Revolution against attacks by the United States government. In Canada, the first FPCC was formed in February 1961.

were repaid with juicy bribes to the countries' leaders, and Washington rewarded their submission by propping up their regimes" (Nieto 2003: 108). In his book Masters of War, author Nieto relates some of the "horrendous crimes" committed by those regimes mostly against workers and *campesinos*. Many of the Latin American military officers involved in those actions were trained against "counterinsurgency" tactics – reportedly including torture – in the School of the Americas (SOA) at Fort Benning, Georgia. SOA continues its questionable work today in spite of being renamed in 2001 to Western Hemisphere Institute for Security Cooperation (WHINSEC). The strong organized opposition to SOA is just as relentless (SOA Watch 2014, March).

Cuba's involvement in Africa, on the other hand, met with more success particularly in Southern Africa (Sweig 2009: 114-115). Characteristically, Cuban internationalism had no intention of acquiring material gain or interests; no military bases or personnel were left behind, nor unfair deals were forced on those governments. An outstanding example of this comes from Cuba's involvement in Angola in the 1980s, which lead to that country's independence followed by Namibia's, and Cuba's support of the African National Congress, that in turn lead to the end of apartheid in South Africa. After more than 2,000 Cuban lives lost in internationalist actions, the only, and perhaps the highest reward Cubans received was Nelson Mandela's comment to Fidel Castro during his inauguration as first black president of South Africa, "You made this possible." (Quoted in Sweig 2009: 115). Cuba's armed involvement in the world did not last long, ending during the 1970s.

If the demise of the Soviet Union and the socialist block marked the end of the Cold War at the beginning of the 1990s, that same event marked the beginning of a severe period of hardship and challenges for the Cuban Revolution, aptly termed "Special Period". Paradoxically, it also allowed a positive transformation – a maturity of the revolution. "In the realm of foreign policy, the 1991-2007 period was 'special' because it marked Cuba's first real experience with independence since the start of

Nino Pagliccia

Spanish colonization five hundred years earlier. No single foreign power structured Cuba's political, economic, and foreign policy decisions" (Brenner, Jimenez, et al. 2008: 194). However, in practical terms the Cuban leadership needed a short-term plan to overcome the ensuing economic crisis while maintaining the gains of the revolution, and its highest achievement, the socialist system. In the absence of access to international financial institutions, Cuba quickly and appropriately transformed its economy from a dwindling sugar industry to a thriving tourism industry that has attracted selected foreign business partners from many countries, including Canada, and provided the needed hard currency.

In its own unique way, the Cuban government managed to maintain all its social programs and has been able to minimize the social disparity that is usually inevitable at times of dire economic situations. This prompt reorganization of the Cuban economy has achieved economic recovery at a very low social cost domestically; and internationally has opened the doors to the world to visit Cuba, strategically countering the isolationist attempts from the U.S. Indeed, the response from the international community has been very positive with over three million tourists visiting every year; of those, about one third are Canadians.

Using the strength of its successful healthcare sector domestically, Cuba changed the character of its internationalism during this period emphasizing medical cooperation with many countries in Latin America, Asia, and Africa, and as far as Kiribati, an island nation of 100,000 inhabitants in the central tropical Pacific Ocean. The *Ministerio de Salud Pública* (Ministry of Public Health) manages this program that is simply called *misión médica* (medical mission) by Cubans, or *colaboración médica cubana* (Cuban medical cooperation). The official website of this program states that it is based on the "principle of international solidarity" and started with its first medical brigade to Algeria in 1963. Today it covers 76 countries with almost 38,500 healthcare workers (*Enciclopedia Cubana en la Red* n.d.). As part of the same program, Cuba receives international medical students from 122 countries (including the U.S.) at the *Escuela Latinoamericana de*

Medicina (ELAM, Latin American School of Medicine) in Havana with about 1,350 registered students (Infomed n.d.). Author Robert Huish has researched the impact of physicians trained in Cuba on local communities upon their return in a case study of Ecuador. In his dissertation Huish concludes, "ELAM does well to foster the appropriate clinical skills and ethics of service for its graduates to meet the needs of their communities. This is done through an appropriate recruitment process, the building of institutional ethics, clinic-based instruction for core clinical competency, and by forming a culture of service for the public good" (Huish 2008: 271).

The program, in its different facets, has been dubbed doctor diplomacy, medical diplomacy, Cuban soft diplomacy, and oil-for-doctors program (in the case of Venezuela), and is widely seen as part of the country's successful foreign policy strategy. The different labels used for this program should not hide the fact that it has saved thousands of lives and provided relief to the most needy in the most remote corners of the world as a non-profit enterprise. Authors John Kirk, Robert Huish, and others have extensively researched and written about the origin, the scope and the impact of Cuban medical internationalism (Huish 2013, Kirk 2012, Kirk and Erisman 2009, Saney 2009, Huish and Kirk 2007, De Vos et al 2007).

The third period of Cuban foreign policy identified by Sweig is the current period under the presidency of Raúl Castro that began in 2008. No major changes have occurred in foreign policy during this period, in spite of the U.S. expectations following Fidel Castro's retirement from public life. Cuba appears to remain committed to its socialist path and in order to accomplish that, the Cuban government has given priority to domestic economic programs while consolidating its international relations with traditional friends, especially in Latin America.

Cuba continues to view foreign relations as a platform based on cooperation among nations rather than competition. A strategy of competition may be advantageous to countries with strong economies, but weaker economies would have to build a certain critical mass both

Nino Pagliccia

economically and socially in order to counter any undesired hegemonic take over. Under this principle, Cuba has been, together with Venezuela, the co-founder of the *Alianza Bolivariana para los Pueblos de Nuestra América* (ALBA - Bolivarian Alliance for the Peoples of Our Americas), which promotes a Latin American and Caribbean economic integration that accepts social welfare and mutual economic aid as part of the trade agreement. This paradigm of relations among nations epitomizes a drastically different set of values from those frequently displayed by Canada and the U.S.

Perhaps, it is pertinent to quote from the official website of the Foreign Affairs of Cuba to understand the extent of the Cuban outlook on foreign policy:

> Cuba's foreign policy adheres to the basic principles of International Law: respect to sovereignty, independence and territorial integrity of States; peoples´ self-determination; equality of States and peoples; rejection to the interference in the internal affairs of States; the right to international cooperation for the mutual and equitable benefit and interest; the peaceful relations between States, and other principles established in the Charter of the United Nations. Internationalism, anti-imperialism, *solidarity* and unity among Third World countries are also the backbone of Cuban foreign policy.
>
> Cuba condemns all hegemonic, interventionist and discriminatory practices in international relations. It also rejects threats or use of force, the adoption of coercive unilateral measures, aggression and any form of terrorism, including State terrorism. (Ministerio de Relaciones

Exteriores de Cuba n.d.; translation from Spanish: Nino Pagliccia).

What is immediately striking in those two paragraphs is that Cuba squarely and unequivocally states: 1) what "Cuba's values" are: sovereignty, independence and territorial integrity, self-determination, equality of states and peoples, solidarity; 2) what Cuba is willing to do in the international arena: equitable and mutual international cooperation, internationalism and the unity among Third World countries; and 3) what Cuba is not willing to accept: imperialism, hegemonic intervention and discriminatory practices, threats or use of force, coercive unilateral measure, terrorism. Even more important is what Cuba states implicitly: that other government must not question Cuba's social system as precondition to any type of relations. Contrast this with Baird's announced demands for democracy, human rights and economic liberalization prior to his visit to Cuba in February 2013 or Canada's objection to extending an invitation for Cuba to attend the seventh Summit of the Americas in 2015.

Solidarity and International Relations

In any review of U.S. and Canadian foreign policy I have not found a reference to solidarity as a value that characterizes international relations. In Cuba's case on the other hand, solidarity is a predominant value and practice, both domestically and internationally. Cuba has not been shy about enlisting international solidarity not only of governments but also more importantly of people around the world. This is a drastically different tactic in Cuban foreign policy that has proven to be successful as indicated by the continued support for Cuba at the U.N.

yearly vote against the U.S. blockade[8], and the increasing support from Latin America. The hundreds of Cuba solidarity networks around the world is also a clear indication of the result of soft power exerted by Cuba's policy. The people of Cuba deserve a lot of credit for their direct involvement in fomenting ties of solidarity.

Post revolutionary Cuba has a firm tradition of seeking people's involvement as principal actors in building a socialist society city block by city block in urban and rural areas. In fact, popular participation is valued as an antidote to "bureaucratic" tendencies (Fernández Ríos 2011). Canadian author Arnold August gives an extensive account of this unique Cuban process of truly participatory democracy in every aspect of decision-making. "Since 1959 Cuba has been democratizing its society based on socialist principles that allow for a political system founded on participation." (August 2013: 217). August illustrates how on the occasion of the *Partido Comunista de Cuba* (Communist Party of Cuba) 6th Congress in 2011, Cubans (not required to be party members) were called to participate in debates about "concerns, expectations, demands and dissatisfaction", and to propose suggestions to address them. In the three months prior to the congress "There were 163,079 meetings with 8,913,838 participants. They contributed to 3,019,471 separate inputs…[as a result of which] 68 percent of the original 291 guidelines [resolutions] were modified…and 36 new guidelines [were added]" (August 2013: 124).

This intensity of participatory democracy requires a very well informed population with a high level of analytical and political skill. In my personal experience with Cubans of different backgrounds I have often noticed these traits, which have been much more evident in my interaction with those Cubans whom I have met in international forums and who acted as unofficial ambassadors in international

---

8   At the last U.N. vote in 2012, 188 countries voted in favour of ending the U.S. blockade of Cuba. 3 countries voted against and 2 abstained. Compare to 1992 vote, respectively 59, 3, and 71.

relations. Their skills and conviction about the importance of popular participation have largely contributed to engaging support around the notion of solidarity.

I have reviewed the nature of solidarity elsewhere: "Solidarity as originally conceived is – quite contrary to charity work – designed to act upon the social organization in order to change it for the benefit of the larger collective. Solidarity is directed at awareness of the condition and at social change or the redefinition of power relations" (Pagliccia 2008: 121). Given this view of solidarity practice, I contend that a true measure of relationship between Canada and Cuba is not provided "by the analysis of government policies or by measuring the magnitude of the trade exchange between the two countries, but rather by observing how people connect, what people value in each other, and how people-to-people bonds are formed" (Pagliccia 2008: 133).

There is no evidence that Cuba has not lived up to its commitment of solidarity and cooperation in its foreign relations with any nation, organization, or people willing to be engaged. I argue that many have in fact taken notice of Cuba's actions and have responded in kind creating what I call people-to-people international relations based on the principle of solidarity. In fact, this has been the backbone of the (largely unrecognized) bond between Canadians and Cubans in the last five decades. The need for this direct type of connection appears when there is a perception that the state-to-state relationship a) is not achieving a closer association or may even be counter to establishing a closer association; b) is not a sufficiently comprehensive association; or c) is actually producing negative outcomes. Consequently, individuals or civil society rise up to fill the gap and bypass the official state foreign relations.

People-to-people relation is typically desirable and Canada seems to encourage it. In a very thoughtful chapter in *Our Place in the Sun: Canada and Cuba in the Castro Era,* Mark Entwistle, Canadian ambassador to Cuba from 1993 to 1997, speaks of the "familiarity" stemming

Nino Pagliccia

from Canadians mingling with Cubans in their travels, the "mutual affinity" of the two peoples, and the common "search of a unifying narrative for identity" of the two nations (Entwistle 2009: 284, 295).

However, the expectation is that these direct connections are conditioned to promoting state-defined "Canadian values" and therefore leave out the individual's independent initiative and, indeed, values. Ironically, even the U.S. encourages state-sponsored people-to-people connections, in spite of the ban on Americans travelling to Cuba. Similarly, the underlying intent is to introduce an ideology that may be contrary to the internal *status quo* of the recipient country[9].

The notion of non-state foreign policy is not totally new. Involvement by non-state actors with the intention of influencing the established foreign policy has been referred to as "foreign policy from below" (Marsh 1995). This notion may encompass the context I describe, however I have chosen the expression solidarity-based people-to-people international (or foreign) relations for several reasons. First, I prefer to avoid the hierarchical implications of the phrases "from below" and "from above." I consider the direct people-driven foreign policy as running parallel to, and being qualitatively different from, state-driven foreign policy[10]. Second, I aim to identify "people" (to include civil society) explicitly as the actors or agents of this type of grassroots foreign policy. Third, the expression I adopt emphasizes the directionality of the action from people towards

---

9   Pertinent here is the case of the American Alan Phillip Gross who was arrested in Cuba working as a U.S. government subcontractor for the U.S. Agency for International Development (USAID) as part of a program funded under the 1996 Helms-Burton Act. He was prosecuted in 2011 after being accused of crimes against the Cuban state for bringing satellite phones and computer equipment to members of Cuba's Jewish community without the permit required under Cuban law. After being accused of working for American intelligence services in January 2010, he was ultimately convicted for "acts against the independence or the territorial integrity of the state" in March 2011, and is currently serving a 15-year prison sentence in Cuba.

10   I have first learned about this concept of parallel people-driven foreign policy based on solidarity from conversations with Cuban colleagues in 2004 for which I am grateful.

people, although the action may at times be directed to the official state agents of foreign policy.

Finally and most importantly, I want to qualify people-to-people international relations as grounded in the principle of solidarity as defined above. The more generic foreign policy from below may include other features of relationship with other actors. In fact, it will likely include lobby groups that may put pressure on governments to act counter to the interests of another government or people. In the case of Cuba this is particularly true with lobby activities that attempt to interfere with the internal affairs of Cuba. Not surprisingly, the Cuba Lobby in the U.S. has been so exceptionally influential that it is believed to have driven U.S.-Cuba foreign policy. As professor LeoGrande wrote in Foreign Policy Magazine, "the Cuba Lobby isn't one organization but a loose-knit conglomerate of exiles, sympathetic members of Congress, and non-governmental organizations, some of which comprise a self-interested industry nourished by the flow of 'democracy promotion' money from the U.S. Agency for International Development" (LeoGrande 2013: n.p.). Further, in a clear example of how "domestic politics and international relations are often somehow entangled" (Putnam 1988, quoted in Entwistle 2009: 297), "the Cuba Lobby was launched at the instigation of conservative Republicans in government who needed outside backers to advance their partisan policy aims" (LeoGrande 2013: n.p.).

Canada has not been exempt from pressure and it has found itself to be the object of criticism by strong U.S. lobby groups. Former ambassador Entwistle wrote, "Frank Calzon, executive director of the Center for a Free Cuba and the original architect of the Washington lobbying effort of the Cuban American National Foundation, provides a typical hard-line Cuban-American assessment of Canadian business in Cuba" (Entwistle 2009: 288).

In summary, I define solidarity-based people-to-people international relation as a grassroots connection among peoples across borders in the spirit of respect, understanding, co-operation, and support. It is carried out in transparent actions by collectives of well-informed individuals loosely organized, reflecting a broad-base ideology. It aims to align itself in solidarity with just popular struggles and resistance, and by so doing, raises awareness and possibly influences governments to adopt friendly policies. It runs parallel to the official state-to-state foreign policy in its attempt to complement incomplete or unfulfilled international relations.

I believe that this is the notion that has shaped the Cuba solidarity movement in Canada since the beginning of the Cuban Revolution, and I anticipate it will be the substratum of the narrative that follows from some of the actors of a close Canada-Cuba connection that has lasted more than five decades.

Conclusion

This book aims to characterize a special relationship between the people of Canada and the people of Cuba as seen by a sample of Canadians who collectively have been active in Cuba solidarity for more than fifty years. I have proposed in this chapter a framework for this relationship that I have called "solidarity-based people-to-people foreign relations." I suggest that this relationship is grounded at the grassroots and runs parallel to the state-to-state international relations.

I have also highlighted the main differences in outlook to bilateral relations between the U.S. and Cuba, and Canada and Cuba. I notice that the notion of solidarity is missing in the vocabulary of U.S. and Canadian foreign relations and that a strong ideology is present under the misnomer of "values." I believe that this is the foundation of conflictive foreign policies in relation to Cuba.

Ideology is by definition a divisive concept that is also evident in domestic policies. I recognize the fact that a certain amount of ideology will always be present in human relations but I question it when it is used as a pre-condition to establish a rapport between nations. Consequently, while economic dealings - as in the case of Canada and Cuba - may establish a sort of relation between the two countries based on commercial benefits, this is only a narrow connection compared to a broader range of closer possibilities if the barrier of ideology were removed. To fill this gap, people have envisioned a type of relationship among peers that can co-exist with ideology but is based on the more unifying and binding concept of human solidarity.

I believe that Cuba has developed a working model of foreign relations that is not limited to state relations and involves people from the grassroots. We may not, however, be able to appreciate the full potential of this Cuban model due to the obstinate opposition, by a minority number of bureaucrats, to Cuba's internal political autonomy. Sadly we will miss out on the most promising collective experiment in producing social well-being for the majority. As Cuba speaks the language of solidarity, many in Canada - indeed in the world - are listening and have responded to the call through a "solidarity movement" that has established respectful people-to-people relations between Canada and Cuba.

Within the image of parallel foreign relations, I hope the book will give a coherent view of this movement – more than 50 years old – through individual but connected accounts, and that it will provide a complement to the on-going narrative about Canada-Cuba relations.

Cuba solidarity continues to be work in progress. It is part of the larger human pursuit for social justice and the meaning of true solidarity.

References

August, Arnold (2013). *Cuba and its Neighbours –
    Democracy in Motion*. Halifax, Winnipeg: Fernwood
    Publishing; London, New York: Zed Books.
Blanchfield, Mike (2013). Baird to raise Canada's concern over ties
    between Iran and Venezuela on visit to Caracas. *National Post,
    Canadian Press*. http://news.nationalpost.com/2013/02/17/

baird-to-raise-canadas-concern-over-ties-between-iran-and-venezuela-on-visit-to-caracas/ Retrieved August 24, 2013.

Bolender, Keith (2012). *Cuba under Siege: American Policy, the Revolution and Its People*. Basingstoke, Hampshire: Palgrave Macmillan.

Bow, Brian and Patrick Lennox (2008). *An Independent Foreign Policy for Canada?: Challenges and Choices for the Future*. Toronto: University of Toronto Press, Scholarly Publishing Division.

Brenner, Philip, Marguerite Rose Jiménez, John M. Kirk and William M. LeoGrande (Eds.) (2008). *A Contemporary Cuba Reader: Reinventing the Revolution*. Lanham: Rowan & Littlefield Publishers, Inc.

CIA (n.d.). *The World Factbook*. https://www.cia.gov/library/publications/the-world-factbook/fields/2034.html#155. Retrieved April 17, 2014.

Clarkson, Stephen (Ed.) (1968). *An Independent Foreign Policy for Canada? The University League for Social Reform*. Toronto: McClelland and Stewart.

De Vos, Pol, et al. (2007). Cuba's International Cooperation in Health: an Overview. *International Journal of Health Services*, Volume 37, Number 4, Pages 761–776

Enciclopedia Cubana en la Red (n.d.). Colaboración Médica Cubana. *EcuRed* http://www.ecured.cu/index.php/Colaboración_Médica_Cubana. Retrieved April 17, 2014.

Entwistle, Mark (2009). Canada-Cuba Relations: A Multiple-Personality Foreign Policy. In Robert Wright and Lana Wylie (Eds.), *Our Place in the Sun: Canada and Cuba in the Castro Era*. Toronto: University of Toronto Press.

Fowler, Michael Ross and Julie Marie Bunck (1995). *Law, Power, and the Sovereign State: The Evolution and Application of the Concept of Sovereignty*. The Pennsylvania State University Press.

Franklin, Jane (1997). *Cuba and the United States: A Chronological History*. Melbourne, New York: Ocean Press.

Gosse, Van (1993). *Where the Boys are: Cuba, Cold War America and the Making of a New Left.* London: Verso.

Government of Canada (February 2013). *Canada-Cuba Relations.* http://www.canadainternational.gc.ca/ cuba/bilateral_relations_bilaterales/canada_cuba. aspx?menu_id=7. Retrieved April 13, 2014.

Government of Canada, Foreign Affairs, Trade and Development Canada (2013). *Baird to Travel to Latin America: Promoting and Protecting Canadian Interests and Values.* http://www.interna-tional.gc.ca/media/aff/news-communiques/2013/02/13a. aspx?lang=eng. Retrieved August 23, 2013.

Government of Canada, Foreign Affairs, Trade and Development Canada. *About the Department.* http://www.international.gc.ca/ department-ministere/index.aspx. Retrieved August 15, 2013.

Hofstadter, Richard (1996). Cuba, the Philippines, and Manifest Destiny. In Richard Hofstadter, *The Paranoid Style in American Politics: And Other Essays.* Cambridge: Harvard University Press. Reprint edition.

Huish, Robert (2008). *Going where no doctor has gone before: The place of Cuba's Latin American School of Medicine in building health care capacity for Ecuador.* PhD dissertation. Simon Fraser University, Burnaby, British Columbia, Canada.

Huish, Robert (2013). *Where No Doctor Has Gone Before: Cuba's Place in the Global Health Landscape.* Waterloo: Wilfrid Laurier University Press.

Huish, Robert and Jerry Spiegel (2008). Integrating health and human security into foreign policy: Cuba's surprising success. *The International Journal of Cuban Studies* Volume 1 Issue 1 June 2008.

Huish, Robert and John M. Kirk (2007). Cuban Medical Internationalism and the Development of the Latin American School of Medicine. *Latin American Perspectives*, 34; 77

Ignatieff, Michael (Ed) (2005). *American Exceptionalism and Human Rights*. Princeton: Princeton University Press.

Infomed (n.d.). *Historia de la ELAM*. http://instituciones.sld.cu/ elam/historia-de-la-elam/. Retrieved April 17, 2014.

Kilibarda, Kole (2008). *Canadian and Israeli Defense -- Industrial and Homeland Security Ties: An Analysis*. Queen's University, Surveillance Studies Centre, The New Transparency Project, Working Paper II, IRSP IV, November 2008.

Kirk, John M. (2012). An Extraordinary Success - Medical Internationalism in Cuba. *Counterpunch* - http:// www.counterpunch.org/2012/12/14/medical-inter- nationalism-in-cuba/. Retrieved April 17, 2014.

Kirk, John M. and H. Michael Erisman (2009). *Cuban Medical Internationalism: Origins, Evolution, and Goals*. Basingstoke, Hampshire: Palgrave Macmillan.

Kirk, John M. and Peter McKenna (1997). *Canada-Cuba Relations: The other good neighbor policy*. Gainesville: University Press of Florida.

LeoGrande, William M. (2013). The Cuba Lobby. *Foreign Policy Magazine*. http://www.foreignpolicy.com/ articles/2013/04/11/the_cuba_lobby_jay_z?wp_ login_redirect=0. Retrieved May 12, 2013.

McEvoy-Levy, Siobhan (2001). *American Exceptionalism and U.S. Foreign Policy: Public Diplomacy at the End of the Cold War*. Basingstoke, Hampshire: Palgrave Macmillan.

McKenna, Peter and John M. Kirk (2008). Sleeping with an Elephant. In Philip Brenner, Marguerite Rose Jiménez, John M. Kirk and William M. LeoGrande (Eds.), *A Contemporary Cuba Reader: Reinventing the Revolution*. Lanham: Rowan & Littlefield Publishers, Inc.

McKenna, Peter and John M. Kirk (2009). Canadian-Cuban Relations: Muddling through the 'Special Period'. In Robert Wright and

Lana Wylie (Eds.), *Our Place in the Sun: Canada and Cuba in the Castro Era*. Toronto: University of Toronto Press.

McKenna, Peter (2013, February). Canada should engage Cuba. *The Chronicle Herald, Opinions*. http:// thechronicleherald.ca/opinion/696859-canada-should-engage-cuba. Retrieved April 17, 2014.

Ministerio de Relaciones Exteriores de Cuba (n.d.). *Ministerio*. MINREX. http://www.cubaminrex. cu/es/ministerio. Retrieved April 13, 2014.

National Security Archive (2001, April 30). Pentagon Proposed Pretexts for Cuba Invasion. The George Washington University. Digital document. http://www2.gwu.edu/~nsarchiv/news/20010430/. Retrieved April 17, 2014.

Nieto, Clara (2003). *Masters of War: Latin America and U.S. aggression from the Cuban revolution through the Clinton years*. New York: Seven Stories Press.

Obama, Barack (2013). Transcript: President Obama's Address To The Nation On Syria. http://www.npr. org/2013/09/10/221186456/transcript-president-obamas-address-to-the-nation-on-syria. Retrieved September 11, 2013.

Organization of American States (1993). *Charter of the Organization of American States* (A-41). https://www.oas. org/dil/treaties_A-41_Charter_of_the_Organization_ of_American_States.htm. Retrieved March 30, 2014.

Pagliccia, Nino (2008). Solidarity Organizations and Friendship Groups: Internationalist Volunteer Work Brigades and People-to-People Ties. In Anthoni Kapcia and Alexander I. Gray (Eds.), *The Changing Dynamic of Cuban Civil Society*. Gainesville: University Press of Florida.

Parliament of Canada (2006). Canadian Arctic Sovereignty. *Library of Parliament*. http://www.parl.gc.ca/Content/LOP/research-publications/prb0561-e.htm. Retrieved April 17, 2014.

Putnam, Robert D. (1988). Diplomacy and Domestic Politics: The Logic of Two-Level games. *International Organization*, 42, no. 3: 427-60.

Saney, Isaac (2009). Homeland of humanity: Internationalism within the Cuban revolution. *Latin American Perspectives* 36 (1), pp. 111-123

SOA Watch (2014, March). *About SOA Watch*. http://www. soaw.org/about-us. Retrieved April 13, 2014.

Sweig, Julia E. (2009). *Cuba: What Everyone Needs to Know*. Oxford: Oxford University Press.

Weeks, William E. (1996). *Building the continental empire: American expansion from the Revolution to the Civil War*. Ivan R. Dee, Publisher. ISBN 9781566631358.

Weisbrot, Mark (2013, August 5). The more nefarious U.S. foreign policy, the more it relies on media complicity. *The Guardian*. http://www.theguardian.com/commentisfree/2013/aug/05/ media-complicity-us-foreign-policy. Retrieved April 17, 2014.

World Market Index (n.d.). World GDP (Gross Domestic Product). http://www.indexq.org/economy/ gdp.php. Retrieved April 17, 2014.

Wright, Cynthia (2009). Between nation and Empire: The Fair Play for Cuba Committees and the Making of Canada-Cuba Solidarity in the early 1960s. In Robert Wright and Lana Wylie (Eds.), *Our Place in the Sun – Canada and Cuba in the Castro Era*. Toronto: University of Toronto Press.

Wright, Robert (2009). 'Northern Ice': Jean Chrétien and the failure of Constructive Engagement in Cuba. In Robert Wright and Lana Wylie (Eds.), *Our Place in the Sun – Canada and Cuba in the Castro Era*. Toronto: University of Toronto Press.

Zinn, Howard (2005). *The Power and the Glory. Myths of American exceptionalism*. http://bostonreview.net/ zinn-power-glory. Retrieved August 10, 2013.

Chapter 1

Exhilaration, Hope and Inspiration: the Sixties in Cuba through a Canadian's Eyes

LISA MAKARCHUK

In 1960, when C. Wright Mills published *Listen, Yankee: the Revolution in Cuba* and both Jean-Paul Sartre and Bertrand Russell came out solidly in support of the revolution, I was one of a young generation that was curious and searching, groomed by a Cold War atmosphere that many citizens rejected. Growing up with MAD (Mutually-Assured Destruction) with the foreboding shadow of the mushroom cloud hanging over us, we perked up our ears at the distant drumming of new ideas for a better life that was emanating from Cuba, and many of us were very receptive to them. There was something delectably and unspeakably daring about a small number of dedicated men and women being able to take on a national government supported by a powerful neighbour - and win! Many Canadians such as I were ready to embrace the rebels' victory in Cuba. About 3,000 *barbudos* (bearded ones) from the Sierra Maestra Mountains had overcome an army of 80,000 regulars who had been trained and equipped by the U.S.

Arriving in Havana in May 1961, I found people there from various parts of the world, mainly Latin America, many of whom had been exiled from their own countries. A large number of Cubans had returned home from the U.S. By October, I was translating, editing, and broadcasting news, interviewing guests, and hosting a midnight jazz program that featured commentary between selections of music at a long wave radio station. For a child of rural Saskatchewan, this opportunity was akin to manna from heaven. Having arrived shortly after the Bay of Pigs invasion,

Lisa Makarchuk

I had unwittingly stepped into a steaming cauldron of energy and activity in a country that appeared to be one big school and provided no end of topics for commentary in my radio broadcasts.

The Literacy Campaign

In Cuba, a country of six million people then, over one in five could not read or write. Jose Marti's words, "To be educated is to be free," echoed in the campaign's aims to wipe out illiteracy and to educate over a million people to a grade three level. An army of approximately one hundred thousand teachers, made up of volunteers of all ages, took part in this most noble of tasks. The volunteer teachers were of all ages and social groups but it was mainly students from ages twelve to eighteen that went into the countryside where most of the illiteracy existed. They were each armed with a guidebook, a notebook, a set of lessons, and a lantern for use in the countryside that was mostly without electricity. In urban areas, parks were filled with tables of people learning to read and write. Peasants, workers, seniors, and others all over the country who had never had the opportunity to learn were now not only learning to read and write but were giving lessons that would last a lifetime to the young people. The volunteer teachers eventually identified and bonded with what used to be the poverty-ridden underbelly of their society, recognizing for the first time its terrible insecurity and exhausting labour.

Many of those leaving the big cities for the countryside had never been away from home. They bid good-bye to their tearful parents in Havana and travelled to their destinations, often in isolated areas. They had to travel on the backs of trucks or mules crossing roads that were rutted or washed out. When they arrived at their destinations, they would live with the peasant families, working with them during the day and holding classes in the evening.

At first, some peasants were suspicious of the attention they were getting from the new government but soon the young people came to be seen as heroes and were treated like family members. As the arriving teachers settled into the various *bohíos* (peasant huts made of thatch), many of which were in the mountains, they had to cope with overwhelming loneliness, and confront superstitions and - in some areas - indigenous practices.

The usually dark countryside began to be lit up by the teachers' lantern lights shining through the windows of the *bohíos* - a poignant symbol of the new enlightenment entering everyone's lives.

The Year of Literacy, as 1961 was known in Cuba, had its share of heroes and martyrs. Early in the year, several young volunteer teachers and their students were tortured and killed by roving counter-revolutionary bands. The teaching brigades were named after one of those killed: Conrado Benitez, tortured and then murdered at eighteen years of age. These horrendous crimes were committed to frighten parents into recalling their children from the countryside and, thus, wrecking the campaign.

Of course, there were a few young people who returned to Havana before their three-month stay was completed; others had to go back to join their parents' exodus to Florida. Some never returned having been drowned in rivers or killed in accidents. While a few of the adult students did not have the capacity to learn, the vast majority of the peasants and urban poor took on the challenge of learning to read and write and became a fount of creative energy and full-fledged participants in the revolution. The literacy campaign was deemed spectacularly successful by international organizations such as the United Nations Educational, Scientific and Cultural Organization and regarded as a model for other countries (Lakhani 2010). By

Lisa Makarchuk

December 22, 1961, Cuba declared itself a country free of illiteracy - the first in the Americas - and every region had a school.[1]

Pro- and Anti-Reform

Entering into this world, I at first wondered, who could ever be against teaching people to read and write? Who would be against providing a daily litre of milk to all children under the age of seven? Who could be against providing those children in the countryside with shoes so that half of them would not die from parasites before the age of six? Who could be against the opening of new schools where before there were none? Putting teachers back to work and educating new ones? Who could be against bringing in the forgotten ones in isolated areas, ignored even by census takers, to rejoin their country and participate in its development? Who would be against lighting up the countryside where it would go dark after the cane-cutting season was over when wages dried up and there was no more oil for the lamps? The anticipation, excitement, and exhilaration over resolving these problems and building a new society, as was taking place before my eyes, were overwhelming.

While a vast majority was in favour of these upcoming reforms, others (many – though not all - of the rich and privileged) were not only averse to re-distributing the riches of the country but, even more importantly, were livid over losing their positions of influence. "I would rather pump gas in Miami than take orders from these *campesinos* (peasants)," one of them said to me.

Professionals, top and middle managers, technicians, business people, and the wealthy were leaving town. Maids disappeared from households

---

1   Conditions were then set up to this day for everyone with a third grade level and up to pursue studies free of charge up to and including the University level.

having found better employment elsewhere and *señoras* complained to me that good help was hard to find. Those whom I met appeared to be suffering from a great deal of anxiety over uncertainty but were also quite sure that the U.S. government would find a way to stop the *locura* (madness) that was going on around them.

The Need for Revolution in the 1950s

People I met spoke of their intense hatred of the U.S.-supported Batista regime, under which anything and everything was for sale in Havana. The Mafia built larger and more luxurious casinos and hotels while running gambling and prostitution operations. Daytime Havana streets with the detritus of life were sun-drenched while at night they were lit up with gaudy, glaring neon lights sometimes hiding the city's underbelly of violence, exploitation, and brutality. The toll gates, which today still stand (unused) after passing through the tunnel from Havana on the way to Varadero, remain as mute reminders of a corrupt past where privileged Batista's son-in-law pocketed all their revenues.

About twenty thousand people, many of them students, were arrested, tortured, and killed by Batista's police for engaging in "subversive" activity. Bodies would be left in ditches or roadsides where modest markers were later erected to show where they had been found. There was a generalized fear of the police; beatings by them were listed in the "In Cuba" section of the weekly magazine *Bohemia*.

Fulgencio Batista had come to power in a coup on March 10, 1952. Although he had declared himself President, Batista, due to his ancestry, was not allowed in the "Whites Only" premises of some of the wealthy clubs. In other cases, no Cubans at all could enter. Even well-to-do Cubans felt undervalued as foreigners were running many enterprises and viewed the Cubans as a lazy people who could not get things done.

Lisa Makarchuk

To the U.S. government Batista was our man in Havana. He was given ample armaments, military training, money and the run of Cuba. Privately financed gangs ran amok at the bidding of the large landowners. Folklore tells of the sons of the head of one of these gangs playing football with the skulls of their father's victims. Jesús Sosa Blanco ruled Oriente province as a private preserve of the United Fruit Company. The company enjoyed a tax-free status and many sweetheart deals. Later in the so-called show trials victims or their relatives were able to confront, accuse, and witness against men such as Sosa Blanco, some of whom were then expeditiously executed by firing squad. When Fidel Castro and others attacked the Moncada barracks on July 26, 1953 most of the deaths resulted from Batista's police torturing to death persons, mostly young, who were taken prisoner after the assault. Horrendous stories of what was done to these idealistic young people also made their way into common folklore. Once the revolution had triumphed, the public wanted and needed a settling of accounts, a show of justice being done for the pain, humiliation, and suffering of the past. While these show trials, as they were referred to by big media in Canada and the U.S., brought a lot of bad publicity to the revolution, in Cuba they established the revolution as a bastion of protection, justice, and hope.

In the countryside, a very small but very rich group of families owned about half of the arable land. While 150,000 families of sugarcane cutters lived as tenants, another 200,000 families lived as squatters and worked sporadically as day labourers. Some families in the countryside were huge, at times numbering over twenty children. Without family planning information or education, women were akin to brood mares providing generations of cheap labour for which the beneficiaries – the landowners - did not have to take any responsibility. This information provided to me palpable evidence of the connection between poverty, exploitation, illiteracy, and women's suffering.

Revolution Manifested

On December 2, 1956, eighty-five men, launched on the boat "Granma" from Mexico, landed at Alegría de Pio, an unintended spot on Cuba's southern shores. With Fidel Castro, his brother Raúl, *Che* Guevara, and Camilo Cienfuegos among them, these men began the armed fight against Batista. After their first skirmish with government forces three days after landing, only a dozen rebels were still alive. In due time, the rebel forces grew, enrolling many of the local *campesinos*, and began to broadcast to Cubans with their clandestine radio station, *Radio Rebelde,* which relayed a steady stream of information to offset lies broadcast by the official pro-government media. By the time a general strike was called in 1958 in cities across the country, the loosely-formed *Movimiento 26 de Julio* (26 of July Movement, shortened to M-26-7), aided by the March 13 Revolutionary Directorate and members of the Popular Socialist Party (Communists), was able to call on an endless well of support.

Having taken Santiago de Cuba and making it the temporary capital on January 1, 1959, Fidel Castro's Liberty Column, as it was called, headed for Havana. The old political parties (never prohibited) simply dissolved. By January 4, workers were told to end their general strike and go back to work as all arms and military installations were in the hands of the revolutionary forces. The power of a people united in support would become an unforgettable historical lesson that Cuba taught the world in those days.

Arriving in Havana, Fidel Castro pronounced a speech to the people of Cuba on January 8, 1959. During this speech, as fate would have it, a white dove flew down and rested on his shoulder signalling to many steeped in the Afro-Cuban religions that the saints had produced the anointed one whom they would protect. Despite 635 documented attempts on Fidel Castro's life, he has outlasted almost a dozen U.S. Presidents, so one cannot help but wonder.

Lisa Makarchuk

Deemed to be a logical transitional figure between the past and the future, a former judge under Batista, Manuel Urrutia, assumed the Presidency but resigned five months later, replaced by Osvaldo Dorticós who remained President until 1976.

Beginning of the Revolution - Defiance and Reforms

If they could not install their own man in Havana then, the U.S. government must have assumed that they could, at least, buy the acquiescence of this apparently new kind of leader that had emerged in Latin America. It did not take them long, however, to realize that the men and women of the revolution were not for sale.

In April 1959, on one of their very early trips abroad, Fidel Castro and his entourage sought an audience with President Eisenhower. He refused to see them, going golfing instead, and sent Vice-President Nixon to meet with them. According to a second hand account of this meeting, Nixon waved a checkbook and asked the entourage, "How much?" Overcome by the insult of this question, Camilo Cienfuegos, one of the most popular of the leaders of the revolution, reportedly had to be restrained from attacking Nixon. That question, however, crystallized the deep divide between the two parties in that room: one representing the old way of doing business in Latin America, the other representing a new kind of leader - firm believer in the sovereignty of his country, its independence and its self-determination, and proud of his mission.

Many terrorist acts against the revolution, emanating mainly from Florida, have resulted in the deaths of thousands of persons and injuring or maiming thousands more. One of the worst occurred on March 4, 1960 when the steamship La Coubre, bearing arms from Belgium to Cuba, had on board two large explosions in Havana harbour; the second and more sinister one killed volunteers who had come to rescue those injured after the first explosion. More than a hundred people were killed and over two hundred were injured. In his speech after these explosions, Fidel Castro coined the phrase *"Patria o Muerte"* (homeland or death), and Alberto Korda, a well-known professional photographer in Havana, captured the ubiquitous and now iconic photo of *Che* Guevara standing beside Fidel during that speech.

The La Coubre explosion was attributed to the CIA, though its French owners imposed a 150-year restriction on releasing the complete file of the investigation into this disaster. It sits in a strongbox of a French maritime foundation.

Diplomatic Relations Between the U.S. and Cuba Broken and Bay of Pigs Attack

By January 3, 1961 the U.S. had broken off diplomatic relations with Cuba, closed its Embassy in Havana, and withdrawn its diplomats and its recognition of the Cuban government. The Swiss Embassy took over as a conduit to deal with affairs arising between Cuba and the U.S. Cuba, too, broke its relations with the U.S. and, alert to any invasion, Cuba's Council of Ministers specified that this break was not with the people of the U.S. but only with their government.

On April 17, 1961, shortly before my arrival in Havana, an invasion force of 1,500 men, trained by the U.S., with its air and naval support, attacked Cuba at *Playa Girón* (Bay of Pigs) and was subsequently defeated within seventy-two hours. In this attack, the people's militia played a heroic role in stopping the first incursions. The U.S. government denied participation in this venture and, consequently, the body of a U.S. pilot was reclaimed only after decades in cold storage in Cuba, because officially he was not there. Many of the invaders, taken prisoner, claimed to be chiefs on the expedition and all those captured were eventually sent back to the U.S. in exchange for baby food and powdered milk.

Cuba, the U.S. and the Central Intelligence Agency

After the ignominious failure at the Bay of Pigs, President Kennedy's focus turned toward organizing activities inside Cuba to overthrow the government by weakening the economy, promoting discontent, and trying to sow division. Basing this on information reported from recently declassified documents, this action went under the name of Operation Mongoose beginning on March 14, 1962. Two days later, President Kennedy approved the preparations to create the conditions that would justify armed intervention of Cuba. About five months later, President Kennedy became convinced there was no way that the Cuban government could be overthrown from within the country. Mongoose was now authorized to carry out more aggressive actions from outside Cuba.

When I arrived in Cuba, I soon became aware of a constant alert to the threat of foreign invasion. Some people argued that this was simply a tactic to distract people from demanding elections. Again, recent documents released by the U.S. State Department confirm that the threat was indeed real. At my workplace, tension was heightened when news arrived that a Cuban sentry, at the boundary between the U.S.-controlled Guantanamo Bay Naval Base and the rest of the country, was shot at and killed.

Reforms

Agrarian Reform

May 17, 1959 marked the First Law of Agrarian Reform, fulfilling the revolutionaries' promises to the *campesinos* of the mountains that first harboured and protected Fidel Castro and the rest of the rebels. To the chagrin of Fidel's own sister, the first land deeds handed out by her brother were to lands belonging to their father. Strategically, the vision was to develop cooperatives organized by small landholders themselves and large-scale agriculture through collective farms.

One of the first tasks of the new revolutionary government was to replace *bohíos* with more formal dwellings. By 1960, more than twelve thousand *bohíos* had disappeared, replaced with simple but sturdy dwellings with concrete floors and windows. Clearly, a mammoth job awaited the new government in confronting the housing shortage. The chosen priority was to concentrate the government's resources in the countryside to answer its crying needs but it also left Havana, 'the engorging monster' as some called it, short-changed, its infrastructure deteriorating and left unattended for many years.

Urban Reforms

With the passage of the Urban Reform Act, rental payments of tenants were halved. By October 14, 1960, all rentals had reverted into ownership; i.e. tenants became owners of their apartments. During my stay in Havana, my room became my property, which I signed over to others upon leaving Cuba. As a foreigner, I technically could not own property in Cuba but this question would be left for future resolving.

Social Reforms

The first two years of revolution saw culture for the masses established as a priority. The Cuban Institute of Cinematographic Arts and Industry was set up in March 1959 under the leadership of Alfredo Guevara (no relation to *Che*) who summed up his approach thus: "Our artists must be non-conformists or we will have no artists." Foreign movies by the foremost directors of the day such as Ingmar Bergman and Luís Buñuel were strong favourites of an appreciative new public. Also, an avalanche of discussion and argument was unleashed. For example, some criticized Bergman's films for being "pessimistic" or "too individualistic;" some condemned the film classic *La Dolce Vita* as decadent art. The music of the Beatles was banned for a short while, though a statue of John Lennon now sits on a bench in a public park in Havana.

The *Imprenta Nacional* (National Publisher) was also established in 1960. Newsprint that had mostly been imported from the U.S. disappeared but was soon replaced by newsprint made from sugarcane in Cuba or imported from the Soviet Union. It seemed that books, sold at a very low cost, became *de rigueur* in most homes - in many they were welcomed for the first time.

Radio Rebelde and Radio Havana Cuba had their own studios. Alicia Alonso, the prima ballerina of Cuba, was personally approached by Fidel Castro to set up the National Ballet of Cuba with adequate funding promised by the government. Among others, this company has since flourished winning great acclaim abroad and at home where people go to see its performances for a tiny fraction of what ballet performances normally cost in Canada or the U.S.

Personal income tax was discontinued. After all, the land was fertile and the factories were now in the hands of the people and Cubans believed they would create enough wealth to be able to provide the populace with its basic needs. They would eliminate unemployment and economic crises. This general optimism was a potent vision that affected most people living in Cuba at that time: after a few years, Cuba would be like a Garden of Eden evolving its people into the most cultured in the world.

Elena Díaz González, a Cuban from that sixties generation, explains: "It was easy to think like that...with the blue of the sky, blue-green of the water and elegant royal palms in almost every glance. We were poor, we had no meat, lost weight, worked seven days a week but we were young, healthy, energetic, with so much to do, impassioned by whatever tasks were before us. We were given over entirely to the cause of a new society and the new person...We were a part of the Revolution and the Revolution was us..."

In that first year of revolution, army barracks, a grisly reminder of past brutality, were renovated and transformed into schools. Private clubs and beaches were opened to the public. Ten thousand new classrooms were opened and, in the rural areas, five thousand young teachers started classes. The casinos were closed and about 60,000 sex workers were given opportunities and scholarships to learn skills and integrate themselves into the revolution. The Cuban Federation of Women (*Federación de Mujeres Cubanas*-FMC) encouraged women in general to enter the work force. Old values and attitudes were surprisingly quick to change: boots for volunteer work replaced daytime stilettos and women's clothing became looser and more comfortable. The conventional idea that men only could be the heads of households was discarded, while the discounting of single mothers and single women in general, the emergence of divorce, women's right to choose regarding pregnancies, and a more positive view of interracial relationships were slowly gaining majority acceptance. The FMC succeeded in getting the government to pass a housework law in 1967, which demanded equal responsibility from both parents in the running of a household and in rearing of children. There is no record of a wife taking her husband to court for reneging on carrying out his share of household duties; however, the law assaulted the nation's patriarchal state of affairs. Everyone did not embrace these new values easily. Even Fidel apparently was given a metaphorical wrist slap by the FMC for inopportune remarks he would make at times regarding women's issues. (The Revolution was teaching him, too). Women integrated into the work force and, albeit reluctantly, husbands undertook "women's work" more and more making sure that they were not within the view of their neighbours as they did it.

Nationalizations and Blockade of Cuba

On July 2, 1960, after the nationalization of some U.S. businesses, President Eisenhower substantially reduced the Cuban sugar quota eventually suspending it entirely. This was Cuba's one and only big cash crop. The USSR stepped in to buy the sugar in exchange for its oil. The U.S.-owned oil refineries refused to process oil from the USSR; the Cuban government nationalized them. First-hand information disclosed that some refinery managers were ordered by their parent companies to destroy the workings of the refineries before leaving Cuba. By September 17, all U.S. banks were nationalized and by October 13, 382 big enterprises, mainly U.S.-owned, were also nationalized. While Cuba had arranged with Canada and other countries for a smooth take-over of foreign-owned property that was being nationalized, the U.S. never agreed to these negotiations.

President Kennedy signed the order for the total commercial blockade of Cuba on February 3, 1962, to start at 12:01 a.m., February 7, closing the door on a 250-year trade history dating back to the time of the Thirteen Colonies. The U.S. referred to these sanctions as an "embargo." On February 4, 1962, over one million people, including myself, converged on Revolution Square to hear the Second Declaration of Havana, which analyzed the political situation in Latin America and outlined Cuba's response to its exclusion from the Organization of American States (OAS) and the imposition of the blockade. Meantime U.S. government circles went on to deny all financing or sending of money to Cuba, thus reducing monetary incomes and real salaries in order to provoke hunger and desperation.

Exclusion of Cuba from the Organization of American States (OAS)

The U.S. government pursued a relentless policy of trying to isolate Cuba. One of these opportunities came with the OAS meeting held in Punta del Este on January 21, 1962 (shortly before the Second Declaration of Havana). The U.S. tried but could not receive an agreement for its proposed sanctions against Cuba. A statement was passed, however, that Marxist-Leninist ideology was incompatible with the principles of the inter-American system; this was the basis for Cuba's exclusion from the OAS. Canada was not an OAS member at this time.

Shortages and Rationing

A consequence of the blockade was to experience shortages of everything immediately after its announcement. Higher employment meant greater consumption but productivity dropped. Spare parts for repairs in factories, garages and other enterprises became unavailable. Food shortages first showed up in restaurants where smirking waiters would reply, *"No hay* (Don't have it)" to most requests for items printed on the menu. At my radio station we began to share stories of great meals in our past. To solve the food shortages Cuba decided on rationing, still in place to this day, in order to ensure basic food sustenance to all.

Lisa Makarchuk

One of the Jewels in the Crown
of the Cuban Revolution

Cuba's healthcare system has received international acclaim. Life expectancy has risen from fifty-seven years of age before the revolution to seventy-nine today. The mortality rate of babies went from thirty-two deaths per thousand live births before the revolution to about five presently, better than the U.S. rate. After the revolution succeeded, many doctors, mostly based in Havana, left the country; the government initiated a fast-track program to graduate doctors who would spend at least two years in the countryside after graduating. By 2011, Cuba had close to eighty thousand doctors (Oficina Nacional de Estadística e Información, Cuba 2012).

Not as well known is the internationalist character of the Cuban healthcare system aiming to assist people in other parts of the world. This policy of sharing whatever Cuba has with over sixty countries in the world has made a profound impact on the lives of millions of people. The first medical solidarity contingent left Cuba in 1963 when it sent 29 doctors, 3 dentists, 15 nurses, and 8 medical technicians to Algeria just after it declared its independence from France. There was no tangible benefit for Cuba and involved substantial material costs.

Since the Chernobyl disaster in 1986, Cuba has treated 26,000 children harmed by its effects most of them at no charge. After Hurricane Mitch, the Latin American School of Medicine (ELAM) was set up to bring students from affected countries to train as doctors and later expanded the program to include students from other countries including the U.S. and one from Canada. In 2011, forty students from the U.S. graduated with the promise to work in poor/isolated areas in their country. The role of Cuba's medical personnel during the cholera outbreak in Haiti soon after the earthquake was imperative to prevent the spread of disease. Within hours of Hurricane Katrina in 2005, Cuba offered its 1,500-strong brigade of doctors to the U.S. to help the people of New Orleans; President Bush never responded to this offer.

Twenty-six Latin American and Caribbean countries have sent patients by the thousands to Cuba or have been treated by Cuban doctors in their own countries to restore their eyesight in a project known as *Operación Milagro* (Operation Miracle). Mario Terán, the Bolivian soldier, who shot *Che* Guevara in 1967, recently had his eyes operated on by Cuban doctors in a project his victim would have been the first to endorse.

Author's Observations

The Cuban Revolution struck a responsive chord with millions around the world, including myself. It confirmed that solving the problems of poverty and exploitation is possible through government planning harmonized with the will of a people united in purpose.

Sharing major historical moments with the people of Cuba was a privilege for me. Not only was this new world intoxicating, electrifying, and unifying, it was a *"revolución con pachanga"* (a revolution with a party). I could always hear music outside the window of my office coming from somewhere. It was the best kind of social whirlwind for me in which to spend five years during my twenties.

Notwithstanding imposing difficult years of scarcity on Cuba through the blockade, coupled with unrelenting military, economic, and social threats, the U.S. government has not prevented Cuba from achieving universal literacy and health care. In hindsight one could point to some mistakes made and dubious decisions taken by the Cuban government. At the 6th Congress of the Communist Party of Cuba in April 2011 Raúl Castro reported on the approved Guidelines of the Economic and Social Policy for Cuba indicating that these were necessary in order to update the economic model by "streamlining the bloated payrolls in the public

Lisa Makarchuk

sector", "increasing labour efficiency and productivity", by reducing subsidies, and by scaling down an "excessive centralized economy" that stifled the "development of the productive forces" (Castro 2011: n.p.). However these have not prevented Cuba from also achieving a sustainable agriculture, a flourishing biotechnology industry, an awareness for historical preservation, and a continuously changing and developing economy despite setbacks, as well as the profound dignity and pride that most Cubans have in their country and in their constant search for a truly democratic and equitable society.

I feel fortunate to have witnessed and taken part in this social experiment of building a new society. The world must applaud Cuba's survival, preserving its independence intact, for over five decades fraught with threats. Who would not feel solidarity with a people so intent on building their country in the face of such overwhelming challenges?

The revolution inspired me to work in solidarity groups not only regarding Cuba but other countries as well. In the 1960s Franco was still in power in Spain and Salazar in Portugal. We worked on the "*Solidaridad*" and "*Amnestía*" conferences in defence of political prisoners in those countries. Both conferences took place in Toronto. Later we organized the "Hemispheric Conference to End the Viet Nam War" in Montréal. I volunteered as a fundraiser and manager for a trade union newspaper and organized a First People's Film Festival.

The "*años de las vacas gordas*" (Years of the Fat Cows, during the Eighties), as they were known, came to a screeching halt with the disintegration of the Soviet Union in the early nineties. The ensuing "Special Period" tested the ingenuity and resilience of the Cuban people but it also demanded solidarity from around the world. Our subsequent activities in the Canadian-Cuban Friendship Association (CCFA) resulted in the organization of the First Canada-Cuba Solidarity Conference in Toronto followed by a second one in Havana. We broadened our outreach to include the City of Toronto, which declared the first Toronto-Cuba Friendship Day that has continued as an annual event since 1995. It was a lump-in-the-throat feeling to see the Cuban flag raised for the first time in Nathan Phillips Square as the national anthems of Canada and Cuba were sung.

Presently our greatest challenge is to gain freedom for the political prisoners known as the Cuban Five, three of whom are currently still in prison in the United States while two, René González and Fernando González, are now back in Cuba. In Toronto, the Lawyers' Committee for the Anti-terrorist Cuban Five and the Friends of the Cuban Five Committee are now organized. It is always a source of pride to be a part of so many dedicated people who organize and move these activities forward toward more justice and more peace in the world.

Sources for this Chapter

Searching my memories of the sixties provided the skeleton for this chapter. The body was fleshed out with interviews with Cubans and information culled from various newspapers and journals, pamphlets, and books, listed below.

Bell Lara, José, Delia Luisa López and Tania Caram
    (2006). *Documentos de la Revolución Cubana 1959*.
    La Habana: Editorial de ciencias sociales..
_____ (2007). *Documentos de la Revolución Cubana 1960*.
    La Habana: Editorial de ciencias sociales.
_____ (2011). *Documentos de la Revolución Cubana 1963*.
    La Habana: Editorial de ciencias sociales.
Castro Ruz, Raúl (2011, April 16). Central Report to the 6th Congress
    of the Communist Party of Cuba. http://en.cubadebate.
    cu/opinions/2011/04/16/central-report-6th-congress-
    communist-party-cuba/ (Retrieved April 1, 2014)
Fair Play for Cuba Committee (June 1964). *The Real Cuba As
    Three Canadians Saw It*. http://www.socialisthistory.ca/
    Docs/1961-/Cuba/RealCuba.htm. Retrieved 17 April 2014.

García Luís, Julio (Ed.) (2005). *La Revolución Cubana - 45 grandes momentos*. Melbourne: Ocean Press.

Lakhani, Nina (2010). Latin lessons: What can we learn from the world's most ambitious literacy campaign? *The Independent*. http://www.independent.co.uk/news/world/americas/latin-lessons-what-can-we-learn-from-the-worldrsquos-most-ambitious-literacy-campaign-2124433.html. Retrieved 31 March 2014.

Oficina Nacional de Estadística e Información (2012). *Anuario Estadístico de Cuba 2011*. Edición 2012. Table 19.3. República de Cuba. http://www.one.cu/aec2011/esp/20080618_tabla_cuadro.htm. Retrieved 31 March 2014.

Sánchez Otero, Germán (2011). *El año de todos los sueños*. La Habana: Ediciones La Memoria Centro Cultural Pablo de la Torriente Brau..

Wright, Robert and Lana Wylie (Eds.) (2009). *Our Place in the Sun - Canada and Cuba in the Castro Era*. Toronto: University of Toronto Press.

Personal Interviews

Beatriz Díaz, professor, Chair Canadian Studies Centre, University of Havana.

Elena Díaz, Ph.D., professor, Facultad Latino Americana de Ciencias Sociales, University of Havana; member of the National Academy of Sciences in Cuba.

Chapter 2

Reaching Out and Building Friendship
– The Beginning of a Movement

ELIZABETH HILL

◇◇◇

Birth of the Movement

Canada was one of two countries, together with Mexico, in the hemi-sphere that maintained diplomatic relations with Cuba after the success of the Cuban Revolution in January 1959. Canadians who took excep-tion to the economic, cultural, and sometimes political domination of their own country by the United States, were impressed and encouraged by Cuba's determination to be truly sovereign and to use its resources and energies to provide fairly for the needs of all Cubans - starting with education, health and culture.

Soon after that January 1959, Canadians began organizing activities in solidarity and friendship with Cuba. Some outstanding Canadians made a personal commitment to support Cuba in its effort to build a different and more independent society by moving with their families to Cuba and participating directly in that effort. Many others added their energies and supporting voices in Canada by speaking up against measures the United States government was taking to overturn the will of the Cuban people.

On October 14, 1961 an organization of friendship with Cuba was founded in Vancouver and since then numerous solidarity organiza-tions have sprung up across Canada. The Canadian-Cuban Friendship Association (CCFA) of Vancouver may well be one of the first such organizations in the world that sprung up together with the Fair Play for Cuba Committees in the U.S. and Canada. The aims of the CCFA are to "promote friendship, respect, co-operation and solidarity between the peoples of Canada and Cuba" (CCFA-Vancouver n.d.). To this day it has maintained direct contact with the Cuban Institute of Friendship with the Peoples (*Instituto Cubano de Amistad con los Pueblos* - ICAP) based in Havana and, together with other supporting work, it organizes one or two "Friendship Tours" to Cuba each year providing the opportunity to many supporters to get to know the changing Cuban reality.

The early supporting role of the CCFA was extended occasionally to the crew of Cuban ships arriving in the port of Vancouver by organizing welcome socials and receptions for them. Recognizing and celebrating important Cuban national holidays, particularly those associated with landmark episodes of the Cuban Revolution such as the anniversary of the attack on the Moncada Garrison in Santiago de Cuba on July 26, 1953, have also showed solidarity with the Cuban Revolution.

And a no less important part of its work has always been the material support brought to Cuba by Canadian travellers. Considering that the U.S. blockade of Cuba extended to the academic and research areas, the CCFA encouraged supporters to take subscriptions to much-needed technical and medical journals to be forwarded to Cuba.

The full cruelty of the U.S. blockade was observed early on by CCFA members during a visit to the Abel Santamaría School for the Blind in Havana in the early 1970s. The visitors realized that the school could not buy Braille machines, as they were manufactured in the United States. Immediately the organization raised funds to buy the machines that cost about $200 each from a supplier in the U.S. and one by one they were brought to Cuba with delegations and friendly tourists. Eventually the CCFA of Toronto helped the Vancouver project by individually ordering the Braille machines from the U.S. and delivering them to Cuba. To this day the CCFA maintains a supporting role with the school for the blind in Havana (Canadian-Cuban Friendship Association -Vancouver n.d.).

In a letter to this author in May 1977, outlining the many activities of the Vancouver association, its then President Claude Crosby summed it all up stating: "It is all well worthwhile as the Cubans are the friendliest people in the world and totally devoted to making this a better world for all to live in!"

Solidarity Actions

On April 11, 1977 a group of 17 individuals met and established a group in Toronto similar to the one in Vancouver. A public launch was held on May 24 at the International Student Centre of the University of Toronto. Three singers of Inca folk songs entertained the guests, followed by a performance by a Chilean song group who were recent refugees from the repressive Pinochet dictatorship in Chile. This author spoke about the new CCFA organization and its plans for the future. A Cuban film was shown, followed by refreshments and dancing. The gathering lasted till three in the morning! It was a resounding success with 150 participants, three times more than expected, and established a strong membership base for the organization (Canadian-Cuban Friendship Association-Toronto n.d.).

CCFA membership is open to all Canadian residents who support the aims of the organizations. Currently it includes people from different points of view but sharing their solidarity for Cuba. On this broad basis, support has grown over the years There are several prominent Canadians actively involved, such as David Warner, former speaker of the Ontario Legislature; world renowned mathematician Lee Lorch; John Kirk, professor at Dalhousie University in Halifax; and Canadian Juno award winner and Officer of the Order of Canada Jane Bunnett, along with numerous other professionals, writers, actors, trade unionists, and elected officials.

From October 30 to November 6, 1977 the two CCFA organizations from Vancouver and Toronto participated in a delegation to Cuba where a protocol of friendship was agreed to and signed with ICAP. The accord formalized mutual exchanges and cooperation such as celebration of national holidays, exchange of books and materials, and the exchange of study groups and delegations. Based on this protocol the CCFA-Toronto outlined an ambitious plan of work for its first year that included the celebration of José Martí's birthday in January, the anniversary of the Bay of Pigs victory on April 19, and Cuba's National Day (Moncada day) on July 26. The first of many annual José Martí celebrations in Toronto was a Dinner and Dance at the Winchevsky Centre in North Toronto. The admission tickets were only $5.00, hardly enough to cover the costs, however, it was a sold out crowd that filled the hall. The guest speaker was, Gloria Shephard, a journalist who had written about the achievements of the Cuban healthcare system in spite of the challenges of the U.S. blockade. Everyone opened their wallets for a collection that raised over $500 to buy and send medical journals and subscriptions.

The next big event, and the beginning of an annual tradition, was Moncada Day to celebrate the 1953 attack on the Batista army barracks of the same name in Santiago de Cuba. The event was held in a community centre in Toronto. So many people arrived that many had to wait outside in the hot sun until someone left to make space. One of our volunteers brought out trays of cut up watermelon to offer those lining up.

Several cultural tours of Cuban musicians such as Noel Nicola, Vicente Fileau, and Sara González, were organized to different Canadian cities for the first time. The eight piece popular Cuban band *Grupo Moncada* made five tours to Canada, and performed at Expo in Vancouver in 1986. Cuban poet Pablo Armando Fernández did a five-week tour from Halifax to Vancouver, speaking at universities and social events. Numerous film festivals took place, sometimes with Cuban filmmakers such as Tomás Gutiérrez Alea to show Canadians Cuba's accomplishments through film.

On the political front, in 1981 the United States government under President Ronald Reagan tightened the blockade against Cuba and re-established the travel ban for Americans, and a military intervention was perceived as a possibility. That same year an epidemic of dengue fever affected more than 300,000 people, killing 156 including 101 children in Cuba. Cuba accused the United States of biological warfare, an accusation the U.S. denied.

Under the assumption that the United States was considering aggression against Cuba and Nicaragua that included a military invasion, after observing reports that U.S. forces in the region had been put on military alert, CCFA sent the following telegram to U.S. President Ronald Reagan on November 10, 1981: "Demand you abandon plans for military invasion of Cuba. The Caribbean is not a U.S. lake and any United States action there is a criminal violation of sovereignty and endangers peace in the Caribbean and the whole world. U.S. attempts to dictate its policies through blockades, economic blackmail, and even military aggression will fail now as they have in the past. World peace is at stake – hands off Cuba! Canadian-Cuban Friendship Association – Toronto."

In the same month, several Friendship organizations in Toronto organized a Hands Off Cuba demonstration at the U.S. consulate to condemn U.S. plans for military aggression against Cuba.

The Vancouver CCFA also sent a letter to Mark McGuigan, then Canadian Minister of External Affairs, about its concerns of possible U.S. military intervention against Cuba and Nicaragua, stating: "We are sure you must realize how tense and dangerous the situation is becoming in this area, and urge that you do everything possible in your official capacity to dissuade the United States government from taking any bellicose action."

A letter was then hand delivered to the U.S. Consulate from Vancouver CCFA President Peggy Chunn, "to convey our alarm about the tense and dangerous situation developing between the United States and the Latin American countries of Cuba and Nicaragua." It goes on to say: "Any military intervention or blockade initiated by you directly or otherwise, would create, in our opinion, a most dangerous situation and would further jeopardize world peace."

Western European friendship organizations also issued statements condemning the U.S.'s aggressive policy.

Over the years, friendship organizations were courageous and strong in their public protests and demonstrations to condemn U.S. policies on Cuba and to alert Canadians to the dangers of such policies and the need for recognizing Cuba's right to self-determination.

Expansion of the Movement

Many other friendship and solidarity groups have sprung up across the country, in Halifax, Hamilton, Kingston, Niagara, Ottawa, Windsor, Winnipeg, Calgary, Edmonton, and Victoria. Some have specific aims such as Free the Cuban Five campaign (see Chapter 5), sports exchanges, and gathering material aid for Cuba.

During the deep economic crisis in Cuba known as the Special Period in the early 1990s a group of activists who called themselves *Friendshipment* collected material donations across Canada such as powdered milk, medicines, computers, and school supplies to be shipped to Cuba. They continue working directly with the U.S.-based organization Pastors for Peace[1], which, beyond sending material aid to Cuba, aims to educate Americans about Cuba and openly challenges the U.S. policy that requires applying for a permit in order to travel to Cuba and bring goods. Another Canadian organization, Worker to Worker, is solely dedicated to exchanges between Canadian and Cuban unionists (see Chapter 6).

---

1   Pastors for Peace is an ecumenical agency whose mission is to help forward the struggles of oppressed peoples for justice and self-determination. (http://www. ifconews.org)

An organization in Québec, called *Carrefour Culturel de L'Amitié Québec-Cuba* (Cultural Crossroads of Friendship) was formed. It had a regular newsletter called "Québec-Cuba Sí!" and in 1979 joined a delegation with reps from Vancouver and Toronto and signed a similar protocol with ICAP.

Vancouver Communities in Solidarity with Cuba was organized in 2004 partly in response to U.S. President George W. Bush's increased aggression against Cuba. Wayne S. Smith wrote: "President George W. Bush then appointed a Commission for Assistance to a Free Cuba with the goals of bringing about 'an expeditious end of the dictatorship,' and developing a plan to achieve that goal. In May 2004, the Commission came out with a near-500-page plan whose basic premise was that the Castro regime was near collapse and that another shove or two would bring it down—a few more Radio Martí broadcasts, a few more travel restrictions, another economic sanction or two and it would all be over. The plan also read like a blueprint for an American occupation that would make the trains run on time, show the Cubans how to run their school systems and grow their crops—so much so that it offended many Cubans who read it, even those who didn't necessarily agree with the Castro government." (Smith 2006).

In 2002 the Canadian Network on Cuba (CNC) was formed bringing together different groups to coordinate solidarity efforts. Its mission is to strengthen friendship and solidarity between the peoples of Canada and Cuba. The CNC mission statement says:

> We are committed to the strengthening of friendship and solidarity between the peoples of Canada and Cuba. To this end, we work with the Cuban Institute of Friendship with the Peoples and (ICAP) and other international and national partners in order to promote

social, cultural, political and economic relations between Canada and Cuba on the basis of mutual respect and non-interference. We:

- initiate, co-ordinate and co-operate in cultural, educational, political and aid campaigns and projects involving Canada and Cuba.

- counter media and other distortions of Cuban reality by disseminating information about the achievements of the Cuban Revolution in areas such as education, public health, culture, democracy and human rights.

- work to improve Canadian foreign policy on Cuba (Canadian Network on Cuba n.d.).

In its coordinating role for national campaigns, the CNC has organized cross-country campaigns such as a very successful speaking tour of major cities in Canada with Aleida Guevara, a paediatrician and daughter of *Che* Guevara, and Irma González, the daughter of René González[2]. They presented the case of the Cuban Five to many who heard about them for the first time.

Another successful campaign initiated by the CNC was the fundraising for hurricane relief in 2004. Following three devastating hurricanes that hit the western part of Cuba the Canadian government announced $400,000 in relief, but refused to hand it over to the Cuban government as is usually done in disaster situations. Instead the relief was to be administered by a non-Cuban recipient. This was seen as a snub and deemed unacceptable by the Cuban government. The CNC decided

---

2   René González has since been released and is now living in Cuba. He speaks now for the release of his comrades still in prison.

to launch its own campaign to raise funds for hurricane relief with the hope of surpassing the amount offered by the Canadian government. The CNC not only succeeded in raising over $402,000 dollars from generous Canadians through individual donations, fundraising dinners, and other public events, but also delivered all funds raised to Cuban organizations.

The campaign chair, Keith Ellis, a former professor of Spanish at the University of Toronto commented in a letter on the first phase of the fundraising effort: "This achievement is due to the enthusiastic, imaginative and efficient work done by groups from Victoria to Halifax under the umbrella of the Canadian Network on Cuba. They managed to elicit the generous participation of many organizations and individuals who took the opportunity to thank Cuba for its demonstrated readiness to assist other countries, whether their needs be chronic or arising from natural disasters." (Personal communication).

Again when an earthquake devastated Haiti in 2010 and left millions homeless, the CNC organized a Cuba for Haiti campaign, to raise funds to assist the Cuban Henry Reeve medical brigade. This brigade was already on the ground as part of the medical missions sent by Cuba to many countries. Following the earthquake, additional doctors were sent from Cuba, including many of the students from the Medical School of the Americas, to be added to the contingent already in Haiti. This ongoing campaign has raised and sent $40,000 to Cuba to support its efforts in Haiti. Cuban Doctor Jorge Balseiro, who worked in Haiti, travelled across Canada on a speaking tour about the humanitarian efforts of Cuban trained medical personal in Haiti. See Chapter 11 for an account of this by Keith Ellis.

Conclusion

For over fifty years solidarity and friendship between Canadians and Cubans has been growing in its many forms – social, cultural, material aid, tourism, and political. With over a million Canadian tourists

Elizabeth Hill

travelling to Cuba each year there is a huge potential for ever-increasing understanding and support.

To sustain and improve Canada's longstanding diplomatic and economic relations with Cuba following the Cuba revolution, and to educate Canadians about the reality in Cuba, friendship groups have developed in Canada, and have worked in times when there was very little information available about Cuba. Today even with wide Internet access and with more than a million Canadian tourists travelling to Cuba having first hand experience with life in the island nation, humanitarian and political work is still necessary. Frequently mainstream media remain silent on important justice issues such as the Cuban Five, or spread misinformation about human rights and democracy in Cuba.

Canadian solidarity with Cuba has grown over time and has covered many aspects. Efforts made by Canadians did not go unnoticed in Cuba. In December 1995, during a refuelling stop in Vancouver on his way back to Cuba from a trip to Asia, then-President Fidel Castro took the opportunity to meet with many supporters and personally thanked CCFA-Vancouver President Nazir Rizvi for the Canadian support of Cuba.

Not all actions of support for Cuba have had a political motivation. Some have been strictly humanitarian. Such was the case when six-year-old Elián González was rescued at sea following the drowning of his mother in November 1999, while attempting to leave Cuba with her son and boyfriend to get to the United States. Elián was literally held hostage by anti-Castro distant relatives in Miami against the will of his father in Cuba and against the ruling of a U.S. judge that he be returned to Cuba. Many protests and demonstrations took place in Canada in support of the massive campaign going on in Cuba to have Elián returned to his father and his homeland.

I have met many people who have either been to Cuba or want to go because of the praises they have heard from others who have gone. Their interests vary from outright support of the Cuban Revolution to simply loving the music and beaches. Many make positive comments on the friendliness and hospitality of the Cuban people. In Canada the ongoing diplomatic relationship with Cuba is very important in order to maintain basic channels of contact. However, the solidarity attitude and understanding of individual Canadians toward Cubans is just as important to maintaining and strengthening that relationship, particularly in the face of ongoing U.S. policy against Cuba. The Cuban people deserve no less.

References

Canadian-Cuban Friendship Association-Toronto (n.d). *What is the CCFA?* http://www.ccfatoronto.ca. Retrieved March 30, 2014.

Canadian-Cuban Friendship Association-Vancouver (n.d.). *Welcome page.* http://www.ccfavancouver.ca/welcome.html. Retrieved March 30, 2014.

_____ (n.d.). History of CCFA. http://www.ccfavancouver.ca/history.html. Retrieved March 30, 2014.

Canadian Network on Cuba (n.d.). *Mission and History.* http://www.canadiannetworkoncuba.ca/index.php?option=com_content&view=article&id=63&Itemid=91. Retrieved April 2, 2014.

Smith, Wayne S. (2006, November 6). Bush's Dysfunctional Cuba Policy. *Foreign Policy in Focus.* http://fpif.org/bushs_dysfunctional_cuba_policy/. Retrieved April 2, 2014.

Chapter 3

Projects and Campaigns of the Canada-Cuba Solidarity Movement

DIANE ZACK[1]

◇◇

Every revolution needs friends. So in order to broaden and deepen the great friendship and solidarity of many Canadians towards Cuba, its people and its revolution, the founding of a national network was called for. After a period of concerted effort, the Canadian Network on Cuba (CNC) was founded in September 2002 as an umbrella organization of Canadian solidarity groups committed to the work of raising awareness about Cuba. By 2012, the CNC included among its members regionally-based solidarity groups as well as those focussed on single projects, a national trade union, political parties, arts-based groups, non-profit travel agencies, and others (Canadian Network on Cuba n.d.).

One of the main mandates of the CNC is to organize major national campaigns and projects. Many of these projects had existed before its founding, but they were often based in a city or a region and, without a national network to coordinate, it was more difficult to mount effective campaigns. The founding of the CNC enabled them to be broadened to more parts of the country, thus assisting more local solidarity groups to access speakers and cultural programs than they'd been able to do before. The CNC has also been instrumental in organizing national fundraising campaigns to assist at times of natural disasters, such as recurring hurricanes in Cuba and the major earthquake in Haiti in 2010.

---

1.   With contributions from Evelyn Gervan of the Kingston Canadian-Cuban Friendship Association.

Diane Zack

The CNC has directly organized or assisted in the coordination of national conferences that have brought together activists from across the country, as well as from Cuba, the U.S., Britain, and other countries as well.

Free the Cuban Five Campaign[2]

The Canadian Network on Cuba has held two conferences in order to advance the mission of freeing the Cuban Five. The first "Breaking the Silence" conference was held in November 2007 in Toronto, organized jointly by the CNC and its sister organization in Québec, *La Table de concertation de solidarité Québec-Cuba,* as well as Cuba solidarity organizations in the United States. The second, "Breaking the Silence, Justice for the Five - Peoples' Tribunal and Assembly," was held in Toronto in September 2012 and initiated by the group Worker to Worker Solidarity that had also been a founding member of the CNC. Many Cuba solidarity activists from the United States participated in both these conferences, as did the wives of the Cuban Five along with activists from Britain. The 2012 conference was endorsed by 41 organizations and prominent individuals, including elected politicians such as a member of the Canadian Parliament and a city mayor. The Peoples' Tribunal concluded "that the Cuban Five were unjustly detained" and "in the interest of justice and healing...proposes that the President of the United States should exercise his prerogative of a Presidential Clemency and allow the Five to return home" (Canadian Network on Cuba n.d.).

The resonance of the Free the Five campaign is seen in the number of solidarity groups that have arisen dedicated to this action, most prominently the Free the Cuban 5 Committee in Vancouver, which

---

2   For more information about this campaign see Chapter 5.

has organized monthly pickets without fail since December 2006 to draw attention to this grave injustice (Free the Cuban 5 Committee – Vancouver n.d.).

Canadian solidarity activists have also participated in all the International Colloquia to Free the Cuban Five held each November since 2005 in Holguín, Cuba. This campaign to free the Cuban Five has been one of the most important solidarity campaigns in Canada and will continue to be so until the goal of freedom for those men has been reached.

Humanitarian Solidarity Projects

Other ongoing major projects of the Canadian Network on Cuba include the annual *Che* Guevara Volunteer Work Brigade, which began in 1993, years before the founding of the CNC. More recently, additional cities across the country have sent participants on the Brigade. The Brigade continues to be a major, ongoing campaign of the national network due to its people-to-people focus. See Chapter 4 for details on this project.

Another major campaign has been our Canadian participation in the annual U.S.-based Pastors for Peace *Friendshipment* Caravan to Cuba, which began in 1992 to challenge the inhumane economic, political, and social blockade by the United States against Cuba. So the caravan came about as a political action against the blockade as well as a gesture of humanitarian solidarity towards the Cuban people.

Canadian activists have participated broadly in this caravan by driving vehicles, transporting humanitarian and much-needed donations such as wheelchairs, defibrillators, computers, bicycles, sports equipment, medicines, and other items that Cuba is in short supply of because of the blockade. Currently, five or six routes begin in Canada annually, working their way down through the mainland United States. Along the way *caravanistas* (participants in the caravan) educate people about Cuba and gather momentum and support particularly at the time of crossing the border from Canada into the U.S. The goal is to challenge American law that requires Americans to apply for a permit to travel and to transport goods to Cuba (U.S. Department of the Treasury n.d.).

The founding of the CNC assisted the broadening of this work by providing a national coordinator to work closely with the American organizers as well as raising funds to purchase vehicles for the caravan that would then be donated to Cuba. These have included ambulances, school buses, and vans.

Another campaign established by the CNC is the ongoing fundraising to assist Cuba in the aftermath of devastating hurricanes. Cuba has developed a very effective early warning system in the event of approaching hurricanes that involves drills and simulations: "In the simulations run by the Civil Defence System, the authorities and ordinary Cubans rehearse their roles in prevention and evacuation plans to be implemented in case of disasters like hurricanes, earthquakes, drought, fires or epidemics." (Grogg 2012, May 22). However, while the loss of human lives during natural disasters in Cuba is virtually zero, material losses and damage can be quite crippling for the economy. The advantage of a national network cannot be underestimated in such situations as the groundwork has been laid down and groups and individuals can spring into action more quickly when necessity dictates.

Our most recent effort, the fundraising campaign to assist with reconstruction following the damage in Santiago de Cuba from Hurricane Sandy, raised more than $136,000 in a short period. In a similar vein, our solidarity movement has raised considerable funds to support Cuban doctors working in Haiti in the aftermath of the horrific earthquake that hit that small nation in January 2010. More details about this relief campaign are provided in Chapter 11. The medical assistance through doctors and supplies that Cuba has provided to Haiti has been recognized as the most outstanding of all the international solidarity work in that small nation. The work of the Cuban medical teams in Haiti has been an example of true internationalism – effective, complete and without self-interest; this is entirely dissimilar to the so-called "humanitarian" assistance provided by other parties in Haiti, both governmental and non-, which appear to have been ineffective if not outright designed to create dependency and to undermine and exploit the Haitian people and their dire circumstances.

Four years after the earthquake, most of the rebuilding has gone towards "new buildings all over town: a new airport, new upscale hotels, new private university buildings, new pharmacies and brightly painted boutiques" (Porter 2014). However, "critical needs and acute vulnerabilities remain across the country requiring life and livelihood-saving interventions. An estimated 30 percent of Haiti's ten million people are still suffering from the impact of both chronic and acute needs." (United Nations 2013 p. vii). Health, food and nutrition insecurities in particular are still the highest priority in Haiti today. Most services including schools and hospitals are private and unaffordable to most Haitians who clearly benefit from the presence of Cuban doctors providing free services.

Cultural and Professional Exchanges Projects

Other successful examples of solidarity work for Cuba have been cultural and professional exchanges. For example, in the early 2000s, several exchanges were organized between Canadian prairie farmers and Cuban farmers. Visiting Cuban farmers, a diverse group of agricultural producers, spoke to a large gathering in Winnipeg, and each told their own story about their farming experiences, challenges, initiatives, and hopes. The audience included the largest cross-section of Winnipeggers who had ever come out to a meeting about Cuba and the response was exhilarating. The experience in various cities has shown similar results. This emphasizes the effectiveness of developing relations at the popular level in addition to the other necessary political work that must be carried out.

Diane Zack

Regional cultural festivals and conferences also play an important role. Since 2000, Cuba has been represented at North America's largest multicultural festival, *Folklorama*, in Winnipeg due to the combined efforts of the small Cuban community and the solidarity movement that has always provided volunteers to assist. Toronto hosts its Cuba Friendship Day at City Hall in Nathan Phillips Square every summer, as well as the International Festival of Poetry of Resistance with the participation of Cuban poets. Vancouver also hosts an annual *Che* Guevara Conference with speakers from Cuba and other countries that highlight the current issues at heart in the Cuban society. In fact, one of the key characteristics of all the solidarity organizations across the country is that they provide a wide variety of ongoing educational, political, and cultural activities in order to raise awareness among Canadians about our Cuban friends.

The contemporary Canadian solidarity movement with Cuba really began at the local level, with groups springing up around the country in most major cities. Some were designed to foster relations in specific areas, such as music education. The *Los Primos* project out of Halifax began in 1997 as an outreach of music educators who wanted to organize musical exchanges between Nova Scotia and Cuba as well as to bring Cuban music students to Halifax to work and study. They also collected instruments to bring to Cuba to help support its prominent music education programs, which were and are rich in heritage and skill, but lacking in material resources. The mission statement of the *Los Primos* project states that its purpose is "to inspire, support, and promote live music, music education, and social awareness in Nova Scotia, Cuba, and abroad through cultural exchange, intergenerational learning, and the creation of environments where these elements will flourish" (Los Primos n.d.). *Los Primos* has facilitated trips for Cuban music students to Nova Scotia six times and has taken Canadian music students to Cuba six times also. They have organized the delivery of nearly 500 musical instruments to schools of music in various Cuban cities though partnering with sympathetic individuals and organizations. Over the years, they have raised nearly half a million dollars to support music education in Nova Scotia and Cuba.

Sister Cities Project

Fertile seeds of friendship with Cuba blossomed into a branch of the Canadian-Cuban Friendship Association (CCFA) in Kingston, Ontario in the year 2000. Also dormant within the founding group (a diverse group of artists, professionals, Queen's university faculty members, business people, as well as political activists) was the idea of establishing a Sister City relationship with Cienfuegos, a city on Cuba's south coast bearing many striking similarities to Kingston: a long military history; a natural deep-water harbour; both have national military colleges, RMC in Kingston and the Naval Academy in Cienfuegos; preserved forts, museums; active arts communities and both are home to a large University with a medical school (Canadian-Cuban Friendship Association-Kingston 2013, April).

In November 2004 an agreement to twin Kingston and Cienfuegos was finally signed by Kingston and Cienfuegos. It had been a frustratingly long process with all the hiccups coming from the Canadian side. From the very beginning in 2001, the Cubans had patiently supported and encouraged what was to become the first twinning of a Canadian and a Cuban city. As the Cuban Ambassador to Canada at that time stated in a letter to the Mayor of Kingston, "Solidarity, mutual education and understanding are the strongest tools we have to struggle for justice and for a better world. This twinning is a significant contribution to the historical ties between Canada and Cuba."

The hope is that other Canadian cities and towns will follow Kingston's lead. To that end, CCFA Kingston hosted the first Trilateral Conference in June 2006. The ground-breaking conference brought together people from Canada, Cuba, and the United States to share their experience and interest in twinning with the ultimate aim of fostering further twinning agreements. In 2010, CCFA Kingston's *Cubafest* celebrated the 50th anniversary of the Cuban Revolution by bringing to Kingston Cuban artists of all kinds, many of them from our Sister City. Queen's University's conference "A Measure of a Revolution" brought eminent scholars on Cuba and had in attendance among many other dignitaries Ricardo Alarcón, President of the National Assembly of Cuba.

A member of the Canadian Network on Cuba (CNC) from the time of its founding in 2002, CCFA Kingston has participated in all the campaigns and projects undertaken by the national organization over the years. As hoped, the Sister City arrangement captures the attention of local media and gives extra vitality and a special impetus to projects undertaken. The people-to-people connection can be helpful even in political work such as that undertaken by Canadian solidarity groups on behalf of the Cuban Five and the Pastors for Peace Caravan.

Special Solidarity Actions

Broadly speaking, a large number of the solidarity projects and campaigns organized by Canadian activists for Cuba have been ongoing regularly, in response to natural disasters, or designed to increase the people-to-people contact between Canadians and Cubans. There have been special situations in our solidarity history, however, where sudden action was required to counteract brutal propaganda and other campaigns launched against Cuba.

One such urgent campaign arose during the Pan Am Games in Winnipeg in the summer of 1999, during which Miami-based Cuban-Americans and some media outlets orchestrated a systematic campaign of harassment, intimidation, and misinformation against Cuba and its athletes at the Games. One of the local Winnipeg dailies carried out a non-stop barrage of insults and other demeaning propaganda against Cuba and its athletes, which included a contest to guess how many athletes would defect during the games. This incident prompted an angry response from the Cuban government and became a sore point in official Canada-Cuba relations. It is well known that defection of Cubans are encouraged by the U.S. Cuban Adjustment Act of 1966, which grants automatic refugee status to Cubans who make it to U.S. territory and claim "political persecution" (U.S. government 1966, November 2). From Canada to the U.S. is just a short skip with a little help from Miami. However, it is this Act that has promoted much more dangerous, life-risking sea trips from Cuba to Florida's shores on anything that floats. The Cuba solidarity movement all over the world has strongly condemned what has been termed by Cuba the "killer law" (Lockhart 2009, July 9).

In addition to the relentless media attacks during the Pan Am Games, Cuba's star athlete and the greatest high jumper in the world, Javier Sotomayor, was stripped of his gold medal after allegedly failing a drug test. Many were convinced that this was a clumsy frame-up since Sotomayor had been tested more than 60 times in prior games and had never failed a drug test. Aside from the loss of his gold medal, Sotomayor was also suspended from the sport for two years, which would have led to his being unable to participate in the Sydney 2000 Olympics. This suspension was later reduced to a one-year suspension and he did make it to the Sydney Olympics where he won a silver medal in his sport. Sotomayor's high jump of 2.45 metres has never been equalled and he is still considered to be the world's greatest high jumper. He retired in 2001, remaining true to his country and the high standards of a world athlete, drug-free.

As a result of this perceived unfair treatment of Cuban athletes on Canadian soil, Cuba solidarity activists sprang into action to protest and denounce the harassment against Cuba at the Games. The protest went well beyond the organized solidarity movement and many other supporters came forward as well. In fact, there was a groundswell of support and empathy for Cuba in large part generated by peoples' desire to fight back against the systematic anti-Cuba campaign. One prominent Winnipeg journalist at the newspaper leading the campaign against Cuba distanced herself from the official position of her employer and came to the defence of Cuba. She paid a high price for her defiance by losing her job.

Conclusion

The number of Canadians travelling to Cuba each year is more than one million, being the largest number from a single country. There has been a steady campaign of education throughout Canada by the solidarity groups as well as Cubans living here to let Canadians know that Cuba is more than 'just the beach.' The education campaign consists of two main strands: 1) positive, pro-active information about Cuba's history and achievements, including its education and healthcare systems, its early literacy campaign, which taught all Cubans to read and write within a year in the early days of the revolution, as well as Cuba's rich cultural and social history; and 2) specific responses to direct propaganda misinformation against Cuba on an ongoing basis in most media outlets.

Many misleading reports against Cuba's social system, its government and people have been consistently carried out nationally with blatant disregard for balance and accuracy. For example, at the time when then-president Fidel Castro fell ill in the summer of 2006, some Canadian media outlets simply parroted the barrage of animosity and slander coming out of small but very vocal anti-Cuba groups in Miami. Other media, notably the Canadian Broadcasting Corporation through its radio program The Current, made an effort to get the viewpoint of some representatives of the Cuba solidarity movement by interviewing the co-chair of the Canadian Network on Cuba and other solidarity activists, as well as other Canadian observers about the impact that Fidel Castro's illness might have had on Cuba.

However, that kind of balanced reporting on Cuba is not frequent. More often than not, the Canadian media have simply recycled items from American news services, which reflect the strained U.S.-Cuba relations more than stated Canadian policy of engagement. Calls to the Canadian mainstream media and invitations to attend press conferences when important Cuba events are held have been consistently ignored. That has made it all the more important for the solidarity movement to carry out its work directly amongst Canadians from all walks of life.

Many of the adventurous Canadians who travelled to Cuba in the nineties, during what was called the "Special Period," returned deeply affected by Cuba's struggle to recover from the crushing blow of the collapse of its trade partner, the Soviet Union. Activists or not, many were sympathetic to the besieged nation's critical situation and were angered by the unrelenting interference and hostility coming from the United States. As a result, the turn of the century saw growth in the number of Canada-Cuba friendship groups and a move towards consolidating solidarity work across the country.

We have described some of the most relevant actions carried out in Canada in support of Cuba, but have not presented a full list of activities as there are many more. For instance, the many academic exchanges occurring between universities in Canada and Cuba are as much the result of professional relations among institutions and scholars in different fields as they are an indication of solidarity initiatives. They are signs of solidarity when considering that the country in question is made out to be nefarious solely based on its political system. These exchanges help build relationships among different sectors of society in our two countries. The more institutions of learning and research in Canada reach out to their counterparts in Cuba, and vice-versa, the stronger the bonds between the two countries and people will become. The importance of people-to-people contact cannot be overemphasized. This goes far beyond the parameters of official relations.

All solidarity actions ultimately are undertaken by volunteers and this only points to the level of commitment towards political and social values that is not demonstrated by our government. There are challenges to not conforming with the status quo, but the tenacity of the solidarity movement also reminds us all that the Canadian spirit is one that embraces openness.

References

Canadian-Cuban Friendship Association-Kingston. (April 2013). Kingston, Canada and Cienfuegos, Cuba twinning. http://kingstonccfa.ca/twinning.html. Retrieved April 3, 2014.

Canadian Network on Cuba (n.d.). CNC Member Groups. http://www.canadiannetworkoncuba.ca/index.php?option=com_content&view=article&id=139&Itemid=135. Retrieved April 2, 2014.

_____ (n.d.). The Ruling. http://canadiannetworkoncuba.ca/tribunal/. Retrieved April 18, 2014.

Free the Cuban 5 Committee – Vancouver (n.d.). http://www.freethe5vancouver.ca. Retrieved April 2, 2014.

Grogg, Patricia (2012, May 22). Community Drills Part of Cuba's Top-Notch Disaster Response System. *Inter Press Service*. http://www.ipsnews.net/2012/05/community-drills-part-of-cubas-top-notch-disaster-response-system/. Retrieved April 18, 2014.

Lockhart F., Melissa. (2009, July 9). The killer law: Revisiting Cuban Adjustment. *Foreign Policy Association*. http://foreignpolicyblogs.com/2009/07/09/the-killer-law-revisiting-cuban-adjustment/. Retrieved April 3, 2014.

Los Primos. (n.d.). Mission Statement. http://losprimos.ca/about/governance. Retrieved 3 April 2014.

Porter, Catherine. (2014, January 12). Haitian earthquake: Daunting challenges remain four years after disaster. *The Star*. http://www.thestar.com/news/world/2014/01/12/haitian_earthquake_daunting_challenges_remain_four_years_after_disaster.html. Retrieved April 2, 2014.

United Nations. (2013). *HAITI Humanitarian Action Plan 2014*. Office for the Coordination of Humanitarian Affairs. http://unocha.org/cap/appeals/humanitarian-action-plan-haiti-2014. Retrieved April 2, 2014.

U.S. Department of the Treasury. (n.d.). Resource Center. Cuba Sanctions. http://www.treasury.gov/resource-center/sanc-tions/Programs/Pages/cuba.aspx. Retrieved April 2, 2014.

U.S. Government. (1966, November 2). *Public Law 89-732*. Statute 80, p. 1161. http://www.gpo.gov/fdsys/pkg/STATUTE-80/pdf/STATUTE-80-Pg1161.pdf. Retrieved April 3, 2014.

Chapter 4

The Che Guevara Volunteer Work Brigade: 20 Years of a People-to-People Solidarity Project

NINO PAGLICCIA

◇◇

Many Canadians travel to Cuba every year to enjoy the beautiful sites and beaches. Their drive is to vacation in one of the most pristine and untouched tropical places on earth. They take in the historical sights, the preserved colonial buildings, the exotic fruits, the cheerful music, and they are amused at the vintage cars still running through the streets of Cuba often sharing the streets with horse drawn carriages. Most visitors limit their interactions with Cubans to casual conversations, and their experience is often reduced to a passive observation of sites and people, which they might record on digital cameras. However, Cuba is a country whose real distinctiveness created by the Cuban Revolution can hardly be seen through the camera lens of the most experienced photographer. Its unique and complex social system may require prolonged observation and careful analysis that are not usually part of a typical vacation package to Cuba.

The Cuba solidarity movement in Canada has offered for many years a different opportunity to those who choose to visit Cuba with a spirit of engagement and get a closer and deeper understanding of its society. Why did Cuba decide to break away from capitalism? How is Cuba evolving in the process of perfecting its own brand of socialism? Why is the U.S. relentlessly trying to destabilize Cuba? How does the U.S. blockade impact Cubans? Is Cuba a democracy or a dictatorship? Does Cuba violate human rights? Is criticism of the government allowed?

The *Che* Guevara Volunteer Work Brigade is a yearly project that offers such an opportunity through people-to-people links. The project allows visiting Cuba during three weeks, in the context of doing volunteer work side-by-side with Cubans, with a structured program that promotes learning about the society, the culture, the politics, the hardships, and the aspirations of Cubans. The year 2012 marked the 20th anniversary of this project. Hundreds of Canadians have joined the brigade as volunteers over 20 years of uninterrupted operation.

This project is only one of many different Cuba solidarity projects in Canada and yet it stands out for its inspiration, potential, and endurance. I have coordinated and guided the brigade from 1995 to 2007 and have returned on the 2012 brigade on the occasion of the 20th anniversary. In this chapter I rely on this experience to first reflect on the nature of voluntarism in Cuba and Canada, and then describe the project, which is steeped in this concept as well as in the spirit of solidarity. In the final section I will give a voice to a cross-section of brigade participants (*brigadistas*), who have accepted my invitation to provide their personal statements, in an attempt to gain an insight to their motivation to join the brigade and to their learning from the people-to-people connection. I trust that the experience may have enriched their lives, and their perspectives will enrich our understanding of this project and its impact on the Cuba solidarity movement in Canada and on Cuba.

Volunteer Work in Cuba

It is commonly recognized that Ernesto *Che* Guevara initially inspired volunteer work in Cuba in the 1960s as a way of increasing economic production and creating personal values. The concepts of work and worker are fundamental in the socialist society. Work "acquires a new condition, that of connecting the worker to the object of work and, at the same time, creating the awareness of the importance of creativity" (Ariet 1993: 122). *Che* Guevara believed that it was possible to create a "new man or woman" in a truly socialist society. This new "man of the twenty-first century" would grow out of Cuban youth. "Our... students do physical work during their vacations or along with their studies. Work is a reward in some cases, a means of education in others, but it is never a punishment. A new generation is being born" (Guevara 1965: 157). Students by and large embraced this view of study-work in a revolutionary spirit, with the occasional reluctance to doing physical work. *Che* Guevara himself performed volunteer work as an example to others at the same time that he was a full member of the revolutionary government with ministerial responsibilities. Volunteer work in a socialist context has its roots in the "communist Saturdays" formalized by Vladimir Lenin in Russia in 1920 when community work, as removing garbage and similar tasks, was performed without pay.

Generations of young Cuban students participated in brigades of volunteer workers during their vacation period performing manual work in sugar and coffee plantations, construction and farms. After 50 years, volunteer work in Cuba is an entrenched part of the history of revolutionary sacrifice and commitment of that country. In 2011 the Workers' Central Union of Cuba (*Central de Trabajadores de Cuba*-CTC) agreed to discontinue the practice and reserve it only for special circumstances such as natural disasters or other emergencies. Interestingly, the reasons given for the change are based on the lack of evidence that the work was being really productive, and on the apparent unfair competition on workers seeking needed paid jobs, but not on the formative value for young people as envisioned by *Che* Guevara.

The value of volunteer work was measured in terms of hours contributed rather than the more subtle transformation of revolutionary conscience. In the new Cuban economic model promoted by President Raúl Castro, productivity requires an efficient and not unfair competitive use of human capital. The dream gave way to reality. If *Che* dreamed of

Nino Pagliccia

volunteer work as a sign of solidarity with the revolution and its ideology, now solidarity is requested from Cubans by performing more conscientious paid work. This speaks of a socialist model of productivity in which solidarity is a key part of labour relations.

Volunteer Work in Canada

The concept of volunteer work is not limited to the socialist ideology. In the capitalist system, volunteer work is also encouraged and is more commonly associated with civil society or non-governmental organizations. The reasons to perform volunteer work may range from gaining working experience in a particular field to contributing to a valued project or cause. It is the latter that is generally associated with a sense of solidarity by the volunteer.

The government of Canada has a special website promoting volunteer work for youth. Its first paragraph states: "Work without pay? Yes! Volunteering may be one of the most valuable experiences of your life. It's a double win: your community or cause benefits from your work and you benefit from your experiences" (Youth Canada 2013). Among the stated advantages of doing volunteer work are gaining work experience, meeting people, learning new things, and helping someone else. And among those needing volunteer support are charities, religious organizations, political campaigns, and government agencies.

A Canadian non-governmental organization, Volunteer Canada, states on its website that according to a 2010 survey, "13.3 million Canadians contribute 2.1 billion hours, the equivalent of 1.1 million full-time jobs (Canada Survey on Giving, Volunteering and Participating, 2010)" (Volunteer Canada 2013). Interestingly, they list 33 corporate sector supporters; among others, Enbridge, of the Athabasca oil sand fame, and Wal-Mart Canada, widely criticized for its anti-union policies and practices.

Canadian universities are also great promoters of volunteer work that connect potential volunteers to organizations across Canada seeking volunteers (Canada's Higher Education and Career Guide n.d.).

Using published statistics for the U.S. as a reference for Canada, we also note a great economic contribution of work done by volunteers: "In 2011, the number of volunteers reached its highest level in five years, as 64.5 million Americans volunteered through an organization, an increase of 1.5 million from 2010. Americans volunteered a total of almost 8 billion hours, an estimated economic value of roughly $171 billion" (Corporation for National and Community Service n.d.). With an hourly dollar value for voluntary work in 2011 at $21.79, this sizeable contribution to the economy, without monetary compensation, may well be an explanation why this mode of labour is encouraged over a paid one in a market economy. "If [volunteering] were a company it would be bigger than Ford, AT&T, or Apple" (Baldwin 2012, April 5).

Canadian Volunteer Work Brigade to Cuba

One program for volunteer work outside Canada meets all the advantages stated by the government-sponsored youth program without getting the recognition and promotion as such: this program is the *Che* Guevara Volunteer Work Brigade of the Canadian Network on Cuba.

Volunteer work brigades are generally composed of a group of people committed to travel to Cuba for a period of time to perform manual work alongside Cuban workers. In exchange, volunteers benefit from close contact with Cuban workers and professionals of all walks of life, as well as from meetings with experts and representatives of Cuban mass organizations or civil society. By far this is the most direct means of learning about

Nino Pagliccia

and understanding Cuban society, the Cuban Revolution, and socialism in action. It provides participants with the opportunity to exchange experiences and viewpoints through a Canadian-Cuban dialogue.

The Beginning

A worldwide initiative of Volunteer Work Brigades to Cuba started in the 1960s as a result of the U.S. imposed isolation of Cuba following the success of the revolution. Most outstanding may well be the *Venceremos* brigade from the U.S. that started in 1969 (Venceremos Brigade n.d.). Numerous countries now organize work brigades of volunteers going to different parts of Cuba and in the hundreds at a time. But the largest surge of this type of solidarity with Cuba occurred in the 1990s.

The early 1990s marked the beginning of a particularly harsh economic crisis for Cuba following the demise of the Soviet Union in the late 1980s. The loss of Cuba's principal trade partner caused imports to drop by 80 percent and its economy to shrink by about 34 percent almost overnight giving rise to what Cubans termed the *Período Especial* (Special Period). This devastating situation and its consequences have been documented in detail (Banco Central de Cuba n.d.). It is also well known that the United States government added a new arsenal of stringent policies to the already strangling economic blockade against Cuba, in place since 1962. The ill-termed Cuban Democracy Act of 1992 (also known as Torricelli Act after the name of its sponsor), which prevented food and medicines from being shipped to Cuba, had the sole scope of causing a total paralysis of the Cuban economy disregarding the tragic human impact on the civilian population (United States Department of Treasury n.d.). In addition, two years later The Cuban Liberty and Democratic Solidarity (Libertad) Act of 1996 (also known as the Helms–Burton Act), penalizing foreign companies that traded with Cuba, was supposed to give the *coup de grâce* to the Island nation (United States Congress 1996, March 12).

What is less documented is the massive worldwide response in support of Cuba. The internal solidarity of Cubans, equally sharing the hardship of the Special Period, played a major role in offsetting the external threats mostly coming from the U.S. government. However, the international solidarity with Cuba also contributed in no minor scale at a political level and often at the material level.

Canada's Contribution

Canada participated in that international response in the 1990s and many actions were undertaken in solidarity with Cuba. One advantage that Canadians have had over Americans is that Canada and Cuba have maintained uninterrupted diplomatic relations following the Cuban Revolution, which did not interfere with travel or shipment of goods to Cuba.

Among other solidarity activities, Canada offered an opportunity to witness the real situation in Cuba to all Canadians who were curious enough, wanted to be part of the movement, and were willing to establish a direct connection in solidarity with Cubans. This opportunity was provide by the *Che* Guevara Volunteer Work Brigade (VWB).

Details of the organization of the first Canadian Volunteer Work Brigade to Cuba in 1993 have been lost. I participated in the second brigade in 1994 and have since helped organize, promote and coordinate them for the following 12 years. Since 1993, hundreds of people have been part of the Canadian brigade; many still maintain a connection with Cuba and have become advocates for Cuba.

The VWB is a non-profit people-to-people solidarity project of the Canadian Network on Cuba (CNC) that brings together Canadians and Cubans during three weeks in Cuba to share work, space, time, experience, and ideology. While Cuba's opening to tourism has allowed many Canadians to travel and vacation in Cuba, the VWB provides the means for a more intimate view of Cuba.

"The *Che* Brigade fulfils two main goals. On the one hand, it is a great way to show support for the struggle of the Cuban people to maintain their independence. On the other hand, it is an important opportunity for people from Canada to know and understand the dynamism of all aspects of life in Cuba." (Canadian Network on Cuba n.d.).

Cuban Institute of Friendship with the Peoples

The organization of the VWB is based on principles of partnership with the *Instituto Cubano de Amistad con los Pueblos* (ICAP - Cuban Institute of Friendship with the Peoples). ICAP is an organization that channels most of the international solidarity activities with Cuba. It is a major (but not the only) gateway to Cuba for all international solidarity and friendship activities (ICAP n.d.). In a country where solidarity is a national policy, ICAP represents and carries out that policy. In this sense, it is an informal executor of state policy in all matters of friendship links with the external world, but in its administrative and operational functions ICAP is self-financed and autonomous. The head office, based in Havana, has administrative divisions that cover all areas of the world; ICAP has offices in all provincial capitals of the island that operate as hosts for visiting delegations.

ICAP has a Canada desk that supervises and maintains connections with many solidarity organizations in Canada. It is in partnership with the Canada desk of ICAP that the *Che* Guevara VWB is coordinated. All the logistic work of accommodation and local programming is done in Cuba whereas all the promotion and preparation of the project is undertaken in Canada.

Brigade Participants

Brigadistas, as the brigade participants are called, are a very heterogeneous group. There are students, professionals, workers, immigrants to Canada, young and old, men and women. They represent a cross-section of Canadian society. Similarly, the Cuban counterpart includes workers, students, and various representatives from a cross-section of Cuban society. Cubans are very well educated, have a general knowledge of Canada, and welcome the opportunity to meet Canadians personally. They are genuinely sociable, curious, and interested. They are passionate about their culture and willing to share some of their major cultural assets: music and dance. It is through this basic sharing that friendship and trust starts to grow, but it is through shared work and ideas that a true bonding happens.

Ideologically, there is a wide range of views among Canadian *brigadistas*. Some may not be interested in politics but they may be sympathetic with the Cubans out of human concern for their scarce material goods compared to the affluence of Canada. Others may be left-wing political activists in Canada who visit Cuba to show their solidarity to their Cuban comrades. Still others may be confirmed socialists who hope to live the socialist experience in Cuba, even if it is only for three weeks. It has been my experience that among Cubans there is less ideological heterogeneity. Many may be critical of their condition and the realities in their country, yet they still call themselves *revolucionarios* (revolutionaries). By and large, my observation over the years has been that the cross-section of Cubans I have come into contact with are supportive of their leadership and definitely proud of their achievements.

A Day on the Work Brigade

A typical day on the brigade involves early rising, working until noon, then taking a lunch break and resting; in the afternoon there are visits to organizations and meetings with experts on different topics; evenings are generally free or there may be a cultural activity to participate in. On weekends there may be more visits, a tour of another city or free time for independently exploring the city.

Over the years of the VWB volunteers have done a variety of jobs. They are always relevant to the local community and have social value. One of the toughest jobs that Canadian volunteers have done has been cutting sugarcane, however, some of the most meaningful have been painting a seniors' home, tending trees in a banana plantation, weeding, planting and picking vegetables in organic gardens and farms, painting and repairing the roof of a school, and assisting Cuban construction workers with building a school or a new housing complex.

It is not the motivation of the VWB to provide skilled work that cannot be done by a Cuban worker. More typically Canadian volunteers will have Cuban skilled workers as supervisors and instructors. The goal is learning, sharing and camaraderie. However in the end, Cubans are keen about reporting the actual contribution made by the volunteers, which is invariably very generous towards a high monetary and social value to the satisfaction of all. I like to believe that what Canadians may lack in skill is more than compensated by their enthusiasm.

Visits and meetings are an important part of the program because they give the opportunity for dialogue, questioning and exchange of ideas beyond the one-to-one daily contact. Organizations that are usually visited are mass organizations of which Cubans are very proud and often members. Typically meetings are set up at the nationwide Federation of Cuban Women; schools and hospitals, that show off the two most important achievements of the revolution; political organizations, like the Union of Young Communists; and government structures like the People's Power Assembly – the Cuban Parliament.

Topics discussed with Cuban experts usually cover two general areas: socio-political organization of society and current issues in Cuba. For instance, in the first area, *brigadistas* have a chance to learn about women's role in Cuban society, Cuba's international solidarity with developing countries, and importance of farming cooperatives, the Cuban public health system, the changing Cuban economic model, the legal system and the unique electoral process in Cuba. Among topics in the second area are: the impact of the continued U.S. blockade on the Cuban economy and the case of the Cuban Five. The latter has been a central focus at the highest level of the Cuban government (See Chapter 5).

Reflections from Former Brigadistas

The impact of the *Che* Guevara brigade on individuals can be as varied as the participants in it, and therefore can hardly be appreciated through a brief description of its history and the program. Over the years, I have witnessed deep transformations in awareness and commitment from young, and some older, Canadians that I could not possibly describe. To remedy this in part I have asked some former *brigadistas* to express in their own words what the Brigade has meant to them. The following is what they have written without any editing of their accounts.

Cathy Beharry-Ayanwale

I decided to go to Cuba first and foremost to stand in solidarity with the Cuban people against the illegal economic blockade enforced by the United States. Secondly, to see the victories and understand how Cuba has progressed from the beginning of the revolution.

The voluntary work is an important highlight of the trip. It was great to work side by side with our Cuban friends and learn about their culture and proud history. In my opinion Cuba's greatest resource is its people.

The piece I took away from Cuba that guided my life in Canada is the commitment of the Cuban people in upholding their national sovereignty and self-determination in the face of American imperialism.

Janet Mrenica

Cienfuegos was the destination the year I was the first from Ottawa to participate on the *Che* Guevara Brigade. I was the second person from Ottawa to have ever participated in a brigade to Cuba. Although I thought picking oranges and gardening side by side with Cubans would have been the highlight of my time in Cuba, my first memorable moment was the group excursion to Playa Girón, discovering Caleta Buena, an unforgettable crystal clear water area where one can swim amongst tropical fish. I have since returned there a number of times.

Like all brigades, we spent some time at the ICAP Julio Antonio Mella International Camp in Caimito (near Havana) and from there excursions took us into Havana city. One of those evenings, I experienced one of my life's most memorable moments: I led a group of brave *brigadistas* off the bus at a corner in Miramar to the Karl Marx theatre where they bought last minute tickets to attend the only reunion of the Buena Vista Social Club. I had received my tickets as a birthday present from my girlfriend.

Ten years later now, I remember that on the brigade I wanted to be immersed in a socio-cultural experience while meeting new Canadians and Cubans. My wish was fulfilled. My participation as a *brigadista* broadened my previous decade long experience of Cuba with a new geographical and socio-cultural perspective. On previous visits I had developed Cuban friends but the brigade provided me with a unique cultural context through working hand-in-hand with Cubans and Canadians in a different environment and in a uniquely close way.

Upon my return to Canada I continued to enhance this experience with regular shared reflections on the brigade experience and through studies of Cuba towards my Master's Degree of public policy in international development. My family and I continue to have close ties in Cuba after almost 20 years since we first vacationed on the island.

Vanja Zakanji

Ever since I learned about the Cuban Revolution and *Che* Guevara when I was 17 years old, I decided that I would go to Cuba whenever I got a chance, to pay tribute to the country that sets an example of anti-imperialist struggle. I was very inspired by *Che* and the sacrifice he made for humanity, fighting for a new world led by nothing but his love for justice. My chance to visit Cuba came six years later when I read on the internet about a group of Italian leftists who took part in the volunteer brigade to Cuba where they performed volunteer work, learned about the Cuban revolution, Cuban society, its economy, and culture.

I spent the next few days trying to find out if a similar organization or program existed in Canada and luckily, through the website of the Canadian Network on Cuba, I found out about the Canadian *Che* Guevara Brigade. I contacted them, and on July 27, 2007, I found myself at the international airport in Toronto with the group of Canadian *brigadistas*. These were people of various ages and nationalities, all having a common goal of showing solidarity with one of the few remaining socialist countries that, as a candle in the midst of a storm, is struggling to light up the road for the rest of humanity.

There has been a lot of propaganda against Cuba in the Western media, and many people who didn't know much about the Cuban reality would easily believe it. I was born in Yugoslavia, a country that has been a long time friend of Cuba and that was destroyed by the interests of global capitalism, the same interests that have been attacking Cuba ever since the triumph of the revolution in 1959.

The Yugoslav people lost that battle unfortunately, but Cubans are still proudly fighting. So I felt a great admiration for the strength and courage of our Cuban brothers and sisters in their struggle to protect their independence, their sovereignty and socialism.

My admiration for Cuba was strengthened after the trip because I saw a nation united in solving their ever growing problems with a lot of optimism, solidarity and brotherhood, always smiling in front of the great menace they are facing, not letting it take away their pride and their love for humanity. I learned that Cuba doesn't send soldiers and airplanes around the world to kill innocent people. It sends doctors and teachers to heal them and teach them. I truly believe that Cuba is an example of altruism and humanism at its best.

One of my most pleasant memories happened during a break while we were working in Ciego de Avila on the construction site of a school for children with impaired vision and blind children. Some Cuban workers spontaneously picked up their tools: buckets, shovels, hammers and the like, and started producing a beat. Suddenly, more and more workers joined in, each adding a sound to the rhythm with their own tool. All the *brigadistas* started gathering around them amazed by the musical sound of percussion they were making just using their tools. That was something that I had not seen before. I was impressed to see how good humoured and relaxed workers were on the work site, ready to share their talents.

My time in Cuba marked a great turning point in my life, which led me to understand the importance of commitment of each individual in society towards achieving a common goal and contributing to the struggle for a new humane world by example through whatever abilities the individual possesses. Cuba lit a spark within me, which made me understand that the Cuban Revolution did not end in 1959, but had just started. It is still present today to remind every human being of the importance of ones own effort and dedication in pressing for a better future for humanity, for a new world!

Stephen von Sychowski

For me one of the biggest highlights of the brigade along with activities - like hiking in the Sierra Maestra, or visiting the *Che* Guevara Mausoleum in Santa Clara - was the people. By that I mean both the *brigadistas*, who were great people from across Canada, and even more so the Cuban people. Their determination and strength in building a better way of life in the face of intense pressure from outside is truly inspiring. A lot of people have very distorted perceptions about Cuba. I went on the brigade already as a supporter of Cuba, but the brigade definitely did away with any lingering doubts on that score and strengthened my ongoing support for the Cuban revolution.

Mirko Fernandez

I decided to join the 2002 *Che* Guevara Brigade because I felt it would provide me a more interesting perspective into Cuban society and at the same time allow me to participate and volunteer in an exchange of friendship in a country I always wanted to visit. The highlights for me were the beaches, meeting diverse international medical students, and the *barrio* block party held at the seniors' home. I did not want to go there with any preconceived notions of Cuba, but the beaches were as beautiful as I imagined, and the people just as hospitable and musical.

The values of Cuban society I consider most meaningful to me were the importance given to access to education and health, and gender equality. My most memorable moment with a Cuban co-worker was interacting with the young people where we worked. At such a young age they seemed to be so much more socially aware in conversation than other children of the same age I have meet in other travels.

Upon returning to Canada, my experience from Cuba reminded me about the importance of not getting caught up in consumerism, maintaining an open mind, and enjoying the more basic things in life.

Jessica Bartels

I am happy that the *Che* Guevara Brigade has reached its 20th anniversary. I feel very lucky to have been able to go on the brigade and I have recommended it to all my close friends and family.

My reason for going on the brigade was simple. I believe in the goals of Ernesto *Che* Guevara. I am the daughter of a Vietnam War draft dodger and survivor of the battle for civil rights in the American South. I was raised with a deep respect for all religions, all people, and those on the left. As a teenager, I read about Lily Litvak (Russian female fighter pilot in the Second World War) and *Che*. I admired them so much and learned about *Che's* support of volunteer work from reading his books. It inspired me. I have worked as a volunteer since I was 18 and I work (for pay) for a humanitarian organization. My goal in life is to leave things a little bit better than I found them. The question I grew up with was "what would *Che* do?" and I hope I can achieve this. Joining a Brigade made me feel like I was helping. We were working to renovate a school. I am glad these children will go to a good school and I hope they will have good, productive lives. I hope that the school I helped construct will help these people to support themselves and their country.

There were many highlights for me while on the Brigade. I also really enjoyed having the chance to chat with my Canadian and some Greek comrades that had joined the Canadian brigade. It was a wonderful international experience.

It's hard to say how my perception has changed. I love Cuba. I love being there. I also love Canada, the U.S., the UK, and Russia. I grew up in all of these countries. I love them all and hope that I see the good and bad in all of them. Going on the Brigade introduced me to more real Cuban life. For example, we went to a wonderful Cuban block party. The main "take away" I had from that party was to witness how middle class life was there: good! In these tough economic times in the world, I can only hope that my friends outside of Cuba are supported and have the same quality of life as my Cuban friends.

My perception of Cuba has not really changed. Cuba is just like any other country. People who expect perfection are wrong. People who expect disaster are also wrong. Cuba is a beautiful country with great weather and intense politics. It is a fascinating and successful country.

Ron Murphy

I had been travelling to Cuba yearly and biannually when I finally became aware of the Brigade's existence in 2007. Wanting to learn ever more about the Cuban people and their struggles, I figured that the Brigade would afford me such an opportunity. For once I couldn't have been more correct. The exposure I experienced working alongside everyday Cuban people, the encounters and friendships I made, greatly contributed to a deeper and more meaningful understanding of this wonderful people and country.

I must say that the highlight for me (taken from a list of many) is but a very simple and mundane experience. It was by no means an "epiphany" of sorts, but rather a confirmation that we are all together. It was riding around Ciego de Avila with L., in his old beat up Lada, with only one crank for the windows in the car, doors that only opened from the outside, sputtering along, stopping and seeing all parts of town, meeting his wonderful wife D. and son I., sharing espresso coffees together. I know it doesn't seem like much, but for me it was wonderful and an enjoyment I will not soon forget, if ever.

Mridula Morgan

I did not learn much about Cuba growing up. The popular media claimed it was a mysterious and dangerous place run by a communist dictator. Upon reading and learning more about the details inspiring the revolution, I chose to join a social-educational tour of Cuba in 1996. The place, the people, and the inner workings of a system that was based on principles of equity and social justice mesmerized me. It was the beginning of relearning what is possible when one stands up to oppression and injustice.

Cuban men, women and children shared their personal experiences of residing in a socialist country that was living under a cruel U.S. blockade that denied them basic human necessities. They talked about their country's political system and the continual challenges of racism, sexism, gay rights etc. that needed & received attention from the rigorous political everyday involvement of citizens. They were also quick to emphasize that while the system they lived in was not perfect, it was committed to improving the situation of citizens.

I returned several times to Cuba, twice on volunteer work brigades. The work brigades allowed me to witness the living and working conditions of Cubans as I helped to paint a school and cut sugar cane. One begins to feel the challenges of carrying out the work when working with the old & primitive instruments that Cubans are left with, due to the blockade and inaccessibility of materials.

The most vivid memory I have of my travels to Cuba is of a Cuban woman speaking to our group about life in Cuba. Women, she said, have three roles in Cuba: social, economic, and political. Women are active agents of social change and stand alongside men in maintaining the revolutionary force that inspires the country.

My favourite quote is: *"We are realists, we dream the impossible."* ~ *Che* Guevara.

Concluding Remarks

The *Che* Guevara Volunteer Work Brigade is a project more than 20 years old embedded in the Cuba solidarity movement in Canada. Its main characteristics are voluntarism and solidarity, and it aims at establishing people-to-people connections between Canadians and Cubans. The larger scope is to dispel misinformation about Cuba and learn through a mutual exchange of ideas. Therefore the program is educational as well as recreational. It is a coming together of those who have only experienced the capitalist system and would like to learn about socialism and solidarity, and those who live in a socialist society and practice solidarity. Regardless of the mindset, the exhilaration that all *brigadistas* experience at special sites such as the historical Sierra Maestra, that witnessed resistance against oppression since the time of the indigenous Taínos to the twentieth century rebels of the 26 of July Movement, is indescribable.

Voluntarism, as in work without pay, is an old concept under any ideology, but the lack of pay is the only common feature. The approach to how volunteer work is encouraged and the underlying expectations that go with it, establish the real dividing line between volunteer work in a socialist or a capitalist system. In other words, the nature of voluntarism is a reflection of a country's social system.

Cuba has recently ended the traditional practice of volunteer work by Cubans, choosing to focus on the productivity of paid workers instead in order to strengthen the economy. However, Cuba still encourages volunteers from many countries of the world to bring solidarity and good will to Cuba. In the same spirit Cuba also sends volunteers to the Global South suggesting that international solidarity remains the main underlying motivation behind voluntarism within a socialist society.

The reciprocal nature of solidarity between Canadians and Cubans is manifested at the level of steadfastness to the mutual struggle and continued partnership. I have witnessed expressions of ideological awareness and commitment to a more just cause also shared by many *brigadistas*. I have also often heard from Cubans their promise to continue supporting their revolution as Cuba's contribution to the world struggle, including Canada's.

The range of views about world outlook, political awareness, and approach to solidarity is quite different between Canadians and Cubans due to the different life experiences. Among Canadians, and this can be observed from the cross-section of past *brigadistas* above, solidarity leans mostly towards the humanitarian interest for Cubans and their society; curiosity about Cuba is stronger than the fear of communism. Among Cubans, solidarity has a more political significance: socialist solidarity, which is generally experienced by Cubans internally in their interaction with the state; and political solidarity, which is experienced by Cubans in their interaction with the rest of the world and more openly with those who are perceived to be oppressed by an unfair and unjust social system.

The Canadian participation on the VWB constitutes more of a symbolic gesture of solidarity than real productive labour, but this gesture is highly appreciated by Cubans who marvel at the dedication of foreigners who decide to spend their vacation working in Cuba, and is highly rewarding to Canadians who participate as well. Most significant are the people-to-people links that are clearly reflected by the accounts of former *brigadistas*.

Human connectedness is the best way to peaceful and respectful relationships. As I have stated elsewhere, any people-to-people link is a process rather than an immediate short-term goal. In fact, over the twenty years of being in operation, the *Che* Guevara VWB clearly has focused on the process. In this sense, there is no final single outcome from the coming together of two people representing two different social systems and political views. Rather, we can only expect the establishment of a sustained process of solidarity and friendship based on mutual respect. This process recognizes the differences, bases itself on the common ground of solidarity and operates in the full range of the solidarity space (Pagliccia 2008).

Finally, after so many encounters with Cubans on the *Che* Guevara Volunteer Work Brigade, one is left wondering if the resourceful, political, educated and socially aware Cuban we get to know, appreciate and respect, is not in fact the "new man or woman" that *Che* Guevara envisioned.

References

Ariet, María del Carmen (1993). *Che Pensamiento Político*. La Habana: Editora Política.

Balwin, Greg (2012, April 4). Is Volunteering Worth It? The Economics of Generosity. *Huffington Post*. http://www. huffingtonpost.com/greg-baldwin/is-volunteering-worth-it-_b_1404205.html. Retrieved January 10, 2013.

Banco Central de Cuba (n.d.). *La Economía Cubana en el Período Especial, 1990-2000*. http://www.bc.gob.cu/Anteriores/Otros/economia%20cubana.pdf. Retrieved January 29, 2013.

Canada's Higher Education and Career Guide (n.d.). Canada Volunteer Directory. http://www.canadian-universities. net/Volunteer/index.html. Retrieved January 8, 2013.

Canadian Network on Cuba (n.d.). Che GuevaraVolunteer Work Brigade. http://www.canadiannetworkon-cuba.ca/brigade/. Retrieved April 4, 2014.

Central de Trabajadores de Cuba (2011a). *Cambios Necesarios*. http://www.trabajadores.cu/news/2011/08/01/cambios-necesarios Retrieved January 4, 2013.

_____ (2011b). *Trabajo voluntario: valores y eficiencia*. http://www.trabajadores.cu/news/20111031/255374-trabajo-voluntario-valores-y-eficiencia. Retrieved January 4, 2013.

Corporation for National and Community Service (n.d.). Volunteering and Civic Engagement in the United States. http://www.volunteeringinamerica.gov/national. Retrieved January 8, 2013.

Guevara, Ernesto (1965). *Che Guevara speaks. Selected Speeches and Writings*. Pathfinder Press.

ICAP (n.d.). siempreconcuba.cu. http://www.icap.cu. Retrieved April 4, 2014.

Pagliccia, Nino (2008). "Solidarity Organizations and Friendship Groups: internationalist volunteer work brigades and people-to-people ties". In Antoni Kapcia and Alexander I. Gray (Eds.), *The Changing Dynamic of Cuban Civil Society* (pp 116-139). Gainesville: University Press of Florida.

United States Department of Treasury (n.d.). *Cuban Democracy Act ("CDA")*. United States Code. Title 22. Foreign Relations and Intercourse Chapter 69. http://www.treasury.gov/resource-center/sanctions/Documents/cda.pdf. Retrieved April 4, 2014.

United States Congress (1996, March 12). *The Cuban Liberty and Democratic Solidarity (Libertad) Act of 1996*. Public Law 104-114. http://www.gpo.gov/fdsys/pkg/PLAW-104publ114/pdf/PLAW-104publ114.pdf. Retrieved April 8, 2012.

Venceremos Brigade (n.d). http://www.venceremos-brigade.net/. Retrieved January 24, 2013.

Volunteer Canada (n.d.). About us. http://volunteer.ca/content/about-us. Retrieved January 8, 2013.

Nino Pagliccia

Youth Canada (n.d.). *Volunteer Work*. Government of Canada. Services for youth. http://www.youth.gc.ca/eng/topics/jobs/volunteer.shtml. Retrieved January 8, 2013.

Chapter 5

Building a Consistent and United Campaign Across Canada: the Effective Way to Free the Five Cuban Heroes

TAMARA HANSEN
and ALI YEREVANI

"My main hope is that the nature of the trial is too murky, is too perverse, to withstand the pressure of the best people in the world. I believe that this injustice, this trial, is going to go down in history as one of the worst example of what they call U.S. justice. And I hope that the U.S. government, little by little, is going to feel that the weight of this injustice is costing them more than solving the problem."

- René González, one of the Cuban Five, on
Democracy Now, October 24, 2013.

◇◇

Who are the 5 Cuban Heroes Held in U.S. Jails?

Since 1959, the United States government and its counter-revolutionary allies who left Cuba after the revolution (the majority settling in the state of Florida) have been working together to destroy or distort any gains made by the Cuban people and their revolution. Miami-based terrorist groups such as Alpha 66, Brothers to the Rescue, and others have been responsible for hundreds of terrorist attacks that have taken the lives of nearly 3,500 people in Cuba since 1959 (Lamrani 2005, December 15).

The well-documented list of atrocities committed by these groups and others includes bombings, assassinations, spreading of disease, sabotage, attacks against friends of Cuba and even Cuban diplomats and officials visiting and working in other countries. The most horrendous of these attacks was the bombing of a Cuban airliner in 1976, which took the lives of all 73 people on-board. This included six students from Guyana who had scholarships to study medicine for free in Cuba; five Koreans; and 24 members of the Cuban fencing team returning with gold medals after a great triumph at the Pan American games in Venezuela. The mastermind behind the plane bombing was Luis Posada Carriles who was charged and prosecuted in Venezuela, however Posada escaped from prison before the court gave its verdict. In an article written by attorney José Pertierra, he explains that only a few short weeks after the Cubana airliner was downed, "[Posada] landed a job with the CIA in an operation that later became known as the Iran-Contra scandal. The United States has never bothered to explain how it was possible for an international fugitive charged with 73 counts of first-degree murder to so quickly land a $120,000-a-year job with the CIA, arming Nicaraguan Contras" (Pertierra 2011).

However, there were also many times that this terrorism reached close to home here in Canada. In *Canada-Cuba Relations: The Other Good Neighbor Policy*, Professor John M. Kirk (1997) outlines many acts of intimidation and violence against Cuban diplomats in Canada. For example, Kirk explains that in 1966 and 1967, "a rocket exploded outside the [Cuban] embassy...Threats, both written and by telephone, were received by Cuban diplomats, a Cuban freighter was bombed in Montréal, in March 1967 a bomb exploded at a Montréal auction house that was selling Cuban goods." (p. 76). Additionally, on April 3, 1972 a bomb exploded on the 12th floor of the Cuban Trade Mission in Montréal, Québec killing a Cuban official, and destroying most of that floor. These are but a few examples of attacks that continued throughout the 1970s.

Another case that hits close to home is the murder of Fabio di Celmo, an Italian resident of Canada on vacation in Cuba. Like hundreds of thousands of people living in Canada, di Celmo visited Cuba in 1997 as a tourist to enjoy the warmth and beauty of the island and its people. A bomb planted in his hotel lobby tragically took his life and wounded many others. Posada Carriles virtually admitted to being the mastermind behind this bomb plot.

Of course another tactic used is that of intimidation. At the 2007 DFAIT-NGO (Department of Foreign Affairs Canada and Non-Governmental Organizations) Conference/Consultations in Ottawa, Tamara Hansen (one of the authors of this chapter) and two organizers with *la Table de concertation de solidarité Québec-Cuba* were followed into an underground parking lot and threatened and harassed by members of the Canadian-Cuban Foundation. This was not an isolated incident, as the same people have followed and intimidated activists in the past. These types of incidents show a consistent tactic used by these organizations to scare and threaten those who speak out publicly in support of the Cuban revolution.

It was in this climate of fear and violence that the Cuban Five, Gerardo Hernández, Antonio Guerrero, Ramón Labañino, Fernando González, and René González, volunteered to go to Miami to infiltrate and expose the Miami-based terrorist organizations responsible for these types of crimes against the people of Cuba and the world.

These men were very successful and the information they collected was sent to the Cuban government. This information was then shared with the FBI, in hopes that they would address Cuba's concerns. However, on September 12, 1998, the United States government arrested the group, who came to be known as the Cuban Five, and threw them each in solitary confinement for 17 months, denying them many of their most basic rights. From the time of their imprisonment, those following the case have witnessed gross injustice: from solitary confinement, to the complete media blackout of the trail and case outside of Miami, to their judge refusing a change of venue to move their trial out of the extremely prejudiced city of Miami, to each being convicted as guilty despite a major lack of evidence and receiving very harsh sentences (the most egregious being Gerardo's double-life sentence plus 15 years).

The list of irregularities in their case and trial is too lengthy to fully discuss in this chapter. We hope that those who are interested in the campaign to free the Cuban Five will take the time to research many of the great articles and books that have now been written on their case, some of which are written by authors living in Canada. Two that we particularly recommend are, *Voices from the Other Side: An Oral History of Terrorism Against Cuba*, by Keith Bolender (Pluto Press 2010) and *What Lies Across the Water: The Real Story of the Cuban Five*, by Stephen Kimber (Fernwood Publications 2013).

The main purpose of this introduction is to give our readers a clear sense of the threats and terrorist actions carried out against Cuba, which is needed to fully understand the importance of the work the Cuban Five carried out in Florida. The main focus of this chapter will be on the great work that has been done by volunteer Cuba solidarity activists and their allies across Canada over the past 10 years for the freedom of the Cuban Five. While at first glance, this case seems like one of injustice after injustice, the actions of the U.S. government against the 5 must be contrasted with the strong and courageous response by the 5 themselves (who have been offered money and freedom if they would only denounce the Cuban government and admit their "guilt"). Their determination to prove their innocence and commitment to stop terrorism is celebrated around the world, especially in Cuba where they are known as heroes. Across the globe, thousands of institutions, organizations and individuals are demanding that the U.S. government immediately free these 5 Cubans held in United States' jails.

Beginning the Campaign for the Cuban Five in Canada –its Importance and its Impact

The campaign to free the Cuban Five, began soon after their arrest, however it was not until the formation of the Canadian Network on Cuba (CNC), *la Table de concertation de solidarité Québec-Cuba* (TCSQ-C) and other newly formed regional groups in 2002, that it became an important aspect of solidarity work throughout the country.

This was kicked off with the CNC sponsored national tour of Aleida Guevara and Irma González in the fall of 2003. Aleida Guevara is the daughter of the legendary revolutionary Ernesto *Che* Guevara, she is also a pediatrician. Irma González is the daughter of René González, one of the Cuban Five, and at the time of the tour she was just 19 years old. Having the daughter of *Che* Guevara touring Canada was a creative way to bring attention to the case of the Cuban Five. The two honoured guests visited the country from coast to coast speaking to hundreds of people in Halifax, Montréal, Québec, Kingston, Ottawa, Toronto, Hamilton, Kitchener-Waterloo, Niagara, Winnipeg, Vancouver, and Victoria. For many places across the country, this was the first time anyone had heard of the case of the Cuban Five, as the media in the U.S. and Canada have basically refused to cover this case. According to the report on the website of the Canadian Network on Cuba, the tour received coverage in the Kingston Whig-Standard, Vancouver Sun, Victoria Times-Colonist, Montréal Gazette, Halifax Chronicle-Herald, and on CPAC (the Cable Public Affairs Channel), all of which are major media outlets in Canada.

The tour had a lasting impact. For Tamara Hansen, Aleida and Irma's visit to Vancouver was the first event she attended about Cuba. It so happens that Irma and Tamara are the same age, and the impact of seeing a young woman leader speaking out, not only for her father and the 4 other men held in U.S. prisons, but also against U.S. intervention in her country was powerful. In Vancouver, Irma proclaimed, "That's why we are here, we need you to join our cause...When the trial happened nobody knew about the case, so they felt free to do whatever they wanted. But if these courts see that there are many eyes watching them they will have to apply their laws. We are only asking that the United States apply its own laws, because if they had applied their laws, these 5 men would be free already and home with their families in Cuba" (González 2003). Across Canada Aleida and Irma appealed to all human-loving people to get involved in the campaign for the freedom of the Cuban Five. Many organizations, groups, and individuals around Canada were inspired by these two Cuban women and their appeal for people to roll up their sleeves and get to work.

Successes and Growth of the Cuban Five Campaign

To explain and assess the successes in the campaign to free the Cuban Five over the past decade the authors of this chapter have gone back through archives, websites, and reports over the past ten years to give a full picture of the work that has been done. This is by no means an exhaustive list of events and actions for the Cuban Five. We see it more as an overview of some of the highlights and apologize in advance for any oversights.

In fall 2005, co-directors of the acclaimed documentary "Mission Against Terror," Bernadette Dwyer and Roberto Ruíz Rebo, tour Canada to screen their film on the case of the Cuban Five. The tour is coordinated by the Canadian Network on Cuba (CNC) and *La Table de concertation de solidarité Québec-Cuba.*

In December 2005, the Free the Cuban 5 Committee-Vancouver begins a campaign of monthly picket actions in front of the United States Consulate demanding freedom for the Cuban Five. The 100th monthly picket action took place in March 2014.

In June 2006, the Canadian Federation of Students, a national orga-nization of post-secondary students' unions representing more than half a million students, writes a letter urging then U.S. President George W Bush to release the Cuban Five from jail without delay.

In November 2006, Irma González returns to Canada with the wife of Ramón Labañino, Elizabeth Palmeiro, for a second nation-wide tour to raise awareness about the case of the Cuban Five unjustly held in U.S. jails. The tour was coordinated by the CNC and TCSQ-C.

In May 2007, the TCSQ-C and the *Comité Fabio Di Celmo pour les 5* began monthly picket actions in Montréal for the freedom of the Cuban Five in front of the United States Consulate.

In November 2007, organizations and individuals from across Canada, the U.S. and Cuba unite together in Toronto for the "Breaking the Silence: Solidarity Conference for the Cuban Five." Over 500 people join in for different parts of the program, including speeches by: the Cuban Ambassador to Canada, Ernesto Sentí Darias; Leonard Weinglass, prominent lawyer for the Cuban Five; Livio di Celmo, the brother of Fabio di Celmo; and Elizabeth Palmeiro, wife of Ramón Labañino. The conference is a joint project of the CNC, TCSQ-C, and the National Network on Cuba (U.S.).

In July 2008, efforts by the TCSQ-C and CNC lead Francine Lalonde, a Bloc Québécois Member of Parliament, and 55 other members of Canada's Parliament to sign a joint letter demanding immediate freedom for the Cuban Five. This is a great victory for the campaign in Canada, which partly resulted from a meeting that Elizabeth Palmeiro had with Francine Lalonde in 2007.

In September 2008, groups across Canada and around the world mark 10 years of unjust imprisonment for the 5 Cubans. In Vancouver, there is a special poetry contest held, with over 30 people from across British Columbia writing poems expressing their solidarity with the Cuban Five. The poems are compiled into a special booklet for wide distribution, and will soon be published as a book.

Tamara Hansenand Ali Yerevani

In May 2008, the Canadian Broadcasting Corporation (CBC) features a 13-minute special segment on the case of the Cuban Five. This is a big breakthrough against the mainstream media's wall of silence against this case.

In July 2010, Keith Bolender, a Canadian author and freelance journalist who worked for more than 10 years with the Toronto Star, releases his book, *Voices from the Other Side: An Oral History of Terrorism Against Cuba* (Pluto Press). The book includes over 75 first-person interviews with Cubans who have been victims or have had loved ones killed in U.S.-sponsored terrorist attacks, the same attacks the Cuban Five were trying to prevent.

In September 2012, Toronto hosts another Breaking the Silence conference, "Peoples' Tribunal and Assembly - Justice for the Five." The peoples' tribunal includes over 20 honoured guest speakers from across Canada and around the world. Among them Elizabeth Palmeiro and Adriana Pérez, wives of two of the Cuban Five; Saul Landau, director of *Will the Real Terrorist Please Stand Up?* and other important documentaries; Cindy Sheehan, internationally renowned American anti-war activist; Tony Woodley, Executive Officer of UNITE the Union, UK; Richard Klugh, Lawyer for the Cuban Five and many other distinguished guests.

In August 2013, Fernwood Publications prints *What Lies Across the Water: The Real Story of the Cuban Five* by Stephen Kimber, a professor of journalism at the University of King's College in Halifax and an award-winning writer, editor, and broadcaster.

On March 5, 2014 the Free the Cuban 5 Committee – Vancouver marks 100 monthly picket actions in front of the United States Consulate in Vancouver, British Columbia.

Labour Unions in Canada Take up the Campaign

The union support for this campaign in Canada has grown drastically over the last ten years. Much of this is thanks to the dedicated efforts of the Worker to Worker Canada-Cuba Labour Solidarity Network, led by Heide Trampus (see her Chapter 6). Delegations from unions in Canada have attended many events in Cuba to learn about the case of the Cuban Five. They have then returned to pass resolutions within their unions to raise awareness about the injustice committed by the United States government against the Cuban Five. In 2011, the Canadian Labour Congress, Canada's largest umbrella organization for dozens of affiliated unions, provincial federations of labour and regional labour councils, passed a resolution in favour of the Cuban Five. The resolution, passed at their 26th Constitutional Convention, stated their resolve to, "express our solidarity with the Cuban Five; and write to the United States' President Obama asking him to allow visitation rights for the families of the Cuban Five and urging him to immediately release the Cuban Five" (Canadian Labour Congress 2011).

Later that year, the Human Rights & International Solidarity Committee of the Federation of Post-Secondary Educators (FPSE) in British Columbia organized a tour of campuses across the province with Jorge Soberón, Cuban Consul General in Toronto. Jorge met with hundreds of students and educators on campuses across B.C., to speak about the Cuban Five.

The September 2012, "Peoples' Tribunal & Assembly - Justice for the Five" was sponsored by the United Food and Commercial Workers Union, Canadian Union of Postal Workers, United Steelworkers-Canada, Canadian Union of Public Employees, and the Ontario Federation of Labour. It featured important speakers from the labour movement interested in lending their voices to the campaign for the immediate freedom of all of the Cuban Five.

Tamara Hansenand Ali Yerevani

Most recently, in April 2013, the United Steelworkers' Union (USW) brought Adriana Pérez, the wife of Gerardo Hernández to Toronto and Vancouver. In Toronto, Adriana spoke to a packed event at the Steelworkers' Hall and the visit received media attention with an article published in The Toronto Star newspaper entitled, "U.S. gives Cuba cold shoulder over prisoners and their suffering families" (Ross 2013). Adriana was joined by Julio Garmendía Peña, the Ambassador of Cuba to Canada, during her visit to Vancouver. In Vancouver, Adriana had the chance to speak at a lively solidarity meeting with over 200 people participating. That event was co-sponsored by local solidarity groups, Vancouver Communities in Solidarity with Cuba, The Canadian–Cuban Friendship Association–Vancouver and the Free the Cuban 5 Committee–Vancouver. Adriana also spoke to the USW's national convention where over 600 delegates learned, many for the first time, about the Cuban Five.

There have been many other actions and activities taken on by unions and labour organizations in Canada in favour of the Cuban Five, unfortunately we do not have space to delve deeper into this work, but this is an important part of solidarity that reaches out beyond the progressive and activist community to workers, their unions, and their workplaces.

Fifteen Years of Unjust Imprisonment

September 12, 2013, marks 15 years of unjust imprisonment for the Cuban Five. The chant, "15 years too long! Free the Cuban Five NOW!" rings out around the world. Over 15 years support has been building with Parliamentarians, unions & labour organizations, Amnesty International, 10 Nobel Prize laureates, lawyers & legal experts, award-winning authors & artists, the National Lawyers Guild (U.S.) and others on a list that continues to grow, demanding immediate freedom for all the Cuban Five.

Previously, on October 7, 2011, a big day came for supporters of the Cuban Five around the world. René González, having served his full jail sentence, was released from prison. However, with René being a U.S. citizen he was to remain in the United States on parole in Florida for 3 years. Nevertheless, after a solid campaign demanding he be allowed to return to Cuba with his family permanently, on May 3, 2013, the world learned of an important victory. The Free the Cuban 5 Committee–Vancouver wrote in their statement, "Today, on May 3rd 2013, Judge Joan Lenard signed the order to allow René González to remain in Cuba for the remaining portion of his three-year parole, and of course he can continue to remain in Cuba thereafter. [...] This great victory is felt with joy, happiness, sweat and blood. René has come a long way in this heroic struggle of 14 years against the U.S. injustice system. We feel and understand this great victory. Nevertheless, we must immediately remind ourselves that we still need to go for another four victories until all of our five heroic Cuban brothers are freed" (Free the Cuban 5 Committee – Vancouver 2013).

This victory led to a question: do we start campaigning for the Cuban 4? The resounding international decision is no. We continue to call for the freedom of all 5 Cuban heroes and we still refer to it as the case of the Cuban Five, because René lost 14 and a half years of his life. We believe it is best to let Gerardo Hernández, who has the longest sentence of the Cuban Five, explain. In a letter written from the Victorville Penitentiary in California after receiving the news that René would be able to stay in Cuba, Gerardo (2013) wrote,

> He [René] fulfilled with dignity every day of his sen-
> tence, and came out with his head held as high as when
> he went in, but yet he still had to suffer the loss of his
> brother and his father in solitude. Today each one of the

Five is a little freer. Part of us wanders through the streets of this island with him, and we can almost breathe the air, and bathe under the sun. Someone asked me if we will now say that we are not five, but four, that would be a mistake! We are five and we will continue to be five! Today we have to continue the fight not only for the other four, but for René as well, because we know him, and we know that he will never be really free until we're all back in the homeland. The difference now is that this battle, which will go on until the end for the Five, has from this day on a new standard-bearer. Congratulations René! Your four brothers celebrate with you, proudly!

We cannot forget the injustice committed by the U.S. government against René. He missed watching his children grow up, he missed his eldest daughter's marriage, he missed graduations, he missed time with relatives who passed on before his return to Cuba, he missed the birth of his first grandchild and he was not able to see his wife, Olga Salanueva, for 14 and a half years as the U.S. government denied all of her visa requests. While René is back in Cuba there is still the question of justice, how can the crimes committed against him and his family be undone? This is one of the main reasons we continue to call them the 5 Cuban heroes. Because as Gerardo says, "We know that he will never be really free until we're all back in the homeland." At the time of writing, Fernando González has also been released after ending his full sentence and is back in Cuba. But the work continues.

Campaign for the 5 Cuban Heroes: Our Experience in Vancouver and British Columbia

In recent years there has been a general agreement that Vancouver has established a leading example in the campaign to free the Cuban Five, among more than 300 groups around the world. Nevertheless, we must say that in the last ten years our campaign has gone through a lot of challenges and ups and downs in order to reach this point. Although the Free the Cuban 5 Committee-Vancouver (FC5C-Van) was formed in July 2003 by a group of activists including present activists Nino Pagliccia, Thomas Davies, and Ali Yerevani (one of the authors of this chapter), originally it was Nino Pagliccia, then executive committee member of Canadian-Cuban Friendship Association and Canadian Network on Cuba, who started this campaign in Vancouver and the province of British Columbia. Ali Yerevani, himself a founding member of FC5C-Van, remembers the first time in early 2003 when he received a Cuban Five brochure from Nino. Ali explains that when he looked at the address on the brochure, it was from the National Committee to Free the Cuban Five in the U.S. Ali remembers how it was at that point that it became clear that Vancouver needed a local address and to build a local group.

The desire to create a Free the Cuban 5 Committee in Vancouver became even stronger after a visit by Vladimir Mirabal, the 3rd Secretary at the Cuban Embassy in Canada, who spoke at a forum in Vancouver on July 24, 2003 marking 50 years of the Cuban Revolution and the attack on the Moncada Army Garrison. The new committee formed on July 26, 2003 in order to make the case of the Cuban Five a case known to all people who believe in peace and justice in Vancouver and B.C. Our overall goal was a constant search to find new and dynamic ways of bringing the case of the 5 Cuban prisoners to people. Hence we immediately started to organize many different types of events in a consistent manner in order to do our part in the struggle for their freedom. Our ultimate

Tamara Hansenand Ali Yerevani

goal was very concrete and to the point, as well as simple: make the case of 5 Cubans an issue in Vancouver, B.C., and Canada.

The campaign began with regular petitioning at the Vancouver Public Library to ask people to sign on demanding immediate freedom for the Cuban Five, pretty much no one passing by had heard of the case. Yet through discussions, debates and the enthusiastic energy of petitioners, hundreds of signatures were collected. One of the first events organized was a film showing planned along with a committee in solidarity with Colombia. Many people were familiar with issues in Latin America and interested to learn more about opposing U.S. intervention in Colombia, so it was fitting to also add a short documentary about the case of the Cuban Five to introduce the history of U.S.-sponsored terrorism against Cuba.

Gradually, activists and progressive people in Vancouver learned about the case of the Cuban Five. However, it was clear to the organizers of the Free the Cuban 5 Committee-Vancouver that in order to build the political pressure needed to make this case a real issue in Canadian and American politics, the committee needed to raise awareness about the case with everyone in Vancouver and across British Columbia. In order to understand our successful campaigning for the five Cubans we would like to establish in this section two important and fundamental principles of our work. First, our action program and second, the very hard work of our ongoing activities based on our action program from July 2003 to now.

Our action program is our commitment to building this campaign in a serious way. Our discussions about what strategies to undertake have drawn the following conclusions:

- We need to take on the case of the 5 Cuban heroes as a campaign. A campaign meaning ongoing political activities around them.

- Our work should be consistent; it cannot be casual. Consistency is the key to success.

- Our Cuban 5 committee should have an annual action plan and a political goal to present our perspective, from every little activity to the big ones. In order to have ongoing activities, we need concrete and specific political tasks.

- Our activists should reach out to people beyond activist and progressive communities. We need to find ways of reaching all types of people, working people.

- Our activists should find ways to reach out to politicians too. Whether progressive, liberal or even conservative - simply put - whoever is against this injustice for whatever motivation, we want to include them. This can also include labour unionists, their unions and local councils, religious organizations, city officials, and NGOs.

- We need to popularize the case of the Cuban Five. We believe that all activists should take on the motto, "Let's find a way to make the case of the 5 Cuban heroes a political issue in our region."

- Our work should appeal to the media at all levels, grassroots or mainstream, and especially all possible community and ethnic newspapers that come out in many different languages.

- We need literature in order to educate and bring new people to our activities. This could be booklets, pamphlets, newsletters, postcards, and other audio/video materials.

- Our work should involve ongoing concrete activities with immediate results including, petitioning and information tables, as well as our monthly picket actions in front of the U.S. consulate in Vancouver.

- We should always challenge ourselves to be creative and to work with youth.

In Vancouver alone, since July 2003, we have organized more than 300 different actions and events. This means between 2 and 3 Cuban Five campaign activities each month. This does not include participation in dozens of events and activities in the U.S. and internationally, as well as Cuba.

Needless to say, while Free the Cuban 5 Committee-Vancouver has been the main organizer and promoter of these events, this great workload and activities would not have been possible without the broad support for our work from individuals and groups with their interest to take up the case of the Cuban Five within their own jurisdictions. To begin, the FC5C-Van has greatly enjoyed the support of Vancouver Communities in Solidarity with Cuba (VCSC) that has provided all kinds of assistance including materials and financial. We also received help and support through endorsement, sponsorship, significant solidarity and joint action/events with dozens of organizations in British Columbia such as

- Canadian-Cuban Friendship Association - Vancouver (CCFA-Vancouver), formed in 1961 and the oldest Cuba solidarity organization in Canada

- *Comité de Ayuda para el Desarrollo Social en El Salvador* (CODESES)

- Solidarity Coalition for a United Latin America (SCULA)

- Branches of the Communist Party of Canada

- Communist Party Canada -Marxist Leninist

- Venezuelan Consulate in Vancouver

- Tim Louis, Lawyer and former city councillor

- Colleen Glynn, Chair of the NDP, Richmond East

- Central America Support Committee (CASC) in Victoria

- Goods for Cuba in Victoria

- Friends of Cuban 5 in Nanaimo

- Friends of Cuban 5 in Comox Valley and Courtenay

- Friends of Cuban 5 in Bowen Island

- Thompson Rivers University Socialist Club in Kamloops

Outside of British Columbia, we have worked and collaborated with various groups across Canada and the United States, as well as internationally. In Vancouver, alongside our organizers and local allies, we often invite other groups and individuals to speak at our monthly Free the Cuban Five picket actions, forums, cultural events, film showings, and teach-ins. These include speakers from Pastors for Peace, the International Committee to Free the Five, the National Committee to Free the Five (U.S.), *Comité Fabio di Celmo pour les 5*, Cuban Institute for Friendship with the Peoples (ICAP), and Cuban diplomats. We also invite speakers to connect the Cuban Five to the cases of other political prisoner held in

U.S. jails, such as Private Chelsea Manning, Leonard Peltier, and Mumia Abu-Jamal. Furthermore, war resisters have spoken on the connection between the values of the Cuban Five and their opposition to war. We also often invite musicians and poets to share their cultural participation at our pickets.

International Guest speakers since September 2010 have included:

- Adriana Pérez, wife of Cuban Five Gerardo Hernández

- Aleida Guevara, physician, author and daughter of iconic *Che* Guevara

- Antonio Guerrero, son of Cuban Five Antonio Guerrero

- Manuel Yepe, journalist and professor at the Higher Institute of International Relations in Havana, Cuba

- Basilio Gutiérrez, Esperanza Luzbert, Sandra Ramirez and Raúl Cardoso, representatives of ICAP

- Julio Garmendía Peña, Cuban Ambassador to Canada

- Teresita Vicente Sotolongo, former Cuban Ambassador to Canada

- Jorge Soberón and Laureano Cardoso, former Cuban Consul Generals in Toronto

- Miraly González González, First Secretary of the Cuban Embassy in Canada

- Javier Domokos, Cuban Consul General in Toronto

- Alicia Jrapko, Coordinator of the International Committee to Free the Cuban Five

- Gloria LaRiva, Coordinator of the National Committee to Free the Cuban Five (U.S.)

- Saul Landau, world-renowned filmmaker (recently deceased) and director of "Will the Real Terrorist Please Stand Up?"

- Alberto Antonio Dandolo, director of the documentary film "The Cuban Wives"

- Arnold August, author of *Cuba and Its Neighbours: Democracy in Motion*

- Stephen Kimber, author of *What Lies Across the Water: The Real Story of the Cuban Five*

There were also many other speakers prior to 2010 who lent their voices to the case of the Cuban Five in Vancouver.

Part of the arsenal of literature and materials we have created is a series of six postcards for two parallel campaigns: First, the "Obama Yes You Can!" card, addressed to President Obama, to be sent by people living in Canada demanding that he release the Cuban Five. Second, a series of five artistically designed postcards with information on the case of the Cuban Five and how to get involved in the campaign for their freedom. People are asked to send them to friends and relatives in the U.S. and around the world. FC5C-Van also participates in the International Free the Cuban Five postcard campaign, "Obama Give Me 5!" Our outreach work has included placing information booths in busy places like libraries and other public venues and appeal to people for their support by signing postcards as well as special petitions such as demanding U.S. authorities for visitation rights of the family members of the Cuban Five. All together over time, we reached out to a very large audience and have collected and sent hundreds of postcards to promote the case of the five Cubans.

Most recently, FC5C-Van has also built up the international Yellow Ribbon Campaign in Vancouver and B.C. In May 2013, René González, now in Cuba after finishing his prison sentence, launched the Yellow Ribbon Campaign to appeal mainly to people in the U.S. who would recognize this American folk tradition of tying yellow ribbons to a tree to show hope for the return of a loved one. René asked the people of Cuba to saturate the island with yellow ribbons on September 12, 2013, the day that marked 15 years of their unjust imprisonment. These ribbons are a symbol of the Cuban peoples' desire to see all of their five heroes return home, and Cubans responded in full force. People around the world also took on the campaign, and yellow ribbons have been displayed in hundreds of places across all continents.

The Free the Cuban 5 Committee-Vancouver responded enthusiastically to the call for September 12 and we continue to bring the Yellow Ribbon campaign to the streets of British Columbia. We began with a strong start. From September 12-15, FC5C-Van organized and coordinated 7 events in 4 days in Nanaimo, Bowen Island, Kamloops, and Vancouver. Since then, the yellow ribbons have become a constant part of our work. From banner drops, picket actions, forums, movie presentations, cultural events, and petition drives – the Yellow Ribbon campaign has been an exciting way to generate interest and solidarity with the 5 Cuban prisoners in the U.S. We now even have a continuous presence of yellow ribbons tied in front of the U.S. Consulate in Vancouver! The start of the Yellow Ribbon campaign and its activities has been reflected in major mainstream media, as well as community print media, radio and TV.

As long as the drive for freedom of the five Cubans continues we will be a strong support and fighters against this injustice. The FC5C-Van looks forward to continuing its work full–force as a labour of love until all five Cubans are back in Cuba with their families. We believe that with consistency, determination, unity, and more work this dream will become a reality very soon.

The Prospect of Cuban Five Heroes Campaign in Canada and Beyond

While we are reflecting on the development of the Cuba solidarity movement and campaign to free the Cuban Five in Canada, we must commit this section to looking towards the future.

In a speech given June 4, 2013 at a ceremony held for the "Five days for the Five" campaign, at the José Antonio Echeverría Polytechnic Institute in Havana, Ricardo Alarcón de Quesada, former president of Cuba's National Assembly, gave an inspired and moving speech entitled, "What else can we do?" (2013). In the speech Alarcón de Quesada outlines the need for a deeper strategy to awaken people in the United States about the case of the Cuban Five. He discusses at length the ongoing media blackout against this case and looks at some ways we can begin to break it. He explains, "How do we pierce the wall of silence surrounding this case? […] Gerardo, Ramón, Antonio and Fernando are waiting for Judge Lenard, the same one who initially sentenced them, to rule on extraordinary appeals or habeas corpus, the last legal recourse available to them. It is a complex, difficult, and impossible battle to win if it is not accompanied by solidarity. If it is not fought also outside the courtrooms, if we, those of us who are not prisoners, do not participate." (Fernando González has since been released and is now in Cuba). This call to action is accompanied by references to 9 legal and political documents that prove the innocence of the Cuban Five and their mistreatment in the hands of the U.S. justice system. He concludes his speech with these words, "We must honestly ask ourselves if we have done everything in our power to allow the American people to access to these truths that are jealously guarded by Washington." Of course he also reminds us to keep asking the question, "now, what else can we do?" The answer, we believe, is quite a bit!

While the focus of this chapter has been our work in Canada, Alarcón de Quesada's speech makes it clear that the key to our success lies in building the campaign for the Cuban Five around the world with a focus on bringing the message to the American people. Considering Canada shares a large border with the U.S., people living in Canada seem best suited for working together with institutions, organizations and individuals in the United States on this critical campaign.

Some of this collaborative work has already begun. Groups across Canada have participated in fundraising campaigns with the National Committee to Free the Cuban Five (U.S.) for purchasing ad space in the New York Times, Washington Post, and other mainstream media. Individuals and groups also participated in the 2012 and 2013 "Five Days for the Five" campaign organized by the International Committee to Free the Cuban Five in Washington, D.C. Many are further participating in the "5th of the month for the Cuban Five", by picketing outside U.S. consulates in Canada, sending press releases to U.S. and Canadian media and emailing and phoning the White House. These actions only represent a small fraction of what is possible for the future, if we think creatively and are willing to find new ways to construct this campaign. As Alarcón de Quesada explained during an interview with *Democracy Now* in October 2013, "The case can be solved very easily, simply with a stroke of [Obama's] pen ordering the release of the four brothers [now three] that continue to be in prison. He can do that. [...] If President Obama is really interested in projecting a more positive image of U.S. policy abroad, if he is interested in improving relations with Latin America, he better listen to what many governments in Latin America have been telling him: Simply, free the five."

While we are reflecting on the development of the Cuba solidarity movement in Canada, let us look towards a future where we achieve greater unity by not being limited by the borders that surround us. The great benefit of discussing solidarity in the context of "people-to-people foreign relations" is that borders do not limit us. To paraphrase Cuba's national hero José Martí, 'homeland is humanity'. People in the U.S. and Canada need to work together as one if we are going to succeed in building the political pressure needed to see all 5 Cuban heroes out of U.S. prisons and back with their families in Cuba.

¡Venceremos! ¡Volverán! We will prevail; they will return.

References

Alarcón de Quesada, Ricardo (2013). What else can we do? *Cubadebate.cu*. http://en.cubadebate.cu/opinions/2013/06/17/ what-else-can-we-do/. Retrieved April 18, 2014.

Bolender, Keith (2010). *Voices from the Other Side: An Oral History of Terrorism Against Cuba*. New York: Pluto Press.

Canadian Labour Congress (2011). General resolutions. *Canadianlabour.ca*, Ottawa. http://www.canadian- labour.ca/convention/2011-convention/general- resolutions#HumanRights. Retrieved April 18, 2014.

Dávalos Fernández, Rodolfo (2006). *United States vs. The Cuban Five: A Judicial Cover-up*. Havana: Capitán San Luís Editorial.

Free the Cuban 5 Committee-Vancouver (2013). An Advancement for Human Rights! A Progress for Humanity! René González to Remain in Cuba! http:// www.freethe5vancouver.ca/statements/2013/130503- Rene-statement.html. Retrieved April 18, 2014.

González, Irma (2003). Speech from "Free the Cuban 5! Solidarity Evening in Vancouver". *WorkingTV.com*, Vancouver. http://www.workingtv.com/freethecuban5.html. Retrieved April 18, 2014.

Goodman, Amy (2013a). Exclusive: René González, Lone Cuban 5 Member Freed from U.S. Prison, Speaks Out from Havana. *Democracy Now*. http://www.democracynow.org/2013/10/24/exclusive_René_González_lone_cuban_5. Retrieved April 18, 2014.

_____ (2013b). Ex-Cuban Foreign Minister on Threats by Militant Exiles & Why Obama Should Free the 5. *Democracy Now*. http://www.democracynow.org/2013/10/24/ex_cuban_foreign_minister_on_threats. Retrieved April 18, 2014.

Hansen, Tamara (2010). *Five Decades of the Cuban Revolution: The Challenges of an Unwavering Leadership*. Vancouver: Battle of Ideas Press.

Hernández, Gerardo (2013). We Will Always Be the Cuban Five. *periodico26.cu*. http://www.periodico26.cu/index.php/en/giants/8295-gerardo-hernandez-we-will-always-be-the-cuban-five. Retrieved April 18, 2014.

Kirk, John M. (1997). *Canada-Cuba relations: The other good neighbor policy*. Gainesville: University Press of Florida.

Kimber, Stephen (2013). *What Lies Across the Water: The Real Story of the Cuban Five*. Winnipeg: Fernwood Publications.

Lamrani, Salim (15 December 2005). Fifty years of U.S. terrorism against Cuba. *Voltaire Network*. http://www.voltairenet.org/article132624.html. Retrieved April 4, 2014.

Pertierra, José (2011). The Bombing of Cubana Flight 455: Murder in Paradise. *Counterpunch.org*. http://www.counterpunch.org/2011/10/11/murder-in-paradise/. Retrieved April 18, 2014.

Rodriguez Cruz, Juan Carlos (Ed.) (2005). *Cuba, The untold history*. Havana: Capitán San Luís Editorial.

Ross, Oakland (2013, April 27). U.S. gives Cuba cold shoulder over prisoners and their suffering families. *The Toronto Star*. http://www.thestar.com/news/world/2013/04/27/us_gives_cuba_cold_shoulder_over_prisoners_and_their_suffering_families.html. Retrieved April 18, 2014.

Chapter 6

Canadian Labour Solidarity with Cuba

HEIDE TRAMPUS

◇◇

Worker to Worker

In the early 1990s, following the loss of major trading partners upon the collapse of the Soviet Union and Eastern European countries and having survived 30 years of a U.S. blockade, Cuba faced a very difficult time known as the Special Period.

To make matters worse, the United States, which had tried successively by way of sanctions, sabotage and subversion to overthrow the Cuban government, further strengthened the blockade with the additional Torricelli Law. The bill, officially named the Cuban Democracy Act and presented by U.S. Congressman Robert Torricelli, passed in 1992. It prohibited foreign-based subsidiaries of U.S. companies from trading with Cuba and prevented food and medicines from being shipped to Cuba. In addition the U.S. started the Track II program meant to support anti-Castro groups in Cuba.

In the fall of 1995 U.S. Senator Jesse Helms (R-North Carolina) and U.S. Representative Dan Burton (R-Indiana) co-sponsored the Cuban Liberty and Democratic Solidarity (LIBERTAD) Act known as the Helms-Burton Act. Designed to discourage foreign investment in Cuba and to bring Cuba to its knees, the Act was passed in March 1996 (Cuba Solidarity Campaign n.d.).

Heide Trampus

In 1992, recognizing the unique challenges Cuba was facing in the struggle to assert its sovereignty, a group of Labour union activist led by Sarah Shartel, a member of the United Food and Commercial Workers union (UFCW) formed the Worker to Worker, Canada-Cuba Labour Solidarity Network.

With the slogan "Hands off Cuba," the goal was to present resolutions, demanding an end to the U.S. blockade against Cuba, for debate and vote at the Canadian Labour Congress (CLC) and at national, provincial, and local union convention floors. Getting support from members and the union leadership was a challenge partly due to lack of awareness, partly due to an already busy agenda with labour immediate issues. With the continuing efforts by union activists informing and educating the members, and repeatedly presenting resolutions for Labour to take actions opposing and demanding an end to the blockade, resolutions were finally accepted, brought to the convention floors, debated and voted on. In a short time, resolutions against the U.S. blockade, the Torricelli and Helms-Burton Acts, including resolutions asking for the return of the Cuban child Elián González back to Cuba to be with his father, passed unanimously.

It was during this time that Worker to Worker forged a strong link with the Cuban National Workers' Central Union (*Central de Trabajadores de Cuba*, CTC).

Canadian workers are always surprised to find out that most workers in Cuba are members of a union and that the union movement has a long history there. The CTC originated as the *Confederación de Trabajadores de Cuba* in 1939 representing three million members. Lázaro Peña González was the first elected Secretary General and is still revered by all workers in Cuba. Peña was also an important figure in the founding of the Confederation of Latin American Workers (CTAL) based in Mexico in 1938, and in 1945 was among the founders of the World Federation of Trade Unions (WFTU) and was elected vice president in 1953. When he attended the third WFTU meeting in Vienna, Austria in October 1953,

Cuba's ruling dictator Fulgencio Batista did not allow him to re-enter the country. After the triumph of the revolution in 1959, Peña returned to Cuba and resumed the leadership as general secretary of the CTC until 1966. He died on May 11, 1974 (Pacheco 2011, May 27).

Notable Worker to Worker Solidarity Activities

In the early 1990s the first Worker to Worker Labour Solidarity conference was held in Toronto at the Ontario Federation of Labour building. The invited delegation from the *Central de Trabajadores de Cuba* (CTC) included Pedro Ross Leal, Secretary General of the CTC and Manuel Montero Bistillero, from the International Relations Department, North American section of the CTC.

Union activists, including a group from the Canadian union of Public Employees and John Weatherup, President of CUPE Local 4400, were part of a Worker to Worker delegation attending the International Meeting of Workers against Neo-Liberal Globalization on August 6 to 8, 1997. More than 1300 workers and labour activist representing over 300 unions from 61 countries participated in the event.

From April 27 to May 3, 2000 a Canadian union delegation participated in the "International Meeting of Women and Unionism in the Thresholds of the Third Millennium" and joined in the May Day activities. On November 10 to 14 of that year a Worker to Worker delegation attended the "Second World Meeting of Friendship and Solidarity," held in Havana.

In 2001 a planned U.S.-Cuba Labor Exchange tour to 25 U.S. cities and Puerto Rico had to be cancelled because of visa denials by the U.S. to the Cuban delegation. In a defiant attitude, Worker to Worker and the U.S.-Cuba Labor Exchange organized and held a joint conference in Windsor, Ontario in July 2002. Five labour leaders from Cuba, led by the CTC's general secretary Pedro Ross Leal, attended. Among those representing Canadian Labour were Barb Byers, Vice President of the CLC; Wayne Samuelson, President of the Ontario Federation of Labour (OFL); and Deborah Bourque, National President of the Canadian Union of Postal Workers (CUPW). Attending from the U.S. were the Vice-President of the Service Employee International Union (SEIU) Local 1199, New York, the leader of Black Workers for Social Justice and the director of the Coalition for Immigration Law Reform of Los Angeles. The presence of these important union leaders gave higher relevance to the support for Cuba. The close to 200 delegates attending came from across Canada and the United States. Topics covered were economic, political and social situation in Cuba, the Free Trade Area of the Americas (FTAA), United States-Canada-Cuba relations, and the "Justice for the Cuban Five" campaign. The range of topics was evidence of the mutual and international nature of solidarity but, most importantly, sent a clear signal to the U.S. government that Cuba was not isolated and had a place in labour discussions about typically North American issues.

In November 2002, following the April 2001 Summit of the Americas held in Québec City, a delegation led by Worker to Worker participated in the Second Hemispheric Meeting in the Struggle against the Free Trade Area of the Americas (FTAA) in Havana. Topics of discussion included ways of counteracting the treaty, which was attempting to extend the North American Free Trade Agreement between Canada, the United States, and Mexico (NAFTA) to the entire American hemisphere but undoubtedly to the exclusion of Cuba.

Subsequently, in January 2004 CUPE Ontario President Sid Ryan, other CUPE officials and members, along with a delegation of regional representatives of CUPW were part of a large Worker to Worker contingent attending the "Third Hemispheric Meeting against the Free Trade Area of the Americas (FTAA)."

To strengthen union solidarity, in February 2004, Leonel Gonzáles, a member of the CTC secretariat and Manuel Montero Bistillero from the international relations department of the CTC, arrived from Havana for meetings with Canadian union leaders arranged by Worker to Worker. They were warmly received in Toronto by the leadership of seven large unions: the United Steelworkers (USW), the United Food and Commercial Workers (UFCW), the Ontario Federation of Labour (OFL), the Canadian Union of Public Employees, Ontario Division (CUPE Ontario), and, in Ottawa, by the Canadian Labour Congress (CLC), the Canadian Union of Postal Workers (CUPW), and by the National Union of General Employees (NUPGE). This was followed in November of the same year with a Worker to Worker delegation attending the Seventh International Meeting of Unions Retirees in Havana. In April 2005, the Fourth Hemispheric Meeting of Struggle Against the FTAA (*NO AL ALCA*) took place in Havana and was again attended by a Worker to Worker delegation representing Canada's unions. Following the conference, the delegation stayed in Havana to participate in the May Day and International Solidarity Day activities.

In April of the following year, Venezuela's Hugo Chávez, Bolivia's Evo Morales, and Cuba's Fidel Castro signed the agreement for the establishment of the Bolivarian Alternative for the People of Our Americas (ALBA). A Worker to Worker delegation was present in Havana for this special event and for the May Day celebrations.

In November 2006, Worker to Worker held a Canada-Cuba Labour Solidarity conference at the Steelworkers Hall in Toronto. The conference was sponsored by the Ontario Federation of Labour (OFL), the Canadian Union of Public Employees (CUPE), the Canadian Union of Postal Workers (CUPW) the United Food & Commercial Workers (UFCW), the CUPE Toronto District Council and CUPE, Local 4400. At that conference a well-respected panel of high-level representative

Heide Trampus

from the Cuban Union, presenters from Canadian unions and specialist in the field covered the following topics:

- History of unions in Cuba
- Role of women in unions
- Role of unions in Cuban Society
- Democracy in Cuba
- Struggle against the FTAA and neoliberalism in North, Central, and South America and the Bolivarian Alternative for the Americas (ALBA).
- Health and Education systems in Cuba and Canada
- The truth about the "war on terrorism" and the anti-terrorist Cuban Five with special guest Elisabeth Palmeiro, wife of Ramón Labañino, Olga Salanueva and Irma González, wife and daughter of René González.

A joint statement from the participants was sent to the Attorney General of the United States, Alberto González (no relation to René), demanding that "true justice be served by releasing the five anti-terrorist Cuban men unjustly incarcerated and that Luís Posada Carriles be held accountable for his crimes." A copy was also sent to Canada's Minister of Foreign Affairs, the Honourable Peter McKay. The conference ended with a discussion about future work between Cuban and Canadian Trade unions and workers.

Another Worker to Worker Canada-Cuba Labour Solidarity conference was held in September 2010 at the Steelworkers Hall in Toronto, sponsored by UFCW, CUPW, and the United Steelworkers (USW) covering the following topics:

- The Blockade and U.S. relations

- The pretext of democracy and the U.S. Blockade against Cuba

- The Bolivarian Alternative for the Americas (ALBA). An update on changes taking place in Cuba

On the last day of the conference, a well-attended open forum titled "Solidarity with the Cuban Five," was held with special guest speaker Elizabeth Palmeiro, wife of Ramón Labañino. A joint statement from Worker to Worker and the participants to this forum calling for "Justice and Liberty for the Cuban Five" was sent to the U.S. President Barack Obama with copies to Secretary of State Hillary Clinton, Attorney General Eric Holder, to Canadian Prime Minister Stephen Harper and the Canadian Labour Congress.

All these events and exchanges have been crucial in building the morale of the labour movement both in Canada and Cuba, in strengthening links, and in redoubling the commitment to support Cuba.

Canadian Labour Solidarity Initiatives

Possibly inspired by the keen approach of Worker to Worker to build special ties between Canadian Labour and their Cuban counterpart, or maybe inspired by the intrinsic culture of solidarity within labour, Canadian labour solidarity with the *Central de Trabajadores de Cuba* (CTC) and its provincial and municipal unions developed and strengthened. Nationally and provincially, private and public sector unions and locals formed links of friendship and solidarity with their Cuban counterparts. The following is only a small sample of Canada-Cuba labour solidarity as represented by the initiatives of some of the well-known union leaders.

The Canadian Labour Congress (CLC)

CLC president Bob White began in 1993 to raise concerns about "the Cuban question." A May 1993 CLC statement, published by the CLC's International Affairs Department, called on the United States and other members of the international community to offer guarantees that there would be no foreign interference or intervention in Cuba and that relations with that country would be normalized in an effort to foster progressive internal change. It also called on Canada to use its longstanding relations with Cuba and its international influence to promote the full integration of Cuba into the international community. In a letter to Prime Minister Chrétien on the eve of the arrival of the U.S. President Clinton in Ottawa in February 1995, White officially requested Chrétien to protest the proposed Helms-Burton legislation, while offering suggestions on the expected role of Washington in U.S.-Cuba relations.

In April of 1995 accompanied by two assistants, White left for an official trip to Cuba where he met with government ministers, trade union leaders and workers, human rights activists, Canadian Embassy staff and NGOs. He stated, "Canada has an important role to play in the hemisphere in supporting Cuban workers and in counteracting the destructive role the United States plays through its embargo and recent investment laws." (Kirk and McKenna 1997: 158). In addition the CLC implemented a variety of small projects with its Cuban counterpart ranging from providing advice on foreign joint ventures to translating collective agreements into Spanish, to supporting a CTC collective farm (*finca*).

Further, in a CLC press release, White noted, "the CLC is in Cuba to strengthen our relationship with Cuban workers' organizations...We want to engage constructively with the *Central de Trabajadores de Cuba* (CTC) and Cuban NGOs to explore ways to promote peaceful change." (Kirk and McKenna 1997: 158).

In a continuing effort to maintain close ties with Cuba, in April 2003 CLC president Ken Georgetti, along with the CAW president Buzz Hargrove and treasurer Jim O'Neil, went to Cuba to meet with leaders of the CTC.

In a June 24, 2004 letter to Canadian Prime Minister Paul Martin, CLC president Ken Georgetti issued a vehement condemnation of attempts to destabilize Cuba. The CLC, representing three million workers and being the national voice for 12 provincial and territorial federations, 137 Labour Councils, and most national and international unions inside Canada, called on the Canadian government to reject anti-Cuba measures put forth in the U.S government report "Commission for Assistance to a free Cuba." In that 450-page long report sent from Colin Powell to then-president George Bush was an open call for the overthrow of the Cuban government. Georgetti's letter concludes, "We, as Canadians, must roundly condemn and reject this latest illegal and inhumane U.S. government interference in Cuban affairs, affirm the internationally recognized right to self-determination of countries, and proudly proclaim our independence and sovereignty in pursuing a foreign policy that continues to maintain and develop our friendly relations with Cuba."[1]

The CLC has a constant direct relationship with the CTC and has had many Cuban delegations and invited guests to their conventions. The latest meeting took place in Ottawa in September 2012, when Raymundo Navarro from the CTC International Relations Department was invited on a cross-Canada tour.

In addition to the CLC, other unions and labour organizations have given strong and ongoing support to Cuba.

---

1   Personal communication from the Ken Georgetti.

Heide Trampus

The United Steelworkers, Canada (USW)

With 225,000 members in Canada and more than 800,000 members continent-wide, USW is Canada's most diverse union, representing men and women of every ethnic background working in every sector of the economy in every region in Canada. USW members work in call centres and credit unions, mines and manufacturing plants, offices and oil refineries, restaurants and rubber plants, sawmills and steel mills, nursing homes, legal clinics, social service agencies, and universities.

The United Steelworkers are widely recognized in the labour movement for leading the way in building international solidarity. Fighting for the interest of workers at home and around the world they are active participants in the struggle for workers rights and justice around the globe.

With an incredible "Humanity Fund" the USW has given much support to Cuba. It was created in order to facilitate international worker solidarity, provide emergency relief and humanitarian aid, and fund international development projects.

The most active solidarity work started in the year 2000 with a variety of actions but with a focus to raise awareness about the Cuban Five. For example, following the signing of the agreement between USW and UNITE the Union (UK) in 2008 that created Workers Uniting, the world's first global union, one of the issues agreed to work on immediately as a global union was the freedom of the Cuban Five.

At a bi-annually held conference convention organized by the Canadian Network on Cuba in 2010, Jorge García Orgales, USW staff representative of the Global Affairs and Workplace Issues Department, highlighted the leadership of the USW in mobilizing to step up the work in defence of Cuba. He said that the USW stands for the development of joint actions in Canada and in the world for the release of the Cuban Five and has its own actions to develop closer links between the Steelworkers in the mining and metallurgical sectors and their Cuban counterparts. This work is of mutual benefits so as to learn from each other, support each other, and grow together. For example, USW is keenly interested in learning how Cuba deals with the impact of the global economic crisis without resorting to layoffs and massive destruction of the productive forces as is the case in Canada.

In fact a year later the USW was part of a delegation that met with the leadership of the CTC's Cuban Metalworkers Union and had a private meeting with Ricardo Alarcón de Quesada, President of the National Assembly of People's Power, and the highest ranking Cuban advocate for the Cuban Five.

The United Steelworkers Union stands continually in solidarity with the Cuban workers, sending delegations to the annual May Day activities, celebrating the international day of workers, in Havana.

Canadian Union of Postal Workers (CUPW)

The 54,000 members of CUPW work in large and small communities from Twillingate, Newfoundland to Tappen, British Columbia. A majority of members work for Canada Post as rural and suburban mail carriers. Others represented are cleaners, couriers, drivers, bicycle couriers and other workers in more than 15 private sector bargaining units. The union is divided into Atlantic, Québec, Metro-Montreal, Central, Metro-Toronto, Ontario, Prairie and Pacific Regions.

CUPW has a long-standing history of solidarity with Cuba and the Cuban Postal Workers union "*Sindicato Nacional de las Communicaciones, la Informática y la Electrónica* (SNTCIE)." National union representatives Fred Furlong and Dave Bleakney (one of the original founding members of Worker to Worker), made solidarity with Cuba an issue in their union. National President Deborah Bourque (2002-2008) was very much committed to building and maintaining links with the CTC as is the now National President, Denis Lemelin. Both visited Cuba many times for meetings with their Cuban sister union and the CTC leadership.

In July 2006 Ernesto Freire Cazañas, then Secretary General of the National Union of SNTCIE, underscored during a CUPW sponsored visit to Canada, the need to develop a greater understanding of how to defend worker's interests in Cuba's changing economy and the emergence of foreign ventures: "Cuban workers' priorities are the protection of the country's accomplishments made since 1959; its government-funded education and health care programs, and the provision of the family food basket." He also disclosed that their greatest fear is isolation and twinning is one way to gather moral support in the face of U.S. efforts to roll-back accomplishments.

Freire Cazañas outlined the history of twinning to show that it is not a new concept and that twinning has proven to be an effective way of developing material solidarity, moral support for Cuban workers and providing Cuban workers with the means of expressing support for Canadian workers' struggles.

Atlantic Region CUPW executive officers Wayne Mundle and Fred Furlong started the initiative by twinning CUPW locals in Halifax and Dartmouth with communication workers of the SNTCIE in the province of Santiago, and they were a driving force to get the national union and other regions involved.

Cindy McCallum-Miller, who was the National Director of the Prairie Region of the CUPW from 1996 to 2008, encouraged a number of locals to twin with specific provinces in Cuba. For example, Calgary twinned with Santa Clara, Saskatoon and Regina co-twinned with Camagüey, and Banff twinned with Granma.

In 2004 CUPW locals authorized members to participate in a tour to twinned areas and May Day activities in Havana. This was the first opportunity to make personal connections between the SNTCIE provincial union leaders and workers, and a delegation from CUPW's Prairie Region locals.

McCallum reported: "Delegates found the approach of the Cuban postal workers very interesting. In Canada the union is totally opposed to a team concept or collaborative process with the employer, because the employer's goal is to reduce jobs, benefits, and services, so there are no common goals. In Cuba, it seemed, the employer needed the consensus of the union and workers to make changes and had an obligation to deal with issues raised by the union and workers. Unlike in Canada where the laws support management rights and the struggle of workers is to protect hard won rights in their collective agreements – the revolution in Cuba creates a different dynamic for workers."

Strengthening and building on the existing relationship, CUPW continues inviting representative of the CTC and/or the SNTCIE as guests to their national conventions and participates with the CTC and SNTCIE in conferences, including the biennial Conference of Communication and Postal Unions held in Cuba, where leaders of communication unions from around the world are brought together. For the first time in the last 12 years, a delegation from UNI Americas (a UNI Global Union's regional organization for Communication and Services Unions, representing 4 million workers from the Americas and Caribbean), officially visited Cuba to evaluate the possibility of developing stronger relations with the Cuban counterpart. This visit is a result of the consistent and persuasive work of CUPW within UNI-Americas.

There have been many other CUPW delegations travelling to Cuba to learn about the Cuban reality on the ground including about the case of the Cuban Five. Mark Desgranges, the leader of the CUPW youth group, summarized some of the learning: "The Cuban people take pride knowing we are here to learn the truth about Cuba, its accomplishments and struggles. Unlike us, Cuban workers have a real voice in the government decision making."

At the September 2010 Canadian Network on Cuba convention, CUPW National President Denis Lemelin said that his union considers the fight for workers' rights inextricably linked to the fight for the alternative to neoliberal globalization. He stated that part of CUPW day-to-day work is to inform Canadians about Cuba and defend Cuba.

Heide Trampus

The United Food and Commercial Workers (UFCW)

UFCW is a progressive and inclusive organization dedicated to workers' rights and a better future for members and their families. It is backed by the strength of UFCW International – one of North America's largest private sector unions with over 1.3 million members. The 47 UFCW Local Unions in Canada have a membership 250,000 strong.

The relationship of UFCW towards Cuba and in particular Cuban Workers organizations has developed over the years from being informal until mid-1989 to becoming closer from the mid-1989 to present. The establishment of direct organizational contact and the development of official organizational relations with the *Central de Trabajadores* (CTC) characterize this second period.

January 1999 was a key time in the development of the relationship. This was the time that the first UFCW delegation went to Cuba for an official exchange. Since then the relationship has strengthened and has become one of mutual respect and solidarity with many joint activities. For many years, UFCW has assisted the logistical and structural development of the CTC, the Food Workers Union, Commerce Union and Tourism Union through yearly projects aiming at strengthening their educational, communications, and transportation capacities as a response to the rapidly expanding Cuban tourism sector. For over a decade, UFCW has sent a yearly delegation to Cuba and every two years sponsors Cuban delegations representing the CTC, Food Workers Union, Commerce Union, and Tourism Union for visits to workplaces and meetings with UFCW Locals across Canada.

Future plans of the UFCW are to continue in the same path, to increase the mutual understanding and thus the solidarity of UFCW Canada with the Cuban People and Cuban workers. Members of the United Food & Commercial Workers Union continue to play a significant role in the Worker to Worker, Canada-Cuba Labour Solidarity Network.

The Canadian Union of Public Employees (CUPE)

With 618,000 members across Canada, CUPE is Canada's largest union representing workers in Municipalities, Libraries, Universities, Health Care, Education, Social Services, Public Utilities, Transportation, Emergency Services, and Airlines. A strong union, committed to improving the quality of life for workers in Canada and around the globe, CUPE established the Global Justice fund, supporting work in common causes between CUPE locals and sister unions and activist in other countries. International work in CUPE is not done out of charity, but motivated by principles of solidarity.

Organizationally, there are provincial divisions for each province, as well as the National organization. Labour solidarity with Cuban unions and workers and relations with their Cuban sister union is especially strong in the British Columbia - and Ontario Division of CUPE.

CUPE national has been a long-time supporter of Cuba. Solidarity work with CUPE's sister union "*Sindicato Nacional de Trabajadores de la Administración Pública*" (SNTAP) or National Union of Administration Workers, which represents workers in the Cuban federal ministries, public energy, municipalities, courts and banking sector, began in 1995 when the then National General Secretary of SNTAP, Norma Ortega, attended the CUPE National Convention in Montreal. Since then, an ongoing relationship developed between these two unions and many Cuban union delegations from SNTAP and the CTC National have attended CUPE National conventions and meetings.

For many years an outspoken supporter for Cuba and for justice for the Cuban Five, CUPE National has shown its support through letters and official statements.

In March 2008, national president Paul Moist wrote a letter to Hon. Maxime Bernier, Minister of Foreign Affairs and to Hon. Jim Prentice, Minister of Industry expressing concern about the sale of Canadian credit card service provider, CUETS Financial Ltd. to the Bank of America. With this corporate buyout, CUETS's Canadian credit card services

Heide Trampus

became subject to U.S. laws that apply to its U.S. parent company. A direct outcome of this buyout is that Canadian issued Master Cards used in Cuba are no longer processed by Bank of America, which abides to the U.S. government's more than 50-year-old sanctions against Cuba. This little known fact affects and possibly discourages, thousands of Canadian travellers to Cuba. And insofar as American laws prevent Canadians from using a credit card issued by a Canadian bank many perceive this as an erosion of Canadian sovereignty. Moist's letter ends with "Let us end any Canadian support for that blockade rather than giving the American administration more encouragement to further ostracize Cuba and its people from world markets."[2]

Aiming to address a more international audience, during an official visit to Havana, Cuba, Moist brought solidarity greetings and called on U.S. President Obama to close American Guantanamo Bay military prison, free the Cuban Five and to open dialogue with the Cuban govern-ment towards ending the economic embargo. Similarly, a delegation of the provincial CUPE of British Columbia in 1996 included, as a specific mandate, a fact-finding mission to assess the impact of almost 40 years under a United States enforced blockade.

At the national level, CUPE has been quick to understand the value of supporting the Cuban brothers and sisters and the project soon expanded with funding from the Global Justice Fund. CUPE National and CUPE BC are currently working on a project with SNTAP called "Strengthening Solidarity between Cuban Public Sector Unions and CUPE." CUPE Ontario has also been very active. Sid Ryan, President of CUPE Ontario, wrote the following: "As part of our International Solidarity Plan, we have made the commitment to continue supporting the Cuban workers and

---

2   Quote from a letter to Raúl Macías Bravo, Cuban Institute of Friendship with the Peoples, Canada Desk, in response to an invitation to the II World Meeting of Solidarity and Friendship, October 18, 2000.

their struggle to defend their right to self-determination and preserve their public social safety net."[3]

Many other Canadian labour organizations have close relationships with counterpart labour groups in Cuba. Among those are the Hospital Employee Union, the British Columbia Teacher's Federation, the Vancouver & District Labour Council, and the Ontario Federation of Labour who signed a twinning agreement with the Havana Provincial Committee of the CTC in May 2008.

Labour Solidarity and the Cuban Five

The case of the Cuban Five has been the most important issue on the Cuban agenda since Gerardo Hernández, Ramón Labañino, Antonio Guerrero, Fernando González, and René González were arrested in 1998 and charged with conspiracy to commit espionage. They were given very harsh sentences and to this day, after many appeals, three of them are still in prison. (See Chapter 5 for more details about the Cuban Five).

Part of labour unions' history has traditionally been fighting for justice, human rights, and dignity. Since hearing about the arrest and unfair trial of the Cuban Five, Canadian Labour has been involved in the struggle for justice and their freedom, by sponsoring resolutions, sending letters to the U.S. President, Secretary of State and Attorney General of the United States, to the Prime Minister of Canada and the Minister of Foreign Affairs, and also sending letters and greetings to the 5 Cuban heroes. The National Executive Board of CUPE, for instance, issued a resolution on Solidarity with the Cuban Five in September 2012.

The list of unions whose actions express support for the Cuban Five is long. Aside from unions mentioned above, others involved have been the Canadian Labour Congress (CLC) through its president Ken Georgetti, the United Steel Workers (USW) and its national director,

---

3   Report "Teacher to Teacher: An Empowering Experience", prepared by Julia MacRae and Dr. Isora Enriques O'Farrill. Presented to Pedagogía 2003, February 3-7, 2003, Havana, Cuba.

Ken Neumann, the Canadian Union of Postal Workers (CUPW) with national president Denis Lemelin, The United Food and Commercial Workers (UFCW) presided by Wayne Hanley.

Together with Worker to Worker, UFCW, USW and CUPW were main sponsors and participated in the September 2012 "Breaking the Silence, Justice for the Five, People's Tribunal and Assembly" held in Toronto. Following this event, USW invited Adriana Pérez to their April 2013 convention in Vancouver and gave their support to public held forums both there and in Toronto.

In addition to the above-mentioned labour organizations, there are others labour organizations involved in Canada-Cuba solidarity with the Cuban Five. Under the motto: "An Injury to One is an Injury to All," unions and union activists from across Canada stand in solidarity with the Cuban people demanding justice and freedom for the Cuban Five, an end to the inhumane U.S. blockade and have assisted in the fundraising efforts for "Cuban Doctors for Haiti" and the rebuilding of hurricane destruction in Cuba.

Conclusion

Canadian labour has a long-standing history of involvement in international solidarity and social and global justice around the world.

Worker to Worker is continuously promoting friendship and solidarity and is assisting in building links between Canadian and Cuban labour unions and workers through Canada-Cuba labour exchanges. Links have been created and maintained by promoting and facilitating the sponsoring of Cuban union delegations to meetings and to Canadian Labour conferences, by organizing labour solidarity conferences in Canada and sending delegations to Cuba to attend conferences. Areas of work cover a variety of topics such as: labour, women, and the FTAA. Delegations attend annual international solidarity meetings and the Holguín-hosted International Colloquia "Against Terrorism and Justice for the Cuban

Five." The exchange of information between Canadian and Cuban labour organizations is crucial to mutual learning.

We have highlighted some of the Canadian labour organizations and their activities that have been carried out in solidarity with Cuban counterparts. These links were established at a time of most need for Cuba, at the onset of the Special Period in the early 1990s, and have endured independently of the Canadian government policies about Cuba. They have certainly been much closer and in a spirit of cooperation as equal partners. Perhaps the Canadian Labour Council more explicitly lays out the nature of this spirit of international solidarity: "The CLC knows no borders with solidarity. That's why we spend a large amount of time and energy supporting workers and unions around the world. From our projects and programs across the globe funded here in Canada, to our supporting International Labour Organizations, we believe in decent work for decent life. What happens to workers in other parts of the world directly affects workers in Canada, we are one world and need to support each other and learn from both mistakes and advancements."[4]

Of all the different activities and exchanges with Cuba, the one that is the closest to the hearts of all workers is the joint participation to the May Day activities in Cuba. Held internationally in commemoration of the 1886 Chicago Haymarket Square rally, where dozens of workers were killed while holding a general strike demanding an eight hour workday, May 1st is recognized and celebrated in more than 80 countries around the world. Canada does not officially recognize May Day although many Canadians across the country celebrate it with marches and gatherings. In Cuba this day is known as *el día del trabajador* (worker's day), and is celebrated in honour of all Cuban workers.

Annually, Worker to Worker has organized May Day tours where participants and delegations from international labour and social organizations join with Cuban workers in celebration and attend the International

---

4   Statement from the Canadian Labour Congress on International Solidarity

Solidarity Meeting on May 2. Many Canadian union leaders have participated over the years with remarkable strengthening of solidarity commitment to the world and Cuban workers' struggle. This is an emotional experience rooted in the historical meaning of solidarity and maintained by a sense of common struggle. We end with a small sample of testimonials of that experience by Canadian workers:

" It was the spirit of defiance and pride of the May Day celebration that inspired me to be involved with Cuba."

"I left Cuba knowing I would be back. I sensed that this day, this experience, would forever be etched in my memory."

"There we were, union members from all over the world, seated up under the statue of José Martí, honoured equally with international diplomats and military attaches. I cannot imagine our government ever treating ordinary working class people with this much respect."

Contributors to this Chapter

Carol Wood – Program Director, Co-Development Canada, Member
     of the CUPE Local 1004, Vancouver, British Columbia
Cindy McCallum-Miller - National Director, Prairie Region
     of the Canadian union of Postal Workers (1996-
     2008), currently Vice President Castlegar Local
Gladys Legal – Retired member of CUPE Local
     500, Winnipeg, Manitoba
Joey Hartman - President of the Vancouver and District Labour
     Council, on leave from her position as a staff representative for
     the Hospital Employees union, which is the Health Services
     Division of CUPE, BC. Her own union is the CEP Local 468
Jorge García Orgales – Staff representative of the Global
     Affairs and Workplace Issue Department of the
     United Steelworkers Canada, Toronto, Ontario

Kelti Cameron – International Solidarity Officer, Canadian union
of Public Employees National office, Ottawa, Ontario

Larry Kuehn – Director of the International Solidarity Program,
British Columbia Teacher's Federation (BCTF)

Linda McDowell – Retired member of OPSEU . Positions held: OPSEU
Executive Board Member, President of OPSEU Local 323,
President of the Orillia, Muskoka and District Labour Council

Marc Desgranges – Member of the CUPW Local
1, Bathurst, New Brunswick

Victor Carrozzino – Education and Communication Director for the
United Food and Commercial Workers, Toronto, Ontario

Yom Shamash – ESL Adult Education and Social Studies Teacher
from Surrey, British Columbia, Retired member of the
British Columbia Teachers Federation (BCTF)

References

Cuba Solidarity Campaign (n.d.). What are the Torricelli Law
and Helms-Burton Act? www.cuba-solidarity.org.uk/
faq-answer.asp?faqid=4. Retrieved April 19, 2014).

Kirk, John and Peter McKenna (1997). *Canada-
Cuba Relations, The Other Good Neighbor Policy.*
Gainesville: University Press of Florida.

Pacheco, M.C. (27 May 2011). Lázaro Peña - La cultura como
arma. *Bohemia.* http://www.bohemia.cu/2011/05/27/
historia/lazaro-pena.html. Retrieved April 8, 2014.

Chapter 7

Sustainable Paths to a Just Economy - Cooperatives in the Land of Martí

WENDY HOLM

Built upon the socialist[1] ideals of José Martí[2] the Batista legacy of powerful *latifundios* and illiterate farmers gave agrarian reform a central place on the agenda of Fidel's new government. By hiding and feeding Cuban revolutionaries, farmers had been key strategic partners in the underground movement leading up to the triumph of the revolution in 1959. It was no surprise that agrarian reform and literacy topped the priority list of the new government.

Within the first year, large tracts of privately-held land were expropriated (with compensation) and divided into state farms. Those who applied were given up to 67 acres of good quality farmland. ANAP (*Asociación Nacional de Agricultores Pequeños* - National Association of Small Farmers) was created in 1961 to represent the interests of these

---

1   As a social movement, socialism is about ensuring human development, equity, and social justice. With attention to people's needs at its core, the purpose of a socialist society is captured in the subordination of capital, in calls for fair income distribution, and in ensuring general access to social security and the provision of basic necessities, such as food, shelter, healthcare and education, among other. Rooted in the labour theory of value (Ricardo; Marx), work is the main source of income in socialism, with labour (rather than capital) as rightful owner of the residual income, i.e. profit. Novkovic, Sonja. How to manage co-operative difference in a socialist economy: Cuba's decentralization of decision-making. 2013. Pending Publication.

2   José Martí, Cuba's National Hero, 1853-95, was a poet an essayist, a journalist, a revolutionary philosopher, a translator, a professor, a publisher, and a political theorist. His writings continue to resonate within the Cuban society.

Wendy Holm

private farmers. Thus began a decade of Cuban agriculture characterized by large state farms (>70 percent of production, predominantly sugar and livestock) and many small private farmers.

After the revolution, Cuba's population began to grow rapidly, increasing the demand for food. In the early 1970's, responding to the need to help small farmers become more efficient through shared infrastructure, training, education and support, ANAP encouraged the growth of farm cooperatives. Two different types of private farmer cooperatives were created in the 1970s: Credit and Service Cooperatives (CCSs or *Cooperativas de Créditos y Servicios* - CCS) and Agricultural Production Cooperatives (CPA's or *Cooperativas de Producción Agrícola* - CPA). Members of a CCS retain individual title to their land but cooperate on things such as transportation, farm market sales, sharing of equipment, access to government credit and services and often some shared infrastructure (e.g. value added facilities). Members of a CPA pool their land (receiving payment when they join their lands) and work it collectively. To reduce transportation costs, new co-ops were encouraged to locate close to population centres; at times this involved ANAP-facilitated land swaps.

In Cuba, all members of Cuba's two types of private farmer cooperatives are also members of ANAP - the National Association of Small Farmers.

Many Cubans describe the 1980s as Cuba's "golden age." Sugar produced on monoculture state farms using Soviet-style, high input, "green revolution" farming methods was sold on favourable terms to the former Soviet Union, exchanged for consumer and industrial goods that were plentifully available. *La libreta* (the ration book) provided every Cuban with a basic monthly supply of food and other items for dramatically subsidized prices. Housing had caught up with population growth and was available for all, although extended families often shared a home. Universities had been built in every province and the population was educated and employed. Access to high quality health care and education was (and remains) free.

With the fall of the Soviet Union in the early 1990s, *"La Tubería"* – the umbilicus that connected Cuba to the former Soviet Republics - collapsed, plunging Cuba's economy into darkness.

From Green Revolution to Sustainable Leadership in One Decade

By the late 1980s, Cuba's farm sector had become one of the most highly industrialized in the world. Within a decade, it all collapsed and had to be re-invented. Only one decade later, Cuba came to be recognized as a world leader in sustainable, organic farming methods and in urban agriculture. Today, Cuba is about to embark on a brand new journey to create a sustainable, worker-led cooperative economy.

The collapse of the former Soviet Union, Cuba's major trading partner, was the catalyst in this transformation. The loss of 70 percent of Cuba's food supply and virtually all agricultural inputs (including tractors, tractor parts, petroleum, machinery, pesticides, fertilizers, seed, feed grains) meant Cuba had to quickly find new ways to produce food for her people.

With crisis as the driver and necessity the mother of invention, Cuba embarked on a remarkable journey: learning to grow food in the countryside without chemicals and pesticides while feeding her cities from within. Large state farms were divided up into a third type of cooperative – a UBPC (*Unidad Básica de Producción Cooperativa* or Basic Unit of Cooperative Production) – and workers were given usufruct[3] tenure

---

3   Essentially, the right to work the land in perpetuity. Similar to a life-long lease (unless the Government needs the land for another purpose).

Wendy Holm

to the land, the opportunity to purchase the means of production and to organize cooperatively. Urban areas that were uncultivated were turned into urban organic gardens or *organopónicos* (organized as UBPC's) and "popular gardens." In the countryside, retired farmers were called back to teach younger ones how to plough with oxen, and rustic micro-labs for the production of biological controls were scattered across the countryside to bring farm extension and solutions to local farmers in their fields.

The result, after only one decade, was world leadership in sustainable and organic agriculture.

Cuba had five very important things going for her that made this transformation possible:

- *Scientific capacity*. Following the revolution, the Cuban government put a priority on the development of a strong science and technology sector. Beginning in the 70s and 80s, Cuban scientists started looking for alternatives to high input agriculture to make Cuba's farm sector more economically and environmentally sustainable. As a result, Cuba had established the scientific knowledge and technical capacity to develop the bio-pesticides and bio-fertilizers needed to produce food in the Special Period.

- *Smart and capable farmers*. Cuba's literate farmers, and a national farmers' organization (ANAP) that puts an emphasis on skills and knowledge transfer, meant new methods were easily adopted.

- *A solid system of agricultural extension*. Professionals moving between the research labs and the countryside to identify and solve problems and help farmers adopt new technology to teach farmers sustainable methods.

- *Large Cooperatives.* Cuba's large agricultural cooperatives made it much easier to "get everyone going in the same direction" quickly and effectively.

- *Excellent soils, water and climate,* which certainly made things much easier.

These factors, combined with the agricultural knowledge, concepts and ideas handed across generations and the persistence of the Cuban people, made the impossible possible: just ten years after the collapse of the former Soviet Union, in a solemn session of the Swedish Parliament in December of 1999, Cuba's *Grupo de Agricultura Orgánica* was honoured over 80 other candidates from 40 countries to receive Sweden's prestigious *Right Livelihood Award* (referred to as the "Alternative Nobel Prize") for world leadership in sustainable, organic farming methods and urban agriculture.

In the words of Mavis Álvarez, founding member of ANAP:

> Sustainable technology is difficult without sustainable economic and social structures. The transition to sustainable techniques has also been easier for Cuban farmers than in other countries because of the security bestowed by the Cuban government: land rights, access to and ownership of equipment, availability of credit, markets, insurance and free health care and education. Cuban farmers are highly organized through the formation of cooperatives with real social and economic power, and the presence of national organizations that can represent the interests of individual farmers at the state level...Property rights include not only land, but

Wendy Holm

also the materials necessary for production, such as farming implements, ploughs, housing and other buildings as well as ownership over the harvest itself. [4]

Organic Farming Practices[5]

Cuba's success in large-scale organic agriculture has been achieved (and is maintained) through the widespread adaptation of sustainable farming practices including:

Organic fertilization and soil conservation. The use of organic and biofertilizers have allowed substitution of organic methods for chemical fertilizers to meet the nutrient requirements of crops previously met through external inputs. The use of manure, sugarcane by-products (*cachaza*), organic fertilizers, compost, bioearth, worm humus, residues from sugarcane collection centres (biomass), waste water, cover crops, mulch, biofertilizers, and other materials produce higher yields and improve the soil's organic and dry matter content.

Ecological management of pests, disease and weeds. Elimination of pesticide use is one of the most difficult tasks in a conversion to organic farming practices. The research into bio-pesticides developed by the

---

4   Alvarez, Mavis D. *Social Organization and Sustainability of Small Farm Agriculture in Cuba*. Sustainable Agriculture and Resistance, Transforming Food Production in Cuba, 2002, Institute for Food and Development Policy, USA. Translated from original Spanish *Transformando el Campo Cubano: Avances de la Agricultura Sostenible, Asociación Cubana de Técnicos Agrícolas y Forestales* (ACTAF), 2001.

5   Much of the information contained in this section was taken from *Sustainable Agriculture and Resistance, Transforming Food Production in Cuba, 2002*, Institute for Food and Development Policy, USA. Translated from original Spanish *Transformando el Campo Cubano: Avances de la Agricultura Sostenible, Asociación Cubana de Técnicos Agrícolas y Forestales* (ACTAF), 2001

Cuban Ministry of Agriculture's National Plant Protection Institute (*Instituto de Investigaciones de Sanidad Vegetal* - INISAV) is made available to farmers through the creation of a national network of 280 Centres for the Reproduction of Entomophages and Entomopathogens (CREEs), which manufacture and distribute biocontrol agents suited to local crops and conditions. CREEs are positioned according to local needs and have work teams comprised of university-educated specialists, lab technicians and auxiliary staff. The products are sold directly to area farmers, reducing transport and storage needs. Production is highly diversified and specialized by region.

Livestock Management. The loss of imported feed grains at the beginning of Cuba's Special Period resulted in sharp production cutbacks in Cuba's livestock production sector. Strong advances in crop rotation and polyculture have been employed to improve soil coverage and quality, control harmful pests and diseases and increase production. Successful use of legume-based livestock systems, silvo-pastoral, and integrated crop-livestock systems have resulted in significant and sustainable increases in dietary protein. Bio-controls are used to treat mites and other insect pests.

Crop Management. As of 2000, one million hectares (20 percent of Cuba's total farmland) were protected by the application of biological controls. Much of this land is in vegetable, tropical vegetable, and fruit production. Most of Cuba's 32,000 hectares of citrus and tree fruits are managed organically. Organic production methods are being tested in sugar and coffee (4,500 hectares), cocoa, coconut, pineapple, and mango production. Crop rotations are used to reduce soil pathogens. Intercropping and the use of crop associations are widely used to keep pest populations low and to reduce disease and weeds; common are corn-bean and cassava-bean associations but more complex planting such as corn-squash-sweet potato-beans-cucumbers are also common. Integrated pest management programs are in place for 27 crops, controlling a total of 74 insect and mite pests and several fungal diseases.

Wendy Holm

Ecological Soil Management. Organic techniques such as the use of living barriers, ground cover with locally adapted pasture species, contour ploughing, and conservation tillage systems are used to manage, conserve, and recover compacted, salinized, eroded, and otherwise degraded soils.

Urban Agriculture. Driven by food and petroleum shortages of the Special Period, Cuba's commitment to the production of food in cities, or urban agriculture was a striking success. Today, *organopónicos* (raised bed organic vegetable production), intensive vegetable gardens, backyard and roof top gardens, small (2-15 hectare) suburban farms, and the self-consumption gardens of large enterprises, institutions, and government offices together contribute an estimated 90 percent of the fresh produce consumed in Havana. The production goal for Cuba's urban agriculture sector has been estimated at 1.4 million metric tons per year to meet the national nutritional goal of 300 grams of fresh vegetables per person per day[6]. Key issues in the development of urban agriculture are conservation and management of soil fertility and integrated pest and disease management. Cuba is investigating the introduction of rabbits in urban agriculture models.

Green Medicines. In 1992, organized production of medicinal plants began in Cuba. Today, there are 13 provincial farms and 136 municipal farms producing organic green medicines on 700 hectares of land. Cuba's current annual production of medicinal plants and of herbs and plants used for dyes is 1,000 tons and growing.

Institutional Framework
Cuban NGOs have played a critical role in Cuba's successful transition to sustainable farming practices through the promotion of projects that incorporate sustainable agriculture principles. These include increasing the efficiency of energy utilization, making the best use of local inputs,

---

6   Ibid.

improving livestock nutrition and herd management, conserving biodiversity, reducing the use of chemical fertilizers, implementing low-input agricultural practices, producing quality seed, promoting the preparation and application of bio-fertilizers and bio-pesticides, rescuing traditional agricultural practices, and supporting the family farm economy.[7]

National Association of Small Farmers

ANAP (*Asociación Nacional de Agricultores Pequeños*[8] Cuba's National Association of Small Farmers), representing private farmer cooperatives and individual farmers, is the most important and powerful of Cuba's agricultural NGOs.

Founded in 1961, ANAP functions much like a worker association or union in that it a) represents 100 percent of Cuba's private farmers; b) is funded by dues from all of its members; c) has democratically-elected leadership at the municipal, regional, provincial and national levels; and d) exists to provide organizational and productive support for training, promotion, marketing, international cooperation and the preservation of Cuba's farming traditions, experiences and culture.

For the cooperatives, ANAP is a critical partner in conveying information to the local, municipal, provincial, or national levels, making them well positioned to achieve a cooperative equilibrium between their

---

7   Nieto, Marcos. *Cuban Agriculture and Food Security.* Sustainable Agriculture and Resistance, Transforming Food Production in Cuba, 2002, Institute for Food and Development Policy, USA. Translated from original Spanish *Transformando el Campo Cubano: Avances de la Agricultura Sostenible, Asociación Cubana de Técnicos Agrícolas y Forestales* (ACTAF), 2001

8   Ibid.

Wendy Holm

"associative" (member related) and "enterprise" (co-op related) need. Examples of ANAP's advocacy work on behalf of its members include[9]:

- In 1993, following the collapse of the former Soviet Union, ANAP turned to international NGOs to help support their educational and training programs. Today, ANAP collaborates with more than 50 NGOs from more than 20 countries.

- In 1996, ANAP began developing models for North-South-South cooperation (triangular aid). One example is a Belgian NGO that funds an exchange between ANAP and the Uruguayan Cooperative Centre. Many NGOs in Latin America have also sought funds from northern NGOs in order to provide scholarships for their farmers to attend Cuban schools and training programs and to participate in meetings and exchanges in Cuba.

These collaborations have served to strengthen the sustainable agriculture movement by building cooperation and solidarity across borders.

Today, ANAP's primary goal is to encourage and develop the use of agro-ecological farming techniques to improve production capacity. Much of ANAP's success can be traced to its reliance on farmer-to-farmer programs for promoting ideas and techniques. This has been particularly

---

9   Ibid

successful in disseminating teachings from scientific and technical institutions throughout its membership. Some of its activities include[10]:

- Nationwide training programs to build capacity among small farmers, cooperative members, grassroots organizations, and ANAP leaders.

- Farmer-to-farmer training programs where farmers teach others about their experiences with sustainable agriculture through direct participation and communication.

- Reorientation of the National Training Centre's education and training curriculum in order to emphasize agro-ecological knowledge.

- Collaboration with international donors and non-governmental organizations (NGOs) to promote sustainable techniques.

- Farmer, extension and researcher participation in regional and national networks to discuss topics related to food security and sustainable development.

ANAP combines traditional knowledge and practices with new technologies in a participatory effort that enables farmers to educate each other. The organization is broad-based and horizontal in structure. With a national headquarters in Havana, the majority of ANAP's activities are decentralized through provincial and municipal offices. Planning meetings and programs are held at regional locations appropriate to the topics

---

10   Alvarez, Mavis D. *Social Organization and Sustainability of Small Farm Agriculture in Cuba.* Sustainable Agriculture and Resistance, Transforming Food Production in Cuba, 2002, Institute for Food and Development Policy, USA. Translated from original Spanish *Transformando el Campo Cubano: Avances de la Agricultura Sostenible, Asociación Cubana de Técnicos Agrícolas y Forestales* (ACTAF), 2001

discussed to ensure that meetings are comfortable, accessible and inclusive - a model of communication that has had great success in Cuba.

Through farmer-to-farmer contacts, ANAP has been able to maintain a strong relationship with and among its members, making it very successful in disseminating teachings from scientific and technical institutions through its national structure, allowing information to reach farmers even in the most remote areas.

Some of ANAP's training is conducted via the media. Nationwide, ANAP hosts regular programs on more than fifty radio stations, most of them community based. ANAP has created television shows specifically for farmers that reflect their lifestyle and cultural heritage and provide technical information and training. ANAP's magazine reports on the latest agricultural news and scientific knowledge, including theories and practices of agro-ecology. Promotional materials provide information on specific pests and diseases, biological pest controls, agro-ecological techniques, natural food preservation and other topics.

In the Special Period, when the economic crisis limited access to printing and publication materials, farmer-to-farmer training schools have remained the crux of all outreach efforts. ANAP's successes in communication and training for rural activism earned them UNESCO's International Communications Development Program Award in 1989.

In 1996, ANAP added sustainability as one of the Farmer-to-Farmer Extension Program's official goals. ANAP defines its commitment to sustainability and agro-ecological agriculture through three basic goals:[11]

- To restore and promote the practices of small farmers through direct farmer-to-farmer exchanges of sustainable agricultural techniques.

11   Ibid.

- To support horizontal technology transfers through participatory methods that encourage the use of appropriate sustainable technologies.

- To conduct the research necessary to carry out successful agroecological extension, public education and appropriate technology transfers.

Other NGOs

Lead NGOs in Cuba's agricultural and food security sector include:

Asociación Cubana de Técnicos Agrícolas y Forestales - ACTAF (Cuban Association of Agricultural and Forestry Technicians) is an umbrella organization that coordinates the efforts of all groups and professionals working in the field of crop production and/or forestry matters.

Asociación Cubana de Producción Animal - ACPA (Cuban Animal Production Association) is an umbrella organization that coordinates the efforts of all groups and professionals working with animals.

Grupo de Agricultura Orgánica – GAO (Organic Farming Group) an organization of Cuban scientists and professors formed in 1993 (through the leadership of the Ministry of Higher Education), which had as its founding principles:[12]

---

12 Funes, Fernando *The Organic Farming Movement in Cuba*. Sustainable Agriculture and Resistance, Transforming Food Production in Cuba, 2002, Institute for Food and Development Policy, USA. Translated from original Spanish *Transformando el Campo Cubano: Avances de la Agricultura Sostenible, Asociación Cubana de Técnicos Agrícolas y Forestales* (ACTAF), 2001

- To develop a national consciousness of the need for an agricultural system in harmony with both humans and nature, while producing sufficient, affordable and healthy food in an economically viable manner;

- To develop local agro-ecological projects, and promote the education and training of the people involved;

- To stimulate agro-ecological research and teaching, and the recovery of the principles on which traditional production systems have been based;

- To coordinate technical assistance to farmers and promote the establishment of organic and natural agricultural production systems.

- To encourage the exchange of experiences with foreign organizations (emphasis on Latin American tropics and sub-tropics) and with specialists in sustainable agriculture and rural development;

- To promote and publicize the importance of marketing organic products.

Centro de Estudios de Agricultura Sostenible - CEAS (The Centre for the Study of Sustainable Agriculture) is part of the Agrarian University of Havana (*Universidad Agraria de la Habana* - UNAH). Since 1998, the National Training Centre and CEAS have supported the Agroecology and Sustainable Rural Development Chair at the University of Havana for professors committed to sustainable agriculture. The impact of this program is multiplied through the national network of research institutions, and the farms and cooperatives that provide practical and demonstrative points of reference.[13]

Federación de Mujeres Cubanas - FMC (Federation of Cuban Women) places a high priority on promoting the role of women in community decision-making with respect to food security. Cuban NGO projects are focused on increasing employment possibilities, improving access to information and promoting a greater participatory role in the family.[14]

Drivers

How were they able to accomplish so much in such a short time? In the words of GAO's Fernando Funes[15], "People came to believe… it was possible to create an agriculture with a different vision. Government put a priority on it and because that priority reflected the interests of the farmers, the capacity of the system and the sustainability of the community, it was accomplished."

---

13 Alvarez, Mavis D. *Social Organization and Sustainability of Small Farm Agriculture in Cuba*. Sustainable Agriculture and Resistance, Transforming Food Production in Cuba, 2002, Institute for Food and Development Policy, USA. Translated from original Spanish *Transformando el Campo Cubano: Avances de la Agricultura Sostenible, Asociación Cubana de Técnicos Agrícolas y Forestales* (ACTAF), 2001

14 Women are equally represented in the Cuban workforce. In agricultural vocational high schools, agricultural capacitation schools, colleges and universities, women are equally represented in the student body across most agricultural disciplines. Women, children and youth typically represent roughly two-thirds of farm co-op communities; women are well-represented on the boards of Cuba's CPA's, and in that role enjoy strong decision-making capacity, particularly as related to the economic affairs of the cooperative. Women constitute an apparent 5 to 10 percent of Cuba's farmers.

15 Funes, Fernando *The Organic Farming Movement in Cuba*.

Wendy Holm

Sovereign decision-making over agricultural and food policy – policy that crosses social, cultural, economic and environmental lines – has also been critical to Cuba's achievement of public policy goals.

Agriculture in Cuba Today

Today, close to 80 percent of Cuba's farm production is cooperative, reversing completely the coop-state ratio of the 1980s.

As of September 2011, under the Cuban government's recent policy to boost food security by increasing the number of new farmers (*Decreto Ley* 259/300), 1.3 million hectares of land were distributed in usufruct to 146,816 individual new farmers (97 percent of applicants), 79.2 of which was in production. With 4,540 new farmers approved and "in process," this brings the total new farmers under this process to 151,356. The average land given per person under this program has been 8.7 hectares. One third of the new farmers are 18-35 years old; 25 percent were unemployed and 13 percent were retired.

The way land is assigned under this program is also uniquely facilitative of good stewardship. When an applicant is approved, the provincial soil lab in the province of the applicant looks for suitable land with a good soil profile. The agricultural extension specialists from the soil lab meet with the new farmer to explain the soil capability and crop suitability of the land s/he is receiving and provide two years of direct support to make them successful.

All new farmers are required to become associated with an area CCS (Credit and Service Cooperative) that provides them with further incubator support. It also is a way of screening applicants – acceptance by a local farmers cooperative is a good indicator of character and capacity.

Cuba's New Cooperative Path

As my elevator speech notes: if you are impressed with Cuba's success in sustainable agriculture, just wait until you see what they are about to do to create a sustainable economy.

In April 2011, after almost a year of grassroots discussions in communities across Cuba, the Sixth Congress of the Communist Party released *Los Lineamientos* - The Guidelines - a set of comprehensive guidelines spread across 12 economic sectors:

- economic management policy

- macroeconomic policy

- external economic policy

- investment policy

- science, technology, innovation & environment policy

- social policy

- agro-industry policy

- industry and energy policy

- tourism policy

- transportation policy

Wendy Holm

- construction, housing & water resources policy

- trade policy

Prior to being finalized, a draft of *Los Lineamientos* was widely distributed throughout the country and a strong attempt was made by government to undertake a grassroots consultation with the Cuban people in the crafting of this new economic model. Neighbourhood meetings and meetings in workplaces were held over several months. A good percentage of the guidelines were actually amended to reflect input from the population. Some of the key amendments include the following:

- Government will create new openings for small and medium sized private enterprises, which fits with pending layoff of 1.3 million government workers as it rationalizes its state enterprises.

- There will also be a gradual reduction in inefficient subsidies including food ration books and a search for new ways to fulfil social objectives.

- In terms of regional decentralization, government will give more power to regional and municipal governments to establish their own priorities and utilize their local human and natural resources.

- Cubans now have the ability to buy and sell homes and cars (previously homes would be "swapped" and only some cars could be sold).

- Government is also looking at ways to encourage cooperatives beyond the agriculture sector.

These policy changes have the power to transform the Cuban economy and society into a model of 21st century socialism. Seven of these policy statements specifically widen the opportunity for cooperatives as a form of non-state enterprise, delivering the socialist objectives of human development, equity and social justice called for by José Marti and embedded in the tenets of the Cuban Revolution.

According to Saint Mary's University Sobey School of Business economist Dr. Sonja Novkovic:

> The key principles include the preservation of socialism and an economic system based on the 'people's socialist ownership over the fundamental means of production, governed by the socialist principle of distribution: from each according to his/her capacity, to each according to his/her contribution.' Planning continues to be the allocation mechanism, but will be informed by market trends. The Cuban model will consist of diverse enterprise forms: 'In addition to socialist state-run enterprises, which will be the main national economic structure, the Cuban model will also recognize and promote other modalities; namely, foreign investment forms (franchises, joint ventures, etc), cooperatives, small farming, usufruct, franchisement, self-employment and other forms that may emerge and contribute to increased labor efficiency.' Also important and reflected in the *Guidelines* is the principle of security for all citizens in the statement that 'no one will be left behind'. The main thread in these general guidelines seems to be the overarching goal to achieve social development (the socialist purpose), with

decentralizing economic decision-making and thereby increasing productive efficiency as a means to achieve that goal. Socialist Cuba has succeeded in reaching a high level of human development[16] and there is an ongoing concern and effort not to erode that achievement with economic restructuring.[17]

The specific *Lineamientos* (guidelines) relating to co-ops are the following (original numeration):

25. Grade 1 cooperatives shall be established as a socialist form of joint ownership in various sectors. A cooperative is a business organization that owns its estate and represents a distinct legal person. Its members are individuals who contribute assets or labor and its purpose is to supply useful goods and services to society and its costs are covered with its own income.

26. The legal instrument that regulates the cooperatives must make sure that this organization, as form of social property, is not sold or otherwise assigned in ownership to any other cooperative or any non-state organization or any natural person.

27. A cooperative maintains contractual relations with other cooperatives, companies, State-funded entities and other non-state organizations. After satisfying

---

16   The Human Development Index consists of three components: income, health and education. HDI for Cuba was 0.78 in 2011, well ahead of economies with similar levels of income per capita. http://hdr.undp.org/en/statistics/hdi/

17   Novkovic, Sonja *How to manage co-operative difference in a socialist economy:* Cuba's decentralization of decision-making. 2013. Pending Publication.

its commitment with the State, the cooperative may pursue sales operations free from intermediaries and in accordance with the business activity it is authorized to perform.

28. Subject to compliance with the appropriate laws and after observance of its tax and contribution obligations, each cooperative determines the income payable to its employees and the distribution of its profits.

29. Grade 2 cooperatives shall be formed, the partners of which shall be Grade 1 cooperatives. A Grade 2 Cooperative shall represent a separate legal person that owns assets. The purpose of this cooperative is to pursue supplementary related activities or conduct operations that add value to the goods and services of its partners (such as production, service and marketing operations) or carry out joint sales and purchases for greater efficiency.

180. Make sure that the management of the different forms of cooperatives is autonomous and agro-industrial service cooperatives are formed at local level.

200. Develop a comprehensive training plan in keeping with structural changes. The purpose of this plan will be to train and re-training managers and workers in the fields of agronomy, veterinary medicine, industrial and food technologies, economics and business management. This plan must also cover cooperative and environmental management.

Wendy Holm

Cuba's new cooperative policies as established in *Los Lineamientos* align well with international cooperative principles:

Voluntary and open membership. (Guidelines 25 and 29)

Democratic Member Control. (Guidelines 25 and 27)

Economic participation of members. (Guidelines 25 and 27)

Autonomy and independence. (Guidelines 25, 27, 28 and 180)

Education, training and information. (Guideline 200)

Cooperation among cooperatives. (Guidelines 27, 29 and 180)

Commitment to the community. (Guidelines 25 and 180)

In December 2011, a series of workshops was organized in Havana that brought together a cohort of co-op academics and practitioners from 3 countries for discussions with their Cuban counterparts on where Cuba is going in this widened cooperative path.[18]

In October 2012, pursuant to recommendations that arose from this workshop, four Cubans were brought to Québec City to attend IMAGINE 2012/ Québec International Summit of Cooperatives. These two conferences, marking 2012 International Year of Cooperatives, drew over 2,800 delegates from 100 nations.

---

18   The proceedings of those workshops are posted at http://www.theholmteam.ca/ HAVANA.WORKSHOPS.Dec.2011.pdf

In August 2013, the first Cuban student will enter Saint Mary's University's Masters of Management, Cooperatives, and Credit Unions Program on full scholarship. University ties are being strengthened at the academic and student level.

Conclusion

The Cuban Communist Party has committed to a transition from state socialism to co-operative control in many sectors of Cuba's economy. Cuba could be the first nation to get this right.

With the exception of China and Vietnam - and they are different in their own right - no socialist economy in transition (post 1989) has made a concerted effort to remain socialist.[19] This is why Cuba does not want to be termed 'in transition' – they are instead transforming, or reforming their (socialist) economy.

Because agricultural cooperatives have a long tradition of working well in the Cuban economy, farmers will lead the way down this wider co-operative path - joining to form "second tier" cooperatives to provide, for example, further-processing, value added services to the members.

A child of Cuba's Revolutionary agrarian reforms, Cuba's cooperative roots are again poised to deliver a cutting edge defence of democratic socialist principles in a world of global indifference.

Imagine...

---

19   Transition economies all deliberately moved to outright capitalism, selling of assets to employees was a (small) part of their privatization efforts for a number of reasons - none of which were ideological. Employee-ownership is still marginally present in some countries; none of them introduced a co-operative economy. (Novkovic, personal communication)

Chapter 8

North of Havana: Canada-Cuba Solidarity and the Canadian Polity - A Brief Overview

ISAAC SANEY

◇◇

The Canadian solidarity movement with Cuba has a history almost as long as that of the Cuban Revolution itself. Canada-Cuba solidarity has tried to mobilize Canadians around the cause of Cuba: from opposing U.S. aggression against the island to supporting Cuba's right to self-determination; from advocating that Canada-Cuba relations remain based on mutual respect and equality to upholding the goals of the Cuban Revolution. Central to these goals has been the effort to ensure that the government of Canada maintains relations with Cuba based on established diplomatic norms as opposed to the aggressive policy of destabilization of the United States.

Of course, while the Canada-Cuba solidarity has found allies and supporters in various major political parties, it has never had the power or strength to directly shape or change Ottawa's policy. Nevertheless, the movement has acted as an important monitor of the Canadian government, and through its efforts at engagement has been able to make its concerns known. This work has been conditioned and influenced by changing historical contexts as the character and position of the Canadian government has varied at given times. At the time of writing, the Conservative government of Stephen Harper poses a particularly unique challenge given Ottawa's increasingly alignment with the overall foreign policy objectives of Washington. With Ottawa-Havana relations now on uncertain and somewhat unpredictable grounds, the

Isaac Saney

Canada-Cuba solidarity movement have reaffirmed its commitment to the principles outlined at the founding of the Canadian Network On Cuba (CNC): "strengthening of friendship and solidarity between the peoples of Canada and Cuba...in order to promote social, cultural, political and economic relations between Canada and Cuba on the basis of mutual respect and non-interference" (CNC 2002).

Historical Background

The foundational elements of Canada-Cuba Solidarity are embedded in historical links between the two nations that stretch back to the 18th century. These early links were based in the trade in codfish, sugar, and rum, which tied the Atlantic Provinces to Cuba via shipping routes. As these commercial relations continued and deepened, in 1945 Canada chose Cuba as the location for its first diplomatic mission. Alongside the commercial relationship, Cubans and Canadians also have a long common history dealing with governments and business interests from the United States of America. In both societies, going back into the 19th century, a relatively tiny handful enjoyed considerable economic benefit from commercial relations with U.S.-based business entities while many others have frequently experienced the sense of being disadvantaged by the U.S. side of such commercial dealings.

At the same time in both societies, U.S. interests also frequently asserted themselves by bringing many sources of extra-economic pressure, raging from the bribing of politicians to intimidating challengers and opponents into silence, in order to ensure U.S. economic dominance. This was reflected in the affinity that Canadians developed towards Cuba, best exemplified by the participation of Canadians in Cuba's wars of independence. In the 20th century, after the First World War, U.S. commercial and diplomatic interests became much more aggressive towards both

Cuba and Canada as the U.S. displaced British and other foreign interests in both countries. Nevertheless, the Canadian trading relationship with Cuba had grown to encompass a considerable presence in the financial sector. For example, the Royal Bank of Canada and the Bank of Nova Scotia played a significant role in the Cuban economy – even occupying a dominant position- as they ranked first and fourth, respectively, in the number of personal accounts held in the country. At the end of World War Two, the commanding heights of Canadian industry in mining and forestry were entirely in the hands of U.S. industrialists and Wall Street banks. This was more extremely mirrored in Cuba. The extensive U.S. presence in Cuba into the cancer of U.S. gangster cliques from Las Vegas and Chicago, led by the Lansky-Siegel group, which dominated casino gambling, converted Cuba in to the Caribbean's brothel and the Cuban government into a criminal organization.

When the Cuban Revolution succeeded in 1959, the Canadian government along with Mexico retained relations with Havana. However, Canada has not been a disinterested party, an innocent bystander. In 1963, at the request of Washington, the Pearson government used the Canadian Embassy in Havana as an instrument of espionage. This activity continued into the 1970s. Canada's refusal to join in the U.S. attempt to diplomatically isolate Cuba has often been viewed as evidence of Ottawa's desire to pursue a course independent of Washington (see, for example, Basdeo & Nicol 2002). This was epitomized in the 1970s and 1980s during Pierre Trudeau's tenure as prime minister when he became the first Western leader to visit Cuba after the triumph of the Cuban Revolution. Indeed, Fidel Castro and Trudeau developed a long-lasting personal friendship, with Castro serving in 2000 as an honourary pallbearer at Trudeau's funeral. However, by maintaining relations with Havana, Ottawa was not indicating affinity or support for the Cuban Revolution but pursuing what Mark Entwistle, former Canadian ambassador to Cuba, described as "calculated engagement," aimed at bringing about changes in Cuba through exerting influence through

Isaac Saney

diplomacy as opposed to the Washington's policy of aggressive isolation and destabilization.

Notwithstanding Ottawa's motives, many Canadians were quite sympathetic and empathetic to the social justice and independence objectives of the Cuban Revolution. This sympathy and empathy found expression in the emergence of an organized movement of solidarity. Following what had occurred in the U.S. Fair Play for Cuba Committees (FPCC) were established in the 1960s across Canada. The first FPCC was founded in Toronto February 1961 (Wright 2009: 96). While the U.S. FPCCs would eventually disappear within a few years, the Canadian FPCCs proved more resilient, persisting in to the late 1960s and 1970s (Wright 2009: 98). The resilience was in part rooted in the resistance of various sectors of Canadian society (particularly sections of the intelligentsia) to the massive U.S. propaganda campaign against Cuba. The founding of several Canadian FPCC branches poignantly illustrates the Canadian resistance to this disinformation barrage. After the February 1961 founding of the Toronto branch, Vernel Olson (a principal FPCC leader) spoke in the western cities of Winnipeg, Regina, Edmonton, and Vancouver to audiences ranging from 75 to 400 (Wright 2009: 104).

Eventually, the FPCC branches that were founded in Toronto, Vancouver, and Montréal proved to be the most active. In the years that followed, while the FPCC formally disappeared, a number of Canada-Cuba solidarity organizations were established, eventually exceeding the scope and country coverage of the FPCC. At present, more than twenty organizations are members of the Canadian Network on Cuba (CNC), the formal umbrella framework for Canada-Cuba solidarity. Founded in 2002, the CNC is an attempt to give more coherent and concentrated expression and focus to the Cuba solidarity movement by drawing together the various local groups across Canada so that national campaigns and initiatives can be organized and coordinated. In Québec, the CNC is complemented by *Table de concertatión de solidarité Québec-Cuba*. This support for Cuba from below – so to speak – springs from the common sentiment of Cuba solidarity activists as expressed by the prominent Canadian activist and Cuba specialist Keith Ellis, who stated that "Cuba has given so much to the world, it now deserves to receive something back" (Interview, 2004).

Equality and Mutual Respect!
The Challenge of the Harper Regime

The breadth and diversity of Cuba solidarity activities across the country encompass the political, social and cultural spheres. The main objective of these activities is to mobilize Canadian public and political opinion to end the U.S. economic blockade of the island. One of the preoccupations of the movement is ensuring that Canada-Cuba relations remain based on the international norms of mutual respect and equality between nations. Since election of a minority Conservative government in 2006, a particular challenge on this front has been posed. This challenge became more pronounced with the assumption of majority government status by the Conservatives in 2011. The Stephen Harper regime's attitude to Cuba represents a departure from previous approaches by Ottawa and contrasts sharply with the high esteem that many Canadians hold Cuba in.

Until the ascension of Harper to power, Ottawa took great pains and expended much rhetoric to distance and distinguish its policy towards Cuba from that of Washington. Under Harper, however, the situation has changed. His government has adopted a profoundly ideological approach to foreign relations. The socialist nature of the Cuban Revolution - its commitment to keeping the economic commanding heights in the hands of the state and condemnation of neo-liberalism - are diametrically opposed to the ideological and philosophical principles and strictures of the Conservative Party. However, Peter McKenna and John Kirk argue that an outright rupture with the previous approach

Isaac Saney

is not feasible, as Ottawa cannot "tinker with the current policy in any fundamental way without somehow negatively affecting public opinion in Canada" (McKenna and Kirk 2009: 180). Nonetheless, while Ottawa has continued to vote in support of the Cuban resolution at the United Nations condemning U.S. economic sanctions against the island, there have been some very disturbing developments.

On May 21, 2008 then Minister of Foreign Affairs, Maxime Bernier, released a statement "encouraging the Cuban people to continue their struggle towards democracy" (McKenna and Kirk 2009: 178). In other words, it was a call to end the Cuba's socialist project. The statement was released on the day after the odiously misnamed "Day of Solidarity with the Cuban People," organized and sponsored by the regime of U.S. President George W. Bush. The statement was an open endorsement of the U.S. campaign of destabilization against the sovereign and legitimate government of Cuba. Bernier, in his capacity as Foreign Minister, stated: "Canada engages Cuban society through our diplomatic presence, which is aimed at helping to lay the groundwork for a Cuba that upholds freedom, democracy, human rights and the rule of law... It is our hope that recent shifts will open the way for the Cuban people to pursue a process of political and economic reform." This apparent alignment with U.S. policy was denounced by the Canada-Cuba solidarity movement, which viewed Bernier's as an open endorsement of the U.S. campaign of destabilization against the sovereign and legitimate government of Cuba, in effect throwing the weight of the Canadian state behind the Bush scheme to re-establish U.S. dominion over Cuba. Bernier's pronouncement constituted an unconscionable interference in the internal affairs of Cuba, the violation of the inalienable right of the people of Cuba - and all other peoples - to determine their future and their political, economic and social system without external interference: a right enshrined in the United Nations Charter and numerous international legal treaties. If the Harper government was truly interested in assisting the Cuban people then it would have insisted on the end of U.S. aggression - which includes sponsoring and giving safe haven to anti-Cuba terrorists - and the economic war being waged against the island. The Canada-Cuba solidarity movement called on Canadian government to immediately retract and repudiate Minister Bernier's statement and to respect international law (see, for example, Saney 2008).

Bernier's pronouncement was not an aberration. In the run-up to the April 2012 Colombia Summit of the Americas, Diane Ablonczy, Minister of State of Foreign Affairs (Americas and Consular Affairs) issued a statement opposing Cuba's participation and declaring that the country "doesn't comply with democratic conditions." While previous Canadian governments had expressed concern that Cuba did not "meet the standards" for summit participation, none had issued official statements. The CNC condemned the statement as reeking of the discredited colonialist mentality and practice of foisting on independent countries imperial arrangements that they do not want or accept (Saney 2012). It pointed out that Ablonczy's declaration flew in the face of the overwhelming consensus of the nations of Latin America and the Caribbean. Their expressed desire is that no Summit of the Americas can truly be legitimate if Cuba is excluded.

Cuba's exclusion from the 2012 Summit of the Americas was the utterly unprincipled, unilateral diktat of one superpower. Washington's warped logic - which Ottawa apparently endorsed - is that any sovereign state in the Americas can be excluded by its fiat, and its fiat alone. Thus, in reality the United States does not recognize the sovereignty of any other country that has been invited – including Canada's. That the Canadian government did not protest the arbitrary treatment of Cuba was viewed as further erosion and weakening of Canada's sovereignty. It was further pointed out that a potentially historic moment was missed in which a regrettable page in the relations amongst the nations of the Americas could have finally been turned. The government of Canada had failed to seize the opportunity to engage in enlightened statecraft. If Ottawa was truly interested in the cause of democracy, as Ablonczy claimed, then it

Isaac Saney

should have stood with the nations of Latin America and the Caribbean, and insisted that Cuba be included in the Summits of the Americas.

Working with Parliamentarians

It goes without saying that these various entreaties on behalf of the Canada-Cuba solidarity movement went unacknowledged by Ottawa. Nevertheless, despite the recalcitrance of the Harper regime, various initiatives and efforts have been aimed at mobilizing particular members of parliament. The example is the very effective program of work with British parliamentarians by the Cuba Solidarity Campaign (CSC) in Britain. The CSC has been able to create through painstaking work a bloc of MPs who act as an active check on London's policy towards Cuba. Indeed, almost annually more than 100 British MPs have endorsed and signed a declaration defending Cuban sovereignty and right to self-determination, free of any external interference in the island's domestic affairs. Within its limited resources the Canada-Cuba solidarity movement has also endeavoured to work with Canadian MPs. This work has had mixed results. Undoubtedly, the greatest success was the signing of a letter in 2008 by 56 MPs (40 from the Bloc Québécois and 16 from the National Democratic Party) of a letter demanding justice for the Five Cuban heroes imprisoned in the United States since 1998 for defending Cuba from terrorist attacks launched by anti-Cuba groups based in Florida. This letter was forwarded to the Canadian Foreign Minister and the U.S. Attorney General. Central to this success was Francine Lalonde (then BQ Foreign Affairs critic) and Libby Davies (NDP MP for Vancouver East). However, this success has not been repeated or sustained. Since 2008 there has been significant turnover of MPs in the Canadian parliament. The base that supported the 2008 letter was considerably eroded.

One of the vehicles that the CNC has worked with is the Inter-Parliamentary Group on Cuba (IPGC). The IPGC has been in existence for more than fifty years. The current co-chairs are Sen. Pierrette Ringuette (Liberal Senator – New Brunswick) and Maria Mourani (BQ MP for Ahuntsic, QC). However, the 31 members (at time of writing) MPs (members and non-members of the IPGC) are generally not well informed about many aspects of Cuba. Those who are interested in Cuba tend to have a very narrow range of issues they engage with, for example, investment and healthcare. They see their issues often in isolation from the general historical context that has shaped the Cuban Revolution. Notwithstanding these limitations, MPs – particularly, members of the IPGC - are opposed to the U.S. economic blockade of the island. The reasons for this opposition may vary from those who see U.S. sanctions as an ineffective means to achieve regime change to those who view Washington's policy an unacceptable interference in Cuban internal affairs.

The IPGC is the obvious and natural vehicle through which the Canada-Cuba solidarity movement can channel its efforts to extend its solidarity work into the Canadian parliament. On March 29, 2013 five BQ MPs sent an open letter to the U.S. Congress. All five were members of the IPGC, among them Maria Mourani, the IPGC's co-chair. However, while the IPGC has taken these progressive steps, they engage in their work without any reference to or interaction with the Canada-Cuba solidarity movement. Indeed, for the most part the IPGC is generally unaware of the breadth and scope of the activities of the movement across the country. Thus, in practice the IPGC and the Canada-Cuba solidarity movement have worked in isolation from each other.

To address this problem, the CNC as an organization met for the first-time on February 11, 2011 with members of the IPGC. The CNC's national spokesperson participated in a working breakfast with members of the IPGC, including IPGC then co-chairs Mile Allen (CP MP for Tobique, NB) and BQ Senator Pierrette Ringuette, Dianne Bourgois

Isaac Saney

(BQ MP for Terrebonne) and Paul Dewar (NDP MP for Ottawa Centre). The IPGC were informed of the nation-wide work of the Canada-Cuba solidarity movement. Particular emphasis was placed on the very successful CNC's Cuba For Haiti Campaign, which has raised hundreds of thousands of dollars to assist the Cuban medical brigades in Haiti in the aftermath of the 2010 earthquake. What stood out, as noted above, was their lack of knowledge of the numerous and varied activities across the country in support of Cuba.

Concerns regarding Canadian relations with Cuba under Harper were raised and discussed. The discussions centred on Canada-Cuba relations, and the imperative to strengthen these relations and maintain them on the basis of mutual respect and equality. One of the conclusions from this meeting was the need for the Canada-Cuba solidarity movement to work closely with the IPGC by assisting MPs in their work. Members of the IPGC emphasized their need for information. During, this visit to Ottawa more than 100-copies of an eight-page CNC Bulletin for Parliamentarians was distributed to members of the House of Commons and the Senate. The bulletin provided information on the Canada-Cuba solidarity movement and Cuba's ongoing work in Haiti. (CNC 2011).

This area of work presents key challenges. The Canada-Cuba solidarity movement, therefore, needs to develop a plan for consistent and organized work with MPs. Given the need of MPs for appropriate, objective information, specifically designed brochures or pamphlets directly targeted at MPs on various Cuban subjects should be produced. A strategy that combines and harmonizes meetings by local organization with the MPs in their particular areas with CNC work in Ottawa would increase the national political weight and impact of the Canada-Cuba solidarity movement.

Conclusion

Since the triumph of the Cuban Revolution in 1959, Canadians have maintained a strong sense of friendship and solidarity with the people of Cuba. The solidarity movement is crucial in maintaining and deepening those ties, building bridges of solidarity and friendship between the Canadian and Cuban peoples. Although Canadian government policy has cooled and warmed over the decades, Canadians have refused to follow the cruel and unjust U.S. policy toward this Caribbean nation. The election in 2011 of a Conservative Party majority government poses very specific difficulties. While Ottawa voted in favour of the annual United Nations resolutions opposing the U.S. economic war on Cuba in 2011, 2012 and 2013, the Canada-Cuba solidarity movement must remain vigilant.

Over the last 54 plus years, Canadian sympathy and empathy with the Cuban people's struggle has deepened and broadened. Canadian commemorations of Moncada Day are a reflection of this sympathy and empathy. Canadians admire the courageous and rebellious spirit embodied in Moncada, a spirit that today is so powerfully manifested in Cuba's steadfastness against the efforts of the empire to destroy the island's independence. Canadians irrespective of their political or ideological positions, stand in favour of building relations of genuine friendship with the island nation: relations based on mutual respect and equality that uphold Cuba's right to self-determination and sovereignty. Having travelled to Cuba in the hundreds of thousands and having witnessed Cuban reality for themselves, Canadians have come away with a profound respect and admiration for the Cuban people and their efforts to build and defend a society centred on independence, justice, and human dignity.

References

Basdeo, Sahadeo and Heather N. Nicol (2002). *Canada,
    the United States and Cuba: An Evolving Relationship.*
    Miami: North South Centre Press.

Canadian Network On Cuba (2002). *Mission and History.* http://www.
    canadiannetworkoncuba.ca/index.php?option=com_content
    &view=article&id=63&Itemid=91 Retrieved April 19, 2014.

_____ (2011, January). Bulletin Canadian Network On Cuba:
    Information for Parliamentarians. (Available on request).

Entwistle, Mark (2009). Canada-Cuba Relations: A Multiple-
    Personality Foreign Policy. In Robert Wright and Lana
    Wylie (Eds.), *Our Place in the Sun: Canada and Cuba in
    the Castro Era.* Toronto: University of Toronto Press.

Kirk, John (1995). *Back in Business: Canada-Cuba
    Relations after 50 years.* Ottawa: FOCAL.

McKenna, Peter and John Kirk (2009). Canadian-Cuban Relations:
    Muddling Through the Special Period. In Robert Wright and
    Lana Wylie (Eds.), *Our Place in the Sun: Canada and Cuba
    in the Castro Era.* Toronto: University of Toronto Press.

Saney, Isaac (2012, April 10). *Canada Must Support Cuba's Right To
    Self-determination: CNC Rejects Ablonczy's Statement.* http://
    www.canadiannetworkoncuba.ca/index.php?option=com_con
    tent&view=article&id=232:canada-must-uphold-cubas-
    right-to-self-determination&catid=74:cnc-news-and-
    events&Itemid=140. Retrieved April 19, 2014.

_____ (2008, May 24). *Canada Must Support Cuba's Right To Self-
    determination: Statement by the Nova Scotia Cuba Association.*
    http://www.nscuba.org. Retrieved April 19, 2014.

Wright, Cynthia (2009). Between Nation and Empire: The Fair
    Play for Cuba Committees and the Making of Canada-Cuba
    Solidarity in the Early 1960s. In Robert Wright and Lana

Wylie (Eds.), *Our Place in the Sun: Canada and Cuba in the Castro Era.* Toronto: University of Toronto Press.

Chapter 9

Writing About Democracy in Cuba

ARNOLD AUGUST

The movement in Canada for solidarity with Cuba strives to engage the people directly to develop positive relations with Cubans and their institutions. The movement also attempts to influence the Canadian government to maintain and further foster positive foreign relations with the Cuban government. Whether through the grassroots or through the federal government, the solidarity movement is a basis for what this book describes as solidarity-based people-to-people foreign relations.

Writing and speaking about democracy in Cuba is a specific type of solidarity that differs from much of the conventional collective solidarity actions that I have participated in since the early 1990s. I am currently a member for Canada of the International Committee to Free the Cuban Five as well as the *Comité Fabio di Celmo pour les 5* of the *Table de concertation de solidarité Québec-Cuba*. As a writer and lecturer, my main preoccupation since the late 1990s has been to counter the media war being waged against Cuba by the monopoly media in the U.S. and Canada.

Much of the established media in both countries base themselves on a similar outlook toward Cuba's political system. There are a few differences, however, whereby some Canadian media often reject the extremism of their U.S. counterparts and are more open-minded. In this sense, the English- and French-language media at times allow known academic experts on Cuba, such as John Kirk and Claude Morin respectively, to air their views on certain features of Cuban reality and the international situation as it pertains to Cuba.

Arnold August

Yet, in this modern era of technology, Canadians are also target consumers of U.S. media, especially cable television and the Internet. The U.S.–Canada media frontier is quite blurred, especially considering that much of the reporting on Cuba in Canada is taken from U.S. news outlets, if not textually, then in overall orientation. This is also the case in many instances with the French-language media in Québec, such as French-language CBC (Radio-Canada), which often surpass their counterparts in the English language media in falsifying the situation in Cuba and other countries such as Venezuela, Bolivia, and Ecuador.

My effort in taking up the challenge of opposing the media war against Cuba by striving to analyze the Cuban reality is not a solitary endeavour, as some may believe. On the contrary, it is a collective undertaking, just as it is with solidarity groups. First, some Canadian publishers, such as Fernwood Publishing, promote critical thinking of authors like me who go against the grain. In this sense, writing is a social undertaking. Second, some solidarity groups play an important role in encouraging the promotion and sale of books like mine. Third, some solidarity websites, along with many alternative websites that are not part of the solidarity movement, collaborate in publishing articles and interviewing authors on our views. These interviews are not monologues, but rather result in a real exchange of ideas between the interviewer and the interviewee, thus resulting in a collective effort. Between 1999 and the release of my book in Canada in January 2013, I wrote and published more than 40 articles on the Cuban political system, the Cuban Five, and U.S.–Latin America relations, many of them in English, Spanish, and French. During this period, as is the case now, the collaboration of some solidarity websites and general alternative websites necessarily consisted of a collective movement linked by the common goal of opposing disinformation and misinformation. This common evolution is all the more important in this era, when the international attempt to stifle the truth from surfacing through the media is on the increase in opposition to those who dare to defy the status quo.

Thus, my individual work as an author is part of a collective movement that is striving to deal with disinformation regarding democracy in Cuba. This "battle of ideas" is important because, more often than not, especially since the 1990s, the supposed lack of democracy and "legitimate elections" in Cuba are used as a pretext to attempt to isolate Cuba and continue the U.S. blockade. The Canadian government, it should be noted, has consistently voted against the blockade at the annual United Nations General Assembly on this issue. Ottawa also maintains economic/commercial and diplomatic ties with Cuba, uninterrupted even by the 1959 Revolution. (Mexico was the only other country in the Western hemisphere that did not break diplomatic ties with Cuba after its revolution). Canada has exhibited an overall positive policy even though it has had its negative diplomatic moments, such as in 2001 during the Summit of the Americas in Québec City. At that time, Jean Chrétien's Liberal government called out Cuba on the issues of "human rights" and "democracy."[1]

There are two issues. Firstly, Cuba has its own tradition and concept of human rights and democracy. I will be dealing with this later on in this chapter. Secondly, irrespective of whether the Cuban experience and perspective on democracy are valid or not, who is Canada to make a judgment? This is entirely an internal affair of Cuba. No country, in my view, has the right to interfere in the domestic affairs of Cuba by judging it, and thus creating pretexts for intrusion. This is the view that I presented on May 1, 2001 in Havana in front of one million people when I was invited to present the opinion of Canadians in opposition to the Chrétien provocation. I still hold the same view.

Despite the overall positive stands by Canada, we cannot let down our guard. The international arena is fraught with dangers. The U.S. is on the offensive in its attempt to retain its world domination. Thus, Canada

---

1   For the definitive analysis of this subject, see John M. Kirk and Peter McKenna, *Canada–Cuba Relations: The Other Good Neighbor Policy*, University Press of Florida, 1997. http://upf.com/book.asp?id=KIRKMF97

– the U.S.'s closest ally – can also be influenced on the issue of Cuba. In addition, in this period when a new Latin America and Caribbean has emerged to form its own regional blocks that exclude both the U.S. and Canada, one can be assured that the U.S. especially – but Canada as well – is not resting easily with this new situation. We have seen this with the now infamous statement by Harper's Conservative government upon the March 2013 death of Hugo Chávez, the architect of the new Latin America. The Prime Minister appealed for what he termed the need for "democracy" in Venezuela; he likewise summoned the entire region (thus including Cuba) to "build a hemisphere that is more...democratic."[2] This goes to show the importance of this work to juxtapose Cuban reality against disinformation regarding Cuba on the issue of democracy.

Let us take one example of how we can strive to deal with a precon-ceived notion related to democracy. The media and government often characterize Cuba as a "single-party system", as opposed to a "multi-party system," such as exists in Canada and the U.S. Therefore, according to this logic, Cuba cannot belong to the exclusive club of democracies. But it is not necessary to accept this "single-party" versus "multi-party" dichot-omy when evaluating political systems. In fact, it is a false dichotomy. If one looks at political systems from the angle of the growing international movement consisting of peoples taking their destiny into their own hands by wielding political power, then there *is* a dichotomy.

The dichotomy, however, is not one based on the number of parties existing in a particular system. Rather, it is founded on the contrast between a political system that promotes the notion that sovereignty be vested in the hands of the people and one that does not. As I write, the U.S. is often promoted internationally as the epitome of a multi-party system. To this end, there is a constant media campaign in Canada promoting the view that the U.S. political system is characterized by competition

2   "Statement by the Prime Minister of Canada on the death of Venezuelan President Hugo Chávez Frías," March 5, 2013, Office of the Prime Minister of Canada. http://www.pm.gc.ca/eng/media.asp?id=5341

between the Democrats and Republicans, liberals and conservatives, left and right. Thus, the thinking goes, the existence of so-called "free and fair elections" is the self-defined litmus test for a real democracy. However, as many academics and observers testify, the competition covers up the reality that the same or very similar domestic and international policies are followed, irrespective of which of the two parties are in power. I write about this in some detail in a manner acclaimed by some experts as being an original contribution; namely, the U.S. two-party system actually serves to not only recuperate the status quo, but also allows it to go on the offensive, as my case study of the Obama phenomenon illustrates. In addition, in the U.S. Constitution, the word "democracy" and the principle that sovereignty is vested in the hands of the people are nowhere to be found. By comparison, Venezuela has a multi-party system. That said, as long as the Bolivarian Revolution remains at the helm of the country – both in practical terms and through its new 1999 Constitution, one of whose fundamental features is the concept that "the inalienable sovereignty resides in the people"[3]– people's power is maintained and fostered on an ongoing basis despite its weaknesses and drawbacks.

Cuba, for its part, in its 1976 Constitution, as amended in 2002, contains two clauses that touch on the theme being presented. Article 3 stipulates, "sovereignty lies in the people, from whom originates all power of the state." While in Article 5, the Constitution specifies that "the Communist Party of Cuba, the organized vanguard of the Cuban nation, is the highest leading force of society and of the state."[4] Disinformation is created as a result of this Article: the Cuban political system is based on a "single-party" and thus is not a democracy. The principle that sovereignty

---

3   Constitution of the Bolivarian Republic of Venezuela," page 10, Article 5, *Asamblea Nacional Constituyente, Ministerio de Comunicación e Información*, Caracas, 1999.

4   Constitution of the Republic of Cuba, Articles 3 and 5, January 31, 2003. http://anterior.cubaminrex.cu/English/LookCuba/Articles/AboutCuba/Constitution/inicio.html

resides in the hands of the people is completely evaded, thus playing on the preconceived notion that the number of parties in a political system is the unique gauge as to its democratic "credentials." The question, rather, is to what extent the Communist Party of Cuba actually fosters the practical application of the principle that sovereignty resides in the hands of the people.

In some reviews of my book and in the course of lectures it is increasingly appreciated that the Communist Party of Cuba is not to be seen as the epitome of democracy. In fact, as my book details, the current major economic/social transformations involved the direct input of the grassroots over several years. This distinguishing procedure was led by non other than the Communist Party of Cuba. Thus it was this political institution that set the tone for a rejuvenation of contemporary Cuban democracy.

If one takes the examples of Cuba and Venezuela and compares them with the U.S. model, the dichotomy is really between those systems that promote, in juridical and practical terms, the modern principle that sovereignty resides in the hands of the people and those that do not, such as the U.S.

In order to analyze whether the Cuban path to democracy in fact exemplifies the notion that sovereignty lies in the hands of the people, should one compare it to the U.S. approach to democracy? I do not think so. It would be far too easy to tip the balance in favour of Cuba. It is common international knowledge that the U.S. system is entirely money-driven with the oligarchy being on the driver seat. This ruling elite offers the voters to choose between two political parties, one of which is seen by many to be the lesser of two evils. The large voting abstentions in the U.S. may well be a reflection of the perceived lack of real alternatives.

Cuba and Venezuela have to be compared not to the U.S., but rather to the situation that existed before their respective revolutions. For example, the Cuban Revolution of 1959 represented principally a revolt against the U.S. dominated political system from 1901 till 1958. During this period the U.S. intervened by actively endorsing alternating political factions and dictators. To what purpose? To maintain the privileges of the ruling circles. Similarly, the Bolivarian Revolution in Venezuela in 1998 specifically targeted the institutionalized two-party system existing since 1958 that maintained the status quo. In both cases, and to very different degrees, the unlimited accumulation of private property in a few hands was challenged. In its place, social, economic and cultural programs for the vast majority of people were instituted. It was this new orientation that opened up new paths for democracy in both countries, very different to what existed before 1959 and 1998 respectively. Thus the number of parties in existence is not the line of demarcation.[5]

This brings us to the point raised at the beginning of this chapter: writing is a specific type of solidarity that differs from much of the conventional solidarity actions. One enters into a very complex situation when, as in the example above regarding the application of the principle that sovereignty resides in the hands of the people, affirmations of fact give rise to questions. As a writer, I cannot afford to offer blind solidarity with Cuba and its model. To present the Cuban version of democracy as ideal and devoid of flaws is not only inconsistent with reality, but also does a disservice to Cuba. No writer would enjoy credibility among the Canadian public by presenting the Cuban political system in idealistic terms. Nor, in my case at any rate, can an overly critical attitude be pursued, thus feeding into the disinformation media war or potentially encouraging negative Canadian government policies against Cuba. Rather, we are striving for the opposite.

This critical yet balanced approach is appreciated by Cuban scholars and other experts, but perhaps has not been sufficiently promoted. It may be symptomatic of the solidarity movement's tendency to shy away

---

5   For a YouTube video on this issue, see the author's presentation "Cuban Democracy and the Twenty-First Century Latin American Left," Pace University, New York City, June 8, 2013, DemocracyCuba. http://www.democracycuba.com/cuban_democracy_and_the_twenty-first_century_latin_american_left.html

from a critical approach in the name of "solidarity." For example, Cuban scholar Martha Prieto Valdés comments in *Cuba and Its Neighbours* that "the examination of Cuba does not amount to praise on a groundless basis; rather, the author, while recognizing the achievements, is critical, and he identifies the limitations and offers his judgements concerning causes and conditions." Cuban writer Rafael Alhama Belamaric invites the reader to appreciate the publication because it "brings us closer to the contemporary changes that are taking place in Cuba as an expression of the existing potentialities" while at the same time recognizing the attention provided to his country's "contradictions and the necessity for new developments." Fernando González Llort, one of the Cuban Five imprisoned in the U.S. until February 2014 when he was released after serving his entire sentence, sent a review of the book in 2013 indicating that the "critical observations are perceptive, very intelligent, and placed in their contexts."[6]

These and other similar comments by Cuban colleagues amount to a confirmation of one of the main theses put forward in the publication. Contrary to what is promoted in the mainstream media regarding Cuba, it is a hotbed of debate and discussion on the future of the country, including its political system with the goal of improving it. In fact, many of the critical perceptions found in the book find their sources among the Cuban academics and political activists with whom I agree and develop upon their ideas.

Is the counter-offensive confronting the media war being waged in Canada and the U.S. on Cuban democracy effective? After all, the supposed lack of democracy in Cuba is one of the cornerstones used to pressure Cuba to fall into the ranks of what is seen by Prime Minister Harper (quoted above) as the need to "build a hemisphere that is more ... democratic."

---

6   "Reviews" [of *Cuba and Its Neighbours: Democracy in Motion*], DemocracyCuba. http://www.democracycuba.com/reviews.html

It is too early to draw any conclusions. However, among the ruling circles, there is an indication that perhaps there is some concern regarding the reality being divulged in Canada and the U.S. concerning Cuban democracy. For example, on July 25, 2013, Fernwood Publishing published a blog post on its website that revealed an issue that arose when Canadian purchasers of my book *Cuba and Its Neighbours: Democracy in Motion* tried to make their payments through PayPal from the Canadian publisher. The post reads, in part:

Beginning on May 1, 2013, four consecutive orders that were all destined for Canadian addresses were monitored by PayPal. In essence, books purchased by customers in Canada were monitored by U.S. law. With each transaction, we received the following note from PayPal: 'Regulations require us to review selected transactions more closely. This payment is pending while we make sure it meets regulatory requirements.'

When the first of these four orders was flagged as 'pending,' Fernwood Publishing contacted PayPal to inquire as to the reason for this new procedure as it was something we had never before come across. PayPal's response was as follows: 'The transaction has been suspended due to U.S. governmental regulations, which impose sanctions on specific countries and individuals.' The response goes on to say: 'It more or less is random selection and should be completely ignored unless the payment is declined.'

The payments for the four transactions were all approved very quickly. However, we took issue with the fact that PayPal indicated that the selection of said transactions was 'more or less random.' The only time this issue ever came up was when customers ordered the book *Cuba and Its Neighbours*. Coincidence? We think not. Random selection? We think not. Did we ignore it? No, definitely not."[7]

---

7   "PayPal Transactions Regulated by the U.S. Government: Raising the Issue," *Fernwood Publishing*.www.fernwoodpublishing.ca/blog/2013/07/paypal-transactions-regulated-by-the-u-s-government-raising-the-issue/

The blog post concludes by revealing that its content was sent to both the Canadian government's Minister of Trade as well as PayPal. It was forwarded to the Minister of Trade, no doubt because it concerns Canada's sovereignty and the right of Canadian enterprises to conduct business without U.S. interference. However, the Minister of Trade has yet to respond or acknowledge its receipt. Nor did PayPal follow up on the viewpoint and questions raised in the post.

What lessons can be learned from this with regard to the title of this edited volume, *Cuba Solidarity in Canada - Five Decades of People-to-People Foreign Relations*? It coincides with what the whole world learned in May 2013 as a result of the Edward Snowden revelations, namely that the U.S. intelligence services spy on dozens of countries on the planet, including its closest allies. Following our case with regard to PayPal, we can also delineate the spying activities carried out by the Office of Foreign Assets Control (OFAC) of the U.S. Department of the Treasury. It was to this governmental organism that PayPal cited Fernwood Publishing as being responsible for sanctions against other countries such as Cuba and those enterprises in countries in the U.S. and others outside the U.S. in dealing with Cuba. This OFAC activity, however, has been well known for several decades, ever since the U.S. imposed sanctions against not only companies in the U.S., but also non-U.S. enterprises that trade with Cuba, thus making the blockade extraterritorial. This publicly fostered U.S.-policy is nothing new and includes important corporations based in Canada.

With regard to our case, we are dealing with Canadians buying a Canadian book written by a Canadian citizen from a Canadian publisher. Yet, the U.S. OFAC intervened. Moreover, this OFAC interference – and applied temporarily by PayPal, until it rapidly retreated – targeted only one book. Its title includes the two words "democracy" and "Cuba." These two words, according to the status quo criteria, are not supposed to exist in the same sentence or book title in a positive manner. Moreover, the publication had caused a certain amount of buzz in some circles and quite widely on the Internet in the U.S. and Canada by the time that OFAC flagged it in May 2013.

The lack of response by the Canadian government to U.S. interference in Canada on this issue highlights the need for Canadians at the grassroots level to be wary. It is important to make sure that the Canadian government's foreign policy toward Cuba does not regress from its relatively positive diplomatic and trade tradition going back to the 1959 revolution. Therefore, in addition to direct Canada–Cuba people-to-people relations, it is crucial that citizens pressure the Canadian government so that it does not alter its general orientation with regard to the historical relationship between the two countries.

At an Ottawa book launch held in June 2013, one of the four people whose PayPal transaction was delayed raised this publicly in the question-and-answer period. By inserting the problem in Canadian public opinion in this way and by spreading it in other manners through discussion, websites and social media such as Twitter, all of this together can contribute to put pressure on the Canadian government to resist U.S. interference on any issue related to Cuba. In any case, the most important response is to collectively increase propagation among Canadians of the Cuban reality with regard to democracy.

In summary, this reality is two-fold. Firstly, Cuban democracy today is the antithesis of the kind existing before 1959. Political power, rather than being in the hands of the few, now has the capacity to empower the people at the base; we have seen this through the example of the Communist Party's role in the current transformations, involving the grassroots in shaping their own destiny. Another illustration of this popular participation is given by the recent involvement of most Cubans in their workplaces throughout the country contributing to drafting a new bill on Social Security.

Secondly, the reality of Cuban democracy also shows that it is far from being perfect but continually striving for improvements. As mentioned above, social scientists and other analysts are seeking ways to improve democracy so that power being vested in the hands of the people is progressively more relevant. In this discussion, the focal point is the need for the Cuban political system to increasingly involve the people on a daily basis not only in providing input into policy suggestions coming from above, but in formulating new policies from the bottom up. This is a major challenge. However, Cuba has put the bar very high when it carried out its revolution. This pursuit of how to improve democracy is in the end living proof that Cuba practices democracy; a democracy in constant motion.

Chapter 10

Informer et Faire Découvrir Cuba

CLAUDE MORIN

Dans un ouvrage récent, Salim Lamrani (2013), auteur de plusieurs études sur Cuba, analyse la manière dont le quotidien espagnol *El País* rend compte de la réalité cubaine. Ce quotidien, certainement l'un des plus actifs sur Cuba, est un bon représentant de ce qui s'écrit sur l'île. Ses articles et reportages sont souvent cités ou repris par d'autres journaux et contribuent à influencer le regard porté sur l'actualité cubaine. Lamrani s'emploie à déconstruire le discours médiatique. Il montre à quel point *El País* sélectionne l'information qu'il offre à ses lecteurs, s'attardant sur les « problèmes » qu'il présente hors contexte, en les amplifiant, sinon en les créant de toute pièce, alors qu'il passe sous silence les éléments positifs, les réussites. Les sujets abordés, les titres qui coiffent les articles, les faits rapportés, les témoignages retenus démontrent un net parti-pris chez ses journalistes et attestent de la ligne éditoriale de ce quotidien dit « libéral ». Nous sommes très loin d'une présentation équilibrée qui inviterait les lecteurs à un jugement nuancé. Lamrini montre, à l'aide d'autres sources, que ce quotidien n'hésite pas, pour alimenter ses interprétations tendancieuses toujours défavorables à Cuba, à pratiquer les mensonges délibérés, les omissions coupables, les silences complices.

Ce qui vaut pour *El País* vaut malheureusement pour l'ensemble des grands journaux, des agences de presse et des médias écrits et audiovisuels. Lamrani (2009) avait déjà commis un autre ouvrage dans lequel il débusquait nombre de mensonges et de silences. L'évidence s'impose: s'agissant de Cuba, l'équilibre et la nuance ne font pas partie des devoirs

Claude Morin

que s'imposent les journalistes. C'est comme s'ils ignoraient l'histoire de l'île, qu'ils se permettaient de rendre compte de l'actualité sans aucun recul et de juger des événements en dehors de tout contexte, le plus déterminant étant l'hostilité invétérée des États-Unis envers cette expérience originale dans leur voisinage immédiat. Ils s'affranchissent de l'éthique journalistique qui devrait orienter leur pratique.

La Cuba révolutionnaire est ainsi depuis ses origines la cible d'un journalisme éloigné de l'objectivité, comme voué à faire mal paraître les décisions de ses dirigeants, à ajouter encore plus de couleurs sombres à un tableau qui met l'accent sur les manquements, les pénuries, les frustrations. Notre vision de Cuba est amplement affectée par l'image que façonnent journaux et médias de toute sorte, y compris maintenant Internet et toutes les formes de communications qui s'y rattachent.

L'antagonisme de Washington – auquel a répondu la résistance à saveur de défi de La Havane – a beaucoup fait pour polariser la vision qu'on a de Cuba, y compris au Canada qui, malgré des désaccords, n'a jamais rompu les ponts avec La Havane (Kirk et McKenna 1997). Pour les uns, la Révolution cubaine a fait figure d'épouvantail avant d'être perçue, à partir de 1991 et l'effondrement de l'Union soviétique, comme un anachronisme. Pour d'autres, Cuba a été un phare éclairant la route vers une société plus juste, plus fraternelle. La survie de cette expérience de transformation radicale en a fait un exemple de détermination et une source d'espoir. Malheureusement, malgré le développement d'Internet, les Cubains ont moins de poids que les étrangers sur ce qui se discute hors de Cuba, une situation unique en Amérique latine. L'image de Cuba que l'on a à l'étranger est ainsi davantage façonnée par la présentation qu'en font les États-Unis, le gouvernement, les chercheurs, les médias de ce pays. Cette présentation tendancieuse réussit à s'imposer à l'échelle planétaire en raison de la force des moyens de diffusion états-uniens et des pressions qu'exercent les institutions états-uniennes. Mais l'exemple du quotidien espagnol *El País* atteste d'une attitude qui découle moins de la géopolitique que de l'idéologie, laquelle a pour objet la défense du capitalisme face à une expérience qui s'identifie au socialisme.

L'étude universitaire de Cuba révolutionnaire porte également la marque de cette polarisation active dans le champ politique. Elle prend donc une coloration polémique, soit ouvertement, soit subrepticement. Cela fait de la « cubanologie » un domaine relevant de la sociologie de la connaissance. Comment le discours politique influe-t-il sur l'analyse scientifique? Quelle est la portée des valeurs qui habitent le chercheur sur son travail? Quelle position occupe-t-il dans la société susceptible de colorer ses interrogations et ses jugements? Quelles sont les limites de l'objectivité?

La sympathie que nous pouvons éprouver pour la Révolution cubaine ne doit pas se confondre avec la foi. Elle doit se fonder sur la connaissance la plus intime, la plus directe, la plus personnelle de ce que fut et de ce que demeure ce processus en cours qu'est la Révolution cubaine. La quête d'une information honnête doit nourrir notre solidarité. C'est une entreprise difficile dans la mesure où nous sommes submergés dans un flot d'informations ouvertement ou subrepticement partiales, sinon hostiles. Il nous faut constamment demeurer alertes, flairer le mensonge, les demi-vérités, l'exagération. Et nous n'avons pas tous les moyens d'accéder à une information vraie, honnête. La barrière linguistique représente pour beaucoup un obstacle additionnel. Internet a certes ouvert l'accès, mais sur ce plan Cuba est défavorisée en raison du blocus qui élève considérablement les coûts de raccordement aux réseaux externes.

Une autre démarche consiste à découvrir par nous-mêmes ce qu'est Cuba, à aller sur place et à vivre des expériences qui nous font partager le quotidien des Cubaines et des Cubains, à se frotter à leur culture, à comprendre le parcours qui les a menés là où ils sont. Il faut privilégier ces séjours organisés qui nous mettent en contact avec les Cubains, leurs lieux de travail et d'études, leurs milieux de vie, les institutions, les expressions variées de leur culture.

Claude Morin

Ce chapitre se concentrera sur ces deux dimensions. Il rendra compte d'abord d'expériences destinées à contrer la désinformation relative à Cuba en lui opposant une information honnête. Il rendra compte dans un deuxième temps de voyages qui furent à la fois des voies d'accès aux réalités cubaines et des formes de solidarité avec le peuple cubain dans la mesure où ces explorations et rencontres défiaient un des objectifs du blocus, soit isoler Cuba. Je m'en tiendrai dans ces pages à des expériences dont je fus un participant. Ce sera l'occasion de faire état de certaines actions de solidarité qui eurent le Québec comme protagoniste et comme point de départ et d'évoquer rapidement les cadres qui présidèrent à leur réalisation. Le Canada est ainsi fait que la solidarité envers Cuba est souvent vécue dans le cadre des « deux solitudes ». Il convient de le déplorer. L'insertion de ce chapitre dans cet ouvrage est de nature à nous rapprocher dans nos tâches communes.

Combattre la Désinformation et Informer

Cuba fait régulièrement l'objet d'informations tendancieuses, voire trompeuses. C'est le cas de tout ce qui gravite autour des opposants, de ceux que les médias présentent comme des « dissidents ». Le décès d'Oswaldo Payá dans un accident de la route à Cuba en juillet 2012 fut l'occasion d'opérations de désinformation dans l'immédiat, alors que les médias évoquaient un complot possible, puis un an plus tard quand le *Washington Post* publia une entrevue avec le conducteur espagnol, le seul responsable de l'accident en raison d'une vitesse excessive. Angel Carromero prétendit avoir été suivi par une vieille Lada rouge. Le quotidien espagnol *El Mundo* reprit l'article avec un titre plus percutant: « Les services secrets cubains ont assassiné Payá ». Entretemps, la Lada était devenue bleue! C'est une pratique fréquente d'une opération de désinformation que de faire transiter l'information par plusieurs journaux afin de lui insuffler plus de crédibilité. Comme Winston Churchill l'a déjà remarqué avec humour, un mensonge « gets halfway around the world before the truth has a chance to get its pants on. »

J'emploie ici le mot « désinformation » à dessein. Si en anglais on distingue *misinformation* et *disinformation*, en français, on n'utilise qu'un terme pour recouvrir deux sens. Un sens étroit la rattache à l'espionnage, au contre-espionnage, à la guerre. Un gouvernement émet de façon directe ou clandestine des mensonges qu'il veut voir disséminer par des médias en vue d'embarrasser ou de tromper des gouvernements ennemis. L'exemple le plus accompli de désinformation eut lieu juste avant le débarquement en Normandie. Les Alliés réussirent à induire les Allemands en erreur quant au moment et au site du débarquement. La désinformation vise à provoquer des erreurs chez l'adversaire. Ce peut être la transmission secrète de fausses informations à destination des services secrets rivaux. Ce peut être des mensonges destinés aux citoyens pour cacher des actions inacceptables. Le *Contragate/Irangate* en fit usage. La désinformation est ici synonyme de mensonge. Elle est inséparable d'une situation de conflit, d'une guerre en cours, froide ou chaude. Cuba est assez fréquemment la cible de cette forme de désinformation qui émane de la CIA ou du State Department et qui fait partie d'une campagne de discrédit destinée à conditionner l'opinion publique aux États-Unis et à l'étranger.

Il y a un sens nouveau, lié à une critique des médias. Il désigne la conspiration du silence autour de certains faits ou la déformation que les médias font subir aux faits, délibérément ou involontairement, en raison des caractéristiques de production et de diffusion. Les médias sont critiqués pour ce qu'ils disent, ce qu'ils ne disent pas, pour la manière dont ils le disent ou pour les insinuations. La liberté de l'information – celle d'émettre des messages ou d'en recevoir, par la voie de l'imprimé ou par celle des ondes – est subordonnée à des enjeux déterminés par la raison d'État ou par l'influence des groupes de pression (privés ou publics). C'est la plus perfide, parce qu'elle est la plus diffuse. Les acteurs ne sont

Claude Morin

pas toujours conscients de participer à la désinformation. Ici la désinformation se rapproche du « parti-pris », des préjugés non reconnus. C'est une censure qui s'ignore ou une déformation sournoise de l'information.

La démonstration a été faite pour les journaux états-uniens. Tony Platt et Ed McCaughan (1988) ont analysé 331 articles dans 17 grands médias états-uniens. Ils ont noté que « *[the] odd dichotomy between the message of the lead and headlines on the one hand, and the bulk of the story on the other, perhaps indicates editors' attempts to make their correspondents' stories conform to predetermined editorial policy* ». Les titres seraient plus négatifs que les articles eux-mêmes, révélant un parti-pris délibéré de noircir Cuba. À propos de la campagne en faveur des droits de la personne, les auteurs parlent de « désinformation » : « *In many ways, it followed the pattern of a classic disinformation campaign: it asserted political conclusions, which are not supported by reliable evidence; it mixed known facts with unverified gossip; it elevated speculation into proof; it repeated assertions until they became self-perpetuating and self-evident truths; and it used carefully selected experts to legitimate its argumentation* ».

J'ai eu l'occasion en tant qu'universitaire de dénoncer la désinformation à propos de Cuba. Dans une conférence publique, aujourd'hui disponible en ligne, je rassemblais un florilège d'articles qui appartenaient à la désinformation, notamment ceux qui visaient le public québécois (Morin 1995). L'analyse que j'en faisais est toujours valide vingt ans plus tard. Les thèmes ont changé, mais le même parti-pris s'affiche sans vergogne. J'ai constaté au cours des années, depuis au moins 1990, que les journaux ou magazines québécois – je pense ici à *L'Actualité*, un magazine à large diffusion – tendaient à publier des articles négatifs à l'approche de la saison touristique. Cette concentration saisonnière n'est pas fortuite. On croirait que le magazine participe à une opération visant à détourner les voyageurs d'un séjour d'hiver à Cuba afin de priver l'économie cubaine de recettes dont elle a un grand besoin.

Récemment, lors d'une projection publique du documentaire *Playa coloniale*, nous avons été nombreux à critiquer ce portrait-charge du tourisme québécois à Cuba. Les images, le montage, les entrevues avec les Cubains, Yoani Sánchez et les touristes, la bande sonore, tout concourt dans ce film à détourner les spectateurs de la destination cubaine. C'est comme si le film avait été conçu pour donner mauvaise conscience aux voyageurs qui vont à Cuba dans les « tout-inclus ». Le parti-pris de départ apparaît au générique quand on découvre que le traducteur (et conseiller) est Victor Mozo, un anticastriste qui distille son opposition dans les médias québécois depuis plus de 30 ans. Nous comprenons alors que le documentaire participe d'une opération de boycottage sous les dehors d'un film critique d'un type de tourisme. Les deux cinéastes à qui j'ai écrit pour faire part de mes nombreuses critiques ont répondu que tel n'était pas leur objectif. Ils ont néanmoins refusé d'engager le débat sur le contenu de leur film.

En Amérique du Nord, le Québec est une société distincte en raison de la langue. J'ai constaté qu'une part importante de la propagande anticastriste transitait par la France. Ainsi des ouvrages très médiocres trouvent un écho dans les médias québécois au moment de leur sortie en France. Denis Rousseau fut invité sur un plateau de Télé-Québec en raison de son livre (Cumerlato et Rousseau 2000). Serge Raffy (2004), auteur d'un pavé exécrable, eut les honneurs d'une invitation à Radio-Canada en 2013. Le livre de Jacobo Machaver (2004) fut choisi l'ouvrage de la semaine pour un magazine radio[1]. En revanche, on passe sous silence des ouvrages solidement documentés qui sont favorables à la Révolution

---

1   L'ouvrage de Cumerlato et Rousseau constitue un exemple de ce qui se fait de pire en matière de journalisme unilatéral, un montage de propos négatifs, saupoudrés d'anecdotes visant au dénigrement de la Révolution et du « régime ». Celui de Ruffy est un ramassis de ragots, de mensonges afin de construire un portrait-charge de Fidel: le manipulateur, le menteur, le dictateur, le mégalomane, le fourbe, le comédien. Machaver, qui a quitté l'île en 1963, se voue à une seule mission : discréditer l'œuvre de la Révolution. Il fait partie de cette frange d'auteurs qui cherchent à capitaliser sur un intérêt authentique pour Cuba, mais qui en traitent de façons malicieuses, prisonnières d'un rejet personnel passionnel, à moins qu'ils ne soient des mercenaires au service d'une opération téléguidée de dénigrement.

Claude Morin

cubaine (Lamrani 2005, Bovy et Toussaint 2001, Alonso Tejada 2001). Les médias ont deux poids deux mesures, offrant la parole à ceux qui tiennent des propos à l'emporte-pièce.

L'arrestation de 75 opposants en 2003, suivie de leur jugement et condamnation à des peines d'incarcération allant de 6 à 28 ans, a fait les manchettes. L'opinion publique internationale s'est beaucoup émue. Des intellectuels sympathiques à la Révolution cubaine ont dénoncé ces condamnations. L'Union européenne a adopté des sanctions diplomatiques et suspendu des accords de coopération. Tous ont jugé des événements, graves en soi, il faut en convenir, sans égard aux circonstances et aux tensions qui les expliquaient. Les médias ont fait de ces prisonniers des intellectuels. Selon l'organisation *Reporters sans frontières* qui fustige les atteintes à la liberté de presse, 30 des condamnés auraient été des « journalistes indépendants ». Or il s'avère que seulement quatre avaient fait des études en journalisme. L'important était ailleurs. Tous ces gens n'ont pas été sanctionnés pour leurs idées, mais pour leur conduite. Les procès ont démontré qu'ils avaient coopéré directement avec les États-Unis et qu'ils avaient participé à des réunions organisées par la Section des Intérêts Nord-Américains (SINA) à La Havane (qui tient lieu d'ambassade des États-Unis) dont ils avaient reçu argent, conseils et équipement. Pour démontrer le bien-fondé de ces accusations, le tribunal a présenté douze témoins qui ont révélé être des agents de la sécurité cubaine infiltrés dans des organismes supposément voués à la promotion des « droits de l'homme ». Les biens saisis montraient également que les accusés vivaient mieux que la majorité des Cubains et que la « dissidence » pouvait être une activité fort lucrative. J'ai exposé ces faits en les situant dans leur contexte en réponse à une nouvelle campagne de dénigrement en 2004 (Morin 2004).

Plusieurs amis de Cuba ne manquent pas de réagir à la publication d'articles, à la diffusion de documentaires, de reportages ou d'entrevues qui ont en commun d'être trop ouvertement malhonnêtes, voire mensongers. Je pense notamment à Michael Walsh qui a écrit de nombreuses lettres aux journaux et aux responsables de l'information à Radio-Canada. Seules quelques lettres ont été publiées, mais les autres ont circulé entre les amis de Cuba, contribuant à nous informer et à raviver notre vigilance. Les arguments qu'il oppose sont des rappels utiles dans notre travail collectif d'information et d'éducation.

Une autre approche consiste à écrire aux auteurs. Je crois en effet qu'il est contre-productif d'attaquer des journalistes en public. Chacun a son amour propre qui l'empêche de reconnaître son erreur. Beaucoup de journalistes, animateurs, professeurs, politiques ne font que des incursions momentanées sur Cuba. Cuba n'est pas leur spécialité. Ils sont donc exposés à refléter, à véhiculer (et à renforcer par leurs propos) la désinformation ambiante dans laquelle nous baignons tous (y compris nous qui réagissons à partir d'une autre sensibilité) à propos de Cuba. Il convient de leur indiquer qu'il y a une autre face à la médaille que celle qu'ils ont décrite. Il faut éviter l'escalade, demeurer posé, en rester à exposer des contre-arguments. J'ai ainsi à plusieurs reprises communiqué avec les auteurs, ce que facilite le courriel. J'espérais de la sorte non pas les convaincre, mais tout au moins semer le doute et faire en sorte qu'ils soient moins négatifs à l'avenir et qu'ils sachent mieux faire la part des choses. J'ai ainsi pu développer un certain rapport de collaboration avec des journalistes. Certains m'écrivent ou me téléphonent avant de rédiger un papier, ce qui me permet d'exposer ma vision du sujet, laquelle trouvera sa place dans l'article, même si elle côtoiera un point de vue opposé. L'article ne nous satisfera généralement pas, mais nous aurons évité le pire, ce qui est déjà mieux.

J'ai également participé à plusieurs débats contradictoires à la radio et à la télévision. C'est un format inconfortable quand l'animateur démontre une nette partialité dans ses propos et dans ses questions, allant jusqu'à manifester une certaine complicité avec l'invité auquel il nous oppose. J'ai vécu à plusieurs reprises cette situation, alors notamment que j'étais opposé à Victor Mozo, un Cubain venu au Québec dans les années soixante-dix, qui n'est jamais retourné à Cuba et qui tient un discours

Claude Morin

anticastriste sans nuance et sans concession. Comme si son origine cubaine lui conférait d'office une crédibilité sans égard aux dénonciations qu'il aligne à chaque participation. Aucune réforme ne trouve grâce à ses yeux. Tout se résume à la dictature, au totalitarisme, au fiasco. Sa relation personnelle avec la Révolution cubaine a préséance sur l'analyse que je tente d'exposer avec objectivité. J'ai l'impression d'avoir été invité pour justifier sa présence et non l'inverse, que les dés sont pipés et que ma présence sert à donner l'apparence d'équilibre à l'émission. Il n'y a rien de plus frustrant que d'affronter un animateur indisposé par votre point de vue et vos arguments, qui accorde plus d'importance dans sa présentation à vos convictions « fidélistes » qu'à vos travaux comme universitaire, qui cherche à vous faire passer pour un propagandiste du « régime », pour un « porteur de valises »[2]. L'universitaire habitué à jouer de la nuance dans ses analyses n'est pas à son meilleur dans le rôle de contradicteur, de polémiste. Le temps lui est trop compté. Aussi a-t-il l'impression de se battre à armes inégales et de ne pas pouvoir donner sa pleine mesure dans l'éducation du public. Il aurait tort cependant de ne pas relever le défi et de laisser ainsi toute la place au discours dominant.

En revanche, il est beaucoup plus gratifiant d'informer dans le cadre de conférences où c'est nous qui choisissons les thèmes, les arguments. L'auditoire est généralement sympathique, ou du moins il n'est pas hostile. Après tout, il s'est déplacé pour entendre une autre version. J'ai donné ainsi depuis 1979 des dizaines de conférences devant les publics les plus divers et sur des thèmes tout aussi diversifiés à l'invitation d'organismes, les uns militants, les autres neutres. Ce sont des expériences positives comme le sont les participations à des entrevues dans les médias quand l'animateur, au lieu de jouer au contradicteur, vous accompagne dans l'échange, quand l'information a préséance sur le spectacle.

---

2   L'animatrice m'assimilait à ces sympathisants français engagés dans les réseaux de soutien au FLN (Front de libération nationale) durant la guerre d'Algérie.

Ces dernières années, Arnold August a donné plusieurs conférences sur la démocratie cubaine alors qu'il préparait une nouvelle édition de son ouvrage ou qu'il faisait une tournée de diffusion (August 1999; 2013). La démocratie cubaine et la question des droits de la personne sont les sujets pour lesquels il nous faut combattre les préjugés les plus tenaces. Arnold aura fait beaucoup pour élever le débat à la fois par ses conférences et ses écrits. Grâce à lui, la démocratie cubaine n'est plus la boîte noire qui place les amis de Cuba sur la défensive. Son livre est une lecture obligatoire pour qui veut s'affranchir des œillères et de la pensée unique.

Nous avons assuré entre nous un travail d'éducation de l'opinion publique. Y ont également contribué des conférenciers cubains qui ont effectué des tournées au Québec. Plusieurs universitaires ont ainsi pu s'adresser à des publics divers, à l'université et ailleurs (Carlos Tablada, Aurelio Alonso Tejada, Marta Pérez-Rolo, Helena Díaz González, Aleida Guevara – une des filles d'Ernesto Guevara – pour en nommer quelques uns). Ces tournées ont exigé la collaboration de plusieurs institutions afin de faciliter l'octroi de visas et de rassembler des fonds pour défrayer les déplacements et les séjours. Ces conférences connurent toujours un grand succès attirant un large public et révélant le grand talent de communicateur des universitaires cubains. Rarement pourtant trouvèrent-ils dans les grands médias, comme à Radio-Canada, l'accueil réservé à des opposants notoires, telles Alina Fernández Revuelta (une fille de Fidel), la blogueuse Yoani Sánchez, l'écrivaine Zoé Valdés, des professionnels de l'anticastrisme.

Faire Voyager à Cuba

Il n'y a pas de meilleur moyen de s'informer et de se faire une opinion que de voyager à Cuba. Plusieurs sont sceptiques quant à la valeur

Claude Morin

documentaire de ces voyages organisés dans les pays socialistes. Ils parlent de pèlerinages faits par des croyants qui n'ont aucune vision critique face à ce qu'ils voient. François Hourmant (2000) fait le procès de ces « voyages de propagande » organisés pour des intellectuels français plus ou moins célèbres en URSS, en Chine ou à Cuba. Les autorités ne leur montreraient que des « villages Potemkine » et les flatteraient en organisant une rencontre avec le dirigeant suprême, ici Fidel Castro. Pensons au voyage que firent Jean-Paul Sartre et Simone de Beauvoir à Cuba en 1960. Impressionné, Sartre confessa avoir rencontré chez les révolutionnaires cubains ses fils spirituels. Ces visiteurs prestigieux acceptent, par ambition, de jouer le rôle de témoins privilégiés sur une scène où tout est réglé d'avance. Or ce n'est pas ce qui attend l'immense majorité des visiteurs qui ne bénéficie d'aucun avantage. Leurs interlocuteurs sont le plus souvent des gens ordinaires, au mieux des cadres locaux.

Je me souviens d'un voyage que nous fîmes, une vingtaine d'universitaires québécois, en décembre 1979. Le voyage avait été organisé par le Carrefour culturel de l'amitié Québec-Cuba (CCAQC), un organisme fondé onze mois plus tôt. L'Institut culturel d'amitié des peuples (ICAP) était notre hôte. Nous logions à l'hôtel Sevilla, à La Havane. Au circuit touristique classique (la découverte de quartiers, de musées, de la nécropole Colón, etc.) s'ajoutaient des visites à deux usines, une ferme laitière, une école, l'université, l'hôpital Hermanos Ameijeiras, une polyclinique, un projet domiciliaire à Alamar, une fabrique de cigares. Ces visites étaient assorties d'exposés et de rencontres. Nous célébrâmes le Nouvel An dans un CDR (Comité de Defensa de la Revolución) dans Vedado. Ce voyage de 14 jours fut la meilleure introduction aux réalités cubaines. Nous devînmes, à des degrés divers et de notre propre chef, sans incitation aucune, des ambassadeurs.

En août 1991, je fis partie d'un autre type de voyage, une brigade de solidarité organisée par le Canada-Cuba Cultural Interchange, de concert avec le CCAQC[3]. La brigade réunissait 21 membres recrutés depuis la Colombie-Britannique jusqu'à Terre-Neuve, dont sept venaient du Québec. Les camarades de l'ICAP avaient tout mis en œuvre pour que le programme fût à la fois intense et varié. Le séjour se déroula principalement au camp Julio Antonio Mella, à 45 km de La Havane. Cinq matinées furent consacrées à la construction d'un dortoir destiné à loger de futurs contingents de brigadistes. Nous nous retrouvâmes tous engagés dans un travail manuel, aux côtés de camarades cubains, des gens de bureau pour la plupart, sans égard au sexe, à l'âge, à la langue, à la profession d'origine, dans une saine et joyeuse émulation. Ce fut sûrement pour beaucoup d'entre nous une expérience mémorable, enrichissante à plus d'un titre, une leçon sur les réalités du travail à Cuba. Les après-midis étaient réservés à des exposés par des spécialistes sur divers aspects de la vie à Cuba (économie, politique), suivis, en début de soirée, par des rencontres avec des représentants des organisations de masse (jeunesse, femmes). Les soirées se terminaient autour d'un verre (ou d'une bouteille) à discuter, à s'amuser ou à regarder la transmission des Jeux panaméricains qui se déroulaient à La Havane et à voir les prouesses des athlètes cubains. Une chaleureuse camaraderie s'est développée rapidement entre les brigadistes et les camarades cubains du camp. Tout ne fut pas que travail et conférences. Nous visitâmes un projet domiciliaire dans une banlieue pauvre de La Havane, comptant 16 000 habitants. La moitié du quartier avait été reconstruite grâce au travail de micro-brigades. La micro-brigade est comme une école servant à élever la formation culturelle et politique. Nous visitâmes aussi deux coopératives rurales, l'une sylvicole, l'autre agricole (tabac). Le programme comprenait également l'inspection d'un hôpital et d'une usine de transformation du lait. Un des moments forts fut la soirée passée dans un CDR à Pinar del Río.

---

3   Ce type de voyage de solidarité fut l'amorce de ce qui allait devenir, à partir de 1993, le Che Guevara Volunteer Work Brigade, une expérience relatée au chapitre 4.

Plusieurs Québécois se sont rendus à Cuba dans le cadre de voyages d'études. Ainsi une soixantaine ont participé aux cinq éditions d'un cours universitaire organisé à l'Université de Montréal de concert avec l'Université de La Havane. Le cours faisait alterner des conférences par des collègues cubains et des visites de lieux et institutions en rapport avec les thèmes des exposés. Au retour de son voyage, voici ce que m'écrivait Stéphanie Maude Gaudin:

> In Cuba, I have discovered the true meaning of community. [...] The Revolution is not something that 'happened' to the people for better or worst; the people made the Revolution and it is this same spirit that shines through every day activities. [...] Cubans still feel part of the Revolution because they are continuously involved in the process in every day affairs. [...] Cuban socialism itself is worthy of esteem and respect because it has succeeded to a great extent in its fight for equality of all. [...] During my short journey, [...] I learned unforgettable life lessons. For example, true happiness should reside in the success of all, not just my own.

Plusieurs institutions d'enseignement ont organisé des voyages pour faire découvrir les réalités cubaines. Ce fut le cas du collège de Drummondville pendant plusieurs années. D'autres Québécois ont suivi des cours d'espagnol, soit à La Havane, soit à Cienfuegos, généralement en partenariat entre des écoles d'ici et des institutions cubaines. L'apprentissage de la langue comportait toujours des volets visant à familiariser les participants avec la vie locale. Le Centre international de solidarité ouvrière (CISO) a pour sa part réalisé des stages à Cuba pour des syndicalistes venus de plusieurs horizons. Les rapports pour deux de ces stages (CISO 2000; 2004) témoignent de l'impact qu'ont eu ces séjours chez les participants. Ce fut, dans chaque cas, une initiation à la solidarité interne et à la solidarité internationale. CISO avait organisé, en mars 1996, une importante Conférence internationale de solidarité avec Cuba à Montréal. Le moment était grave puisque le Congrès des États-Unis venait de voter la loi Helms-Burton qui renforçait singulièrement le blocus. La conférence réunit plus de deux cents participants, diffusa six documents écrits spécialement pour la réunion et disponibles en trois langues et adopta des résolutions pour dénoncer le blocus. Des invités cubains, notamment des cadres de la Centrale des travailleurs de Cuba, rehaussaient de leur présence ce grand rassemblement, sans doute le plus imposant à s'être tenu à Montréal.

Il convient de réserver une place spéciale à ARO CoopérAction InterNational (http://www.arocoopintl.org/). Depuis sa fondation en 1994, ARO a fait voyager plus de 7000 Québécois à Cuba dans le cadre de camps, de chantiers solidaires, de stages, destinés tant aux jeunes qu'aux retraités. ARO propose de vivre au cœur de la réalité cubaine, au contact direct avec les familles et les communautés, en partageant le travail et le quotidien. L'organisme s'emploie aussi à acheminer médicaments et équipements médicaux. Colette Lavergne, la fondatrice, a acquis au fil de deux décennies une solide connaissance des réalités locales. Elle s'avère une redoutable débatteuse dans les réunions publiques et sur les plateaux de télévision, particulièrement face à des détracteurs de Cuba.

Mon expérience personnelle en tant qu'accompagnateur pour des voyages d'études et plus récemment pour du tourisme culturel m'a appris que l'on ne peut aller à Cuba et côtoyer le peuple cubain sans en revenir transformé par l'expérience. On découvre un peuple digne, résilient, héroïque, solidaire, débrouillard, capable de réaliser beaucoup avec peu. Il ne faut pas s'étonner que beaucoup de Québécois qui vont à Cuba par sympathie, voire par curiosité, en reviennent déterminés à apporter leur contribution, à payer de leur personne, à faire quelque chose, à s'impliquer. L'information, le voyage et la solidarité peuvent ainsi se combiner en une équation dynamique.

Claude Morin

La Solidarité Québécoise et ses Cadres

La solidarité repose sur des individus informés, conscientisés, généreux, mais elle profite de la mise sur pied d'organismes qui facilitent et canalisent les initiatives. L'organisation de la solidarité envers Cuba au Québec ne prend son essor qu'avec la création, le 20 janvier 1979, à Montréal, du Carrefour culturel d'amitié Québec-Cuba (CCAQC). Six délégués de l'ICAP participent à la réunion de fondation. La première année d'existence du Carrefour fut marquée par plusieurs activités dont la tenue d'une fête le 26 juillet, l'ouverture d'un local permanent et le lancement du bulletin *Québecuba Sí*. Une grande célébration eut lieu le 19 janvier 1980 avec orchestre et danses: 400 personnes y assistèrent. Le dynamisme du départ semble s'être vite essoufflé. Les énergies étaient sans doute dispersées entre trop de volets (cours d'espagnol, films, conférences, fêtes). La solidarité avec le Nicaragua sandiniste accaparait aussi beaucoup l'attention. Il y avait trop de causes à soutenir pour le nombre de membres.

La solidarité avec Cuba connaît dans les années 1990 une étonnante diversification. L'effondrement de l'Union soviétique et les rigueurs de la « période spéciale » suscitent de nouveaux besoins pour contrer les effets du « double blocus ». Le CCAQC reprend du service, organise des voyages, facilite la venue de conférenciers cubains, fait campagne pour rassembler des fournitures médicales. Nombre de nouvelles organisations voient le jour à Montréal, à Québec, à Trois-Rivières, à Drummondville, en Estrie, dans les Laurentides: Amitié Québec-Cuba, Brigade Québec-Cuba, Caravane d'amitié Québec-Cuba, Coalition Cuba Si!, Jeunesse cubaine, Solidaridad con Cuba, Association québécoise des amiEs de Cuba, etc. Un effort de concertation se manifeste également. Ainsi, en 1996, le Réseau québécois des groupes de solidarité avec Cuba s'emploie à réunir des représentants des divers organismes actifs au Québec. À partir de 1993, le Québec se joint au mouvement Friendshipment Caravan lancé en 1992 par Pastors for Peace pour la collecte de fournitures et leur transport vers la frontière états-unienne. Des organismes régionaux tissent des collaborations avec des partenaires à Matanzas, à Cienfuegos, à Holguín, ou ailleurs.

La concertation se poursuivra avec la création en 2002 de la Table de concertation de solidarité Québec-Cuba (http://www.solidaritequebec-cuba.qc.ca). En 2010, la TCSQ-C regroupait 22 associations, dont une demi-douzaine vouées à la solidarité envers Cuba. La Table a surtout dirigé ses énergies dans la campagne pour la libération des cinq Cubains « prisonniers de l'empire ». Le Comité Fabio di Celmo en constitue le fer de lance. Une manifestation se tient tous les mois devant le Consulat des États-Unis à Montréal. Mais la Table se consacre aussi à l'information en organisant une journée cubaine à Montréal, en écrivant des lettres au gouvernement canadien en réaction à des déclarations qu'elle conteste, en diffusant par courriel le calendrier des activités et en rassemblant sur son site Internet divers documents en rapport avec la solidarité. Elle anime aussi une émission hebdomadaire à Radio-Centreville (102,3 FM), « Dimension cubaine ». Elle organise enfin la Brigade Madeleine-Parent qui combine des sessions de travail volontaire, des conférences et des visites à plusieurs régions de l'île. La Table est ainsi devenue au fil des années le carrefour québécois pour les actions de solidarité à l'endroit de Cuba. Il convient de souligner ici le travail de coordination qu'accomplit Sean O'Donoghue.

Petit pays aux ressources limitées, Cuba est un géant au plan de la solidarité internationale. Après avoir apporté son appui généreux aux mouvements de libération, particulièrement en Afrique australe, Cuba a mis ses éducateurs et son personnel médical au service de la santé et de l'assistance humanitaire sur trois continents. L'internationalisme désinté-ressé est l'une des valeurs suprêmes mises en pratique par la Révolution cubaine depuis 1959. Plusieurs Canadiens ont été sensibles à cette dimen-sion et ont répondu par leurs actions et leur engagement à cet exemple admirable. Cet ouvrage en témoigne largement. Notre solidarité envers le peuple cubain nous rattache par son entremise à une solidarité planétaire.

Références

Alonso Tejada, Aurelio [et al.] (2001). *Cuba, quelle transition?* Éditions L'Harmattan, Paris.

August, Arnold (1999). *Democracy in Cuba and the 1997-98 Elections.* Editorial José Martí, La Habana.

August, Arnold (2013). *Cuba and its Neighbours. Democracy in Motion.* Fernwood, Halifax, Zed Books, London.

CISO (2000). « Rapport d'un stage de solidarité avec le peuple cubain ». http://www.ciso.qc.ca/wordpress/wp-content/uploads/stage-cuba-2000.pdf

CISO (2004). « Cuba: la solidarité, un mode de vie, une réponse au blocus » http://www.ciso.qc.ca/wordpress/wp-content/uploads/cuba-2004.pdf

Cumerlato, Corinne et Rousseau, Denis (2000). *L'île du docteur Castro. La transition confisquée.* Stock, Paris.

Hourmant, François (2000). *Au pays de l'avenir radieux.* Aubier, Paris.

Lamrani, Salim (2005). *Cuba face à l'Empire.Propagande, guerre économique et terrorisme d'État.* Lanctôt, Outremont.

Lamrani, Salim (2009). *Cuba, ce que les médias ne vous diront jamais.* Prologue de Nelson Mandela. Éditions Estrella, Paris.

Lamrani, Salim (2013). *Cuba. Les médias face au défi de l'impartialité.* Éditions Estrella, Paris.

Kirk, John M. et McKenna, Peter (1997). *Canada-Cuba Relations: The Other Good Neighbor Policy.* University Press of Florida, Gainesville.

Machaver, Jacobo (2004). *Cuba, totalitarisme tropical.* Buchet Chastel.

Morin, Claude (1995). « La désinformation, ou comment peser sur le cours des événements à Cuba » https://www.webdepot.umontreal.ca/Usagers/morinc/MonDepotPublic/pub/CubaDesinfo.pdf

Morin, Claude (2004). « Les droits de l'homme. Un bras de fer entre Washington et La Havane » https://www.webdepot. umontreal.ca/Usagers/morinc/ MonDepotPublic/pub/CubaDroits.pdf

Platt, Tony et McCaughan, Ed (1988). « Tropical Goulag », *Social Justice* 15.

Raffy, Serge (2004). *Fidel l'infidèle*. Fayard, Paris.

Chapter 11

Cuba and the Tradition of Inspiring Humanitarianism

KEITH ELLIS

◇◇

When the horrendous earthquake destroyed densely populated parts of Haiti on January 12, 2010, those of us who were following the news of its immediate impact understood that the Caribbean country would need urgent and efficient help. Our thoughts soon went to the presence of Cuban medical personnel in that country out of concern for their safety and in the context of the help that they could give to victims of the disaster. To our relief, we soon learned that the Cubans were miraculously safe and had already, within the first 24 hours of the earthquake occurring, attended to some 1109 Haitian patients. Naturally, we saw as an effort that had to be sustained, and we wanted to do our part in making it possible. At a meeting of the Canadian-Cuban Friendship Association in Toronto, Paula Larrondo suggested that we launch a campaign to be known as "To Cuba for Haiti", and we thought that solidarity groups throughout Canada would embrace the idea. The Canadian Network on Cuba (CNC) readily endorsed the idea, asking me to coordinate the effort, as I had done for two previous CNC hurricane relief campaigns for Cuba. In those campaigns, the help of Sharon Skup, who administers the Mackenzie-Papineau Memorial Fund, had been indispensable for the imaginative and efficacious manner in which she had carried out the functions of treasurer in hurricane relief campaigns in which every penny collected went to its secure destination, the institution created by the Cuban government to receive the funds.

In the cases of the hurricane relief campaigns, solidarity groups throughout Canada had given generously of their time, energy, and ingenuity to make those campaigns successful. In the second case, when Cuba was battered by three devastating hurricanes in a short period of time, we kept raising our targets successfully from an initial $100,000 to more than $400,000. This latter target was prompted by a certain sense of indignation because, in the face of the enormous damage wreaked by the hurricanes, our national government offered an announced amount of $400,000, with not all of it to be given directly to the Cuban government, which shouldered the responsibility for the recovery from the devastation. Our success in achieving the amount of some $402,000 was greatly appreciated by the Cuban people and recognized as the best effort from any solidarity group worldwide.

Of course, the zeal with which we responded, and the fact that we were not entirely satisfied with the effort, was due to our knowledge of Cuba's generosity to the peoples of countries that are ravished by natural disasters, by the spontaneity with which they assist. This practice demonstrates that Cuba sees the affected simply as human beings and shows no regard for their ideological tenets or political allegiance. Cuba responds with humanitarian imagination that in practice produces miracles, and is limitless in its perception of what needs to be done. Examples of this spirit are numerous.

Cuba suffered the terrible wounds of hurricane Flora in 1963, early in the time of the revolution, with the loss of more than 7,000 human lives as well as the colossal loss of animal life and the widespread destruction of property. It developed from that experience scientific and humanitarian means of protection, which it has continued to refine over the years; and, as is its practice, it has been ready to share this knowledge and this spirit with other countries. When hurricane Mitch wreaked prolonged havoc in Central America in 1998, causing more than 20,000 deaths, the Revolution decided to establish a permanent institution, known as the Henry Reeve Brigade (named for a U.S. doctor who gave outstanding help to Cuba and made the ultimate sacrifice during the first phase of the war of independence against Spain), to give medical and material relief to people wherever in the world the need arose. The Brigade's vital presence was appreciated in the snowy mountains of Pakistan in 2005 when an earthquake made a terrible visit to the people of the Kashmir region during the regime of General Musharraf, the close ally of President George W. Bush.

The help of the Brigade was also offered by Cuba to the United States along with other kinds of help during the time of the crisis provoked by the terrorist attack on the Twin Towers in New York City on September 11, 2001. The assistance by the Brigade was again offered, with notable persistence, when U.S. citizens were suffering and dying, some of them on the streets of New Orleans, in the aftermath of hurricane Katrina in 2005. But the Bush administration rejected it.

Dimensions of this Cuban humanitarianism are manifesting themselves in other ways. For example, in 2003 Cuba undertook to assist the government of the Bolivarian Republic of Venezuela in freeing its people of illiteracy, employing the most efficient system now known to humanity, *"Yo Sí Puedo"* (Yes, I Can), a system developed from Cuban observation of the skill with which illiterate Haitians mastered the use of numbers in their everyday lives. The system "is being applied in over thirty-five countries [including Canada] and has successful completions of over four million people in basic literacy" (ArrowMight n.d.). The Cubans found that some Venezuelans were not able to take advantage of the literacy promotion system, and, on examining them medically, discovered that they suffered from impaired vision. The Cubans saw this as a need that could not be overlooked. Beginning with these Venezuelan patients, the outcome has been the program known as *"Operación Milagro"* (Operation Miracle), which has resulted so far in corrective therapies for nearly 2 million people throughout Latin America and the Caribbean.

Keith Ellis

Cuba's attention to children affected by the Chernobyl nuclear disaster of 1986 and its troubling sequelae is also remarkable, because the disaster occurred when the Eastern European countries were close allies and trading partners of Cuba, giving buoyancy to the Cuban economy. But when that partnership ended, causing a precipitous decline in the Cuban economy, Cuba nevertheless continued the sacrificially expensive gesture of bringing those children, a total of more than 20,000 of them, to the island for treatment.

Another way in which this spirit of Cuba is shown comes from my own experience in administering the "To Cuba for Haiti" campaign. In mid 2010 when we were getting a fairly steady flow of contributions, Sharon Skup brought to my attention the fact that we had received a particularly large donation of more than $40,000 for Cuba. It occurred to me that, in the light of predictions that there would be a season of intense hurricanes in the Caribbean, we might reserve a part of those funds for a possible hurricane relief campaign. I put the matter to Cuba's Consul General in Toronto, Sr. Jorge Soberón, and Cuba's Ambassador to Canada, Sra. Teresita Vicente Sotolongo. In both cases, the reply was unhesitating and immediate: give the whole donation to the Haiti campaign.

One might ask: what is the provenance of the spirit in which Cubans quest after knowledge, particularly scientific? What is it that makes them serve, sharing their education and expertise with such alacrity, even in circumstances in which hostile and powerful forces attempt in every way to keep them from achieving material prosperity? The origins of this spirit are to be found in the beginnings of their long struggle to gain their freedom from slavery and their independence and sovereignty. The first seeds lie in the uprisings against slavery that began in the Cuban copper mines from the early 16th century and occurred sporadically throughout the centuries until they converged with the independence movement of the 19th century. Intellectuals of the Jesuit clergy who were concentrated in the San Carlos and San Ambrosio Seminary played a key role in this convergence that came to be personified in the leading member of the second generation of this grouping: Father Félix Varela (1788-1853).

The Wars of Independence of the South American countries had made him, and some of his contemporaries, dream of and then strive for Cuba's independence, and they felt a parallel responsibility to prepare their country for development in its desired state of independence. This was the essence of Varela's thoughts and deeds. Recognized for the brilliance that he showed at the Seminary where he had studied, been ordained a priest at the age of 23, and then taught philosophy, physics, and chemistry, he was selected to represent Cuba in the Spanish *Cortes* or Parliament. The eminent Cuban scholar Eduardo Torres-Cuevas, in his book *Félix Varela*, has focused incisively on the intimate relationship between thinking and action that characterizes Varela's philosophy (Torres-Cuevas 2002). In so doing he has shown him to be not only "the man who taught us [Cubans] to think" – in the words of José de la Luz y Caballero, one of his famous students (About Educational n.d.) - but also the initiator of a current of thinking that is seen as valid for and prevalent in Latin America and the Caribbean. Torres-Cuevas writes:

> If Varelian philosophy expresses what is autochthonous in an authentic and therefore original way, its validity isn't derived solely from the capacity of that way of thinking to interpret and express its reality, but it goes further; it tries to act on it. This arises from the thinker's commitment to his reality; from this understanding and conviction that thinking has a social function and that the theoretical production should be applied to the reality. This application of ideas to the reality constitutes the *utility* of ideas. (Torres-Cuevas 2002: 207; translation from Spanish: Keith Ellis).

Keith Ellis

Torres-Cuevas then produces this rich quote from Varela's *Lecciones de filosofía* (Philosophy Lessons):

> I deduce then that it isn't useful for anyone to separate himself capriciously from society, renouncing the benefits of this common mother. Nature imposes on human beings the law of making themselves happy by perfecting themselves; hence it must be inferred that we are obliged not to separate ourselves from the sources of these perfections, which lie in the social state.... How absurd it is to say that the misanthrope lives a philosophical life when, attending only to himself, he lives among his fellow beings without interesting himself in the well-being of society! (Quoted in Torres-Cuevas 2002: 278-299; translation from Spanish: Keith Ellis).

Varela's concept of the utility of philosophy is twinned with the moral and ethical tenets he had learned and taught at the Seminary, a combination that ensured that the Spanish authorities would be disappointed in his performance as Cuba's representative in the Cortes. Normally, the appointment of a brilliant young talent to such an office, in a colonial regime, is a co-optive exercise, aimed at winning over the appointee, who could envisage a life of perquisites and privileges, to the colonial cause. But Varela took seriously his mission of representing Cuba, of striving for the good of the society, of making it whole, which it could not be with one part slave and another not fully free precisely because it was colonial. Touched by the hopeful excitement of the spirit of independence that had been sparked by Simón Bolívar's revolutionary wars, he irritated the Spanish authorities by calling on Spain, in the Cortes itself, to put an end to the practice of slavery and to free all its overseas territories from colonial subjugation. The authorities responded by seeking his arrest; and, when he evaded that, fleeing to Gibraltar and then to the United States, they imposed a death sentence on him, making impossible his return to his native land. In the United States he served fellow Cubans and Cuba well, maintaining ties with the progressive sectors and always understanding that the yearned for and anticipated independence had to be sustained by productive knowledge. He forwarded to his friends his readings on contemporary scientific and political developments, translating them into Spanish, if necessary. He translated, for example, Humphrey Davys's *Elements of Agricultural Chemistry*.

Varela died in the United States, precisely a month after José Martí was born, on January 28, 1953. In many ways Martí may be seen as his successor. The two were linked academically by fact that one of Varela's students at the seminary, Rafael Mendive, was Martí's teacher and mentor, helping to make Martí in every good thing useful. At age 12, seeing a slave being hanged, Martí decided to dedicate his life to ending slavery; at 15 his enthusiastic support for Carlos Manuel de Céspedes's declaration of Cuba's independence occasioned the beginning of a series of punishments by the authorities that led to his suffering permanent physical injuries and his banishment from Cuba. These stiffened his resolve to achieve full independence and sovereignty. At 29 with his first book of poetry he changed the course of the genre in Spanish America and Spain. At the same time, in the context of his aspiration for a unified, developing Latin America and Caribbean, while he wrote some of the poems that would constitute his great book *Versos libres* (Free Verses), he began to champion the cause of scientific education.

This simultaneous engagement with science and poetry and science and the arts in general in Cuba was not original with Martí. José María Heredia (1803-1839), himself a highly significant innovator, the first Hispanic Romantic poet—Martí called him "the first poet of the Americas"—also showed an interest in science, bringing it even into his poetry with a work entitled "Progresos de las ciencias." He too had to flee from Cuba under threat of death from the colonial authorities because of his anticolonial activities. Varela's student, Luz y Caballero, sought out equipment in Europe to set up physics and chemistry laboratories in Cuba, worked at establishing a Cuban Academy of Literature and collaborated in journals, such as the *Revista Bimestre Cubana* that supported both the arts and the sciences. Yet no one in any Latin American or Caribbean country in the 19th century showed the zeal, the cogency of argument, and the aptness of phrase displayed by José Martí in promoting culture and education in general and scientific education in particular. Living in New York in the 1880s and being keenly aware of measures being taken in Europe to lift the level of life, with his yearning for economic and cultural development in Latin America and the Caribbean for the benefit of all the region's people, he urged that selected aspects of those measures be applied in those republics. Of course, the *sine qua non* for participation in this development was independence and sovereignty; and that kept his principal focus on the effort to remove his own country from the clutches of colonialism and enabled him to perceive the threat posed to the region by imperialism. He also proposed as insulation against the negative aspects of North American development and as armour for the struggle against colonialism and imperialism the observance of the highest moral and ethical standards and the finest humanitarian sentiments.

Between August 1883 and May 1884 Martí published seven essays dealing with scientific education. These essays are argumentative, tendentious, aiming to persuade Spanish Americans to undertake a radical revolution in education. Together with another contemporary series on World Exhibitions as sites of learning, these essays are replete with fecund aphorisms that speak of the author's deep commitment, his wisdom, his humanism, his Spanish-American patriotism, his passion for freedom and development, his incorruptible ethical sense, and his ardent and boundless faith in the good qualities of his neighbours. These are distinguishing characteristics that make this Cuban highly and widely respected and give resonance and lasting influence to his words; words affirming that the ideal can be achieved (Martí 1963):

> *good teachers, youthful vigour, stimulus and accumulation of learning produce the miracle* (p. 281).

The project has a primary dual mission. The first is the development of the individual within a society that on the basis of knowledge is capable of resisting oppressive external forces. This concept is expressed as:

> *to be educated and cultured is the only way to be free (p. 289).*

The second, in keeping with Martí's view that "homeland is humanity" and, echoing Varela, is expressed as "to be good is the only way to be happy" (p. 289); and a way of achieving happiness is by spreading the benefits of knowledge to those in need. He continues:

> *It is necessary to initiate a campaign of tenderness and science, and create for it a force, that does not now exist, of missionary teachers (p. 291).*

In a similar and more generalized Promethean vein, he adds:

> *let each person be a torch (p. 290),* and sums up:

> *the sun is no more necessary than the establishment of scientific education* (p. 292).

Several of these aphorisms are widely known in Spanish America and the Spanish-speaking Caribbean. They are an embedded part of the culture of Revolutionary Cuba and have always been prominent in the

Keith Ellis

consciousness of the leader of the Cuban Revolution, Fidel Castro Ruz, as John Kirk (1983) has underlined in his book, *José Martí: Mentor of the Cuban Nation*. We may recall that when Fidel candidly faced the courts and was asked who was the intellectual author of the event that started the overt Revolutionary process, the attack on the Moncada military barracks on July 26, 1953, he answered: "José Martí." In elaborating on this answer, he explained that in the year of the centenary of Martí's birth, the country could not abide living the rampant violation of his principles that was being perpetrated by the Batista tyranny and the prevailing social experience of the vast majority of the population.

There is another trait of Martí's literary personality that needs to be mentioned in the context of the inculcation of his values in the Cuban population. This has to do precisely with the supreme intensity with which he presents his worldview. He published two books of poetry during his lifetime: *Ismaelillo* and *Versos sencillos*. His third book, *Versos libres*, which I mentioned earlier, was finally put together and published in 1985 (Martí 1985). All of these books are impressive in their different ways for the sublimity with which they express the views that are peculiar to each book. Not before his *Ismaelillo* (1882), his first book of poetry, had there been in Spanish America or the Caribbean a book that was so tightly unified. In the fifteen poems of this book, the poet, with instructive tenderness, responds to his infant son's inspiration and need for sound constructive guidance, and he displays fitting elevated imagery and music in his verses. In this way he became the first of the Hispanic modernists. In his *Versos sencillos* (1891) all the poems reveal the poet to be sincere and satisfied in his valuing of simplicity and in his commitment to those who are in need. It is amazing that spanning the time in which he wrote *Ismaelillo* he should have been writing many of the poems of the *Versos libres*. The 66 poems of this book (which I have translated for imminent publication in a bilingual edition by Havana's José Martí Publishing House) take the intensity to the level of the individual poems that treat a broad range of topics, each one revealing Martí's deep engagement that requires of him novel concepts and an inevitable complexity of expression. With what desperate force does the Cuban National Hero convey the pain of exile from the homeland that he wants to free from tyrannical hands in the poem *"No, música tenaz, me hables del cielo!"* (No, tenacious music, speak not to me of heaven!). And in *"Flor de hielo"* (Ice Flower) a superb elegy on the death of a close friend, he would take up the sword against death itself and decry the indifference of complacent men of his time who would not join him in the challenge. The poems reinforce the steel-like determination, the uncompromising will, to rectify what is wrong in favour of compatriots and of humanity alike. Martí's prose, evidenced for example in his essay *"Nuestra America"* (Our America), is also compellingly powerful.

In one of his typically incisive comments that give him the status of National Poet, Nicolás Guillén produced the verses: *"Te lo prometió Martí/ y Fidel te lo cumplió"* (Martí promised it to you/ and Fidel carried it out). The verb *cumplió* sparkles with an accumulation of rich jewels. It contains the overcoming of myriad challenges launched by the powerful foe, the fulfilment of many visions that are components of a large guiding vision, the dispersal among millions of an elevated heroic spirit, such as that shown by the Cuban Five, notwithstanding their unjust, cruel and shameful punishment by the implacable foe for their noble effort against terrorism.

As soon as Cuba saw the first signs of recovery from the economic decline of the mid 1990s, it turned its attention to the desperate health-care situation being faced by Haitians, specifically to the high infant mortality rate. Fidel Castro sought the partnership of Canada in facing the challenge of lowering that rate from 120 per 1000 live births at a time when Cuba's was nearing six and Canada's was nearing five. Canada was invited to supply medicines and Cuba would supply the trained medical personnel for the effort. Canada eventually declined the invitation, fearing U.S. reaction; and Cuba decided to undertake the task alone. The island thus became in 1998, when a bilateral agreement was signed between Cuba and Haiti, the first country to show significant solidarity and give meaningful help to Haiti since that country freed itself from slavery and became a Republic in 1804, almost two centuries earlier. This solidarity came as stark contrast to the castigations meted out over two centuries to Haiti by the imperialist gang for the black republic's daring to break the bonds of slavery and of colonialism.

Cuba did not, as is its custom, restrict its medical aid to the area of infant mortality. Once in Haiti, Cuban doctors found it necessary to assume wide responsibilities for health care in that country. And what is more, they also recognized the need and the abilities of young Haitians to be trained as medical doctors. Haitians thus came to be numbered among the 10,000 students of the Latin American School of Medicine established by Cuba to give the opportunity free of charge to intellectually deserving and ethically qualified students from the Americas (including the United States and Canada), the Caribbean, Africa and other parts of the world to contribute to healthcare in their respective countries.

Cuba also administered a School of Medicine in Haiti that had reached an enrolment of some 300 students, when, in 2004, as a consequence of the coup carried out by the United States, France and Canada against President Aristide, the United States billeted their soldiers in the School, putting an end to its functioning. Cuba's response was to transport the students to Santiago de Cuba to continue their studies.

When the earthquake occurred on January 12, 2010, Cuba was prepared and had been preparing others, both technically and ethically, to respond to the crisis. The 300 Cuban medical personnel were quickly joined by hundreds of other Cuban doctors, nurses, technicians, cooks, as well as students, including Haitian and Latin American senior students or recent graduates from Cuban schools of medicine who volunteered to assist in Haiti. And given the Cubans' propensity to understand the broad ramifications of such crises, not only was the spectrum of medical services, such as psychiatry and epidemiology represented, but other areas of Cuban society—painters, musicians and performing artists of various kinds—volunteered to go to Haiti to raise the spirits of the Haitian people, particularly the children.

Nor should the contributions of other countries be ignored in this effort. The United States, ostensibly fearing disorder, increased its military presence and took over the administration of the airport. It also sent the SS Comfort, a hospital ship that during its stay of more than a month off Port-au-Prince served some 871 patients. The governments of Norway and Namibia, recognizing the capabilities of the Cubans, decided to give their help to Haiti through Cuba. In the meantime, with the coming into being of the ALBA grouping, led by Venezuela and Cuba, the aid to Haiti has been expanded. Cuba had already made the huge commitment of providing Haiti with a new healthcare system; and Venezuela, cognizant of its historical debt to Haiti incurred when Dessalines gave crucial help to Simón Bolívar in 1815, making possible the continuation of the war for the liberation of Venezuela, has come to fill some of the wide chasm of need that will be experienced by Haiti for many years to come.

In October of 2011 the Canadian Network on Cuba invited Dr. Jorge Balseiro, who arrived in Haiti five days after the earthquake and who had a long term of service there particularly in the field of psychiatry, to make a lecture tour throughout Canada. Sandra Ramírez, who attends to Canada at the Cuban Institute for Friendship with the Peoples, accompanied him. They had an extensive and very busy tour, and the information they provided was extremely enlightening to audiences. In the course of his visit, on October 30, 2011, he gave an interview to Roger Annis of the Canada Haiti Action Network and provided *inter alia* the following information.

- Since 1998, the Henry Reeve Cuban Internationalist Brigade has treated more than eigteen million cases in Haiti. The Brigade has performed 304,577 surgeries and vaccinated 1,501,076 people.

Keith Ellis

The Brigade estimates that the number of Haitian lives it has saved is 284,239.

- Since the earthquake the Brigade has treated 347,601 people and performed 8,870 surgeries. Its members have delivered 1,631 babies and vaccinated 74,493 people.

- The Brigade has provided rehabilitation services to 75,013 people. Seventy-five people so far have received prostheses to replace lost limbs. Psychosocial treatment is being provided to 116,000 children.

The cholera outbreak has of course added to the burden.

- The Brigade established forty-four cholera treatment units (complete with testing laboratories) and twenty-three cholera treatment centres. The Brigade treated 76,130 cholera patients in the first year of the epidemic and suffered 272 patient deaths. But no deaths have occurred in the 267 days to the end of October 2011. The mortality rate of the patients treated by the Brigade is 0.36 percent, compared to the countrywide rate of 1.41 percent.

The present status is the following:

- Cuba now has 786 doctors and health workers in Haiti, and a further 21 doctors from Latin America are serving with the Cubans.

- The Brigade has twenty-three community hospitals in operation and ten comprehensive diagnostic centres (operated in cooperation with Venezuela).

- The Brigade also has a total of thirty rehabilitation rooms.

- There are twenty-eight active epidemiological surveillance and control programs monitoring such threats as malaria and dengue.

- There are twelve family doctor centres and there are plans to build a laboratory for producing prostheses and three electro-technical workshops.

- There are two Operation Miracle clinics.

- Since the earthquake Cuba has received $23 million U.S. from international donors.

- As of December 17, 2011, the Canadian Network on Cuba had sent CAD$403,278.40 to Cuba. This sum represents the full amount, every penny, of the donations received, with no administrative or mailing costs deducted. We currently have on hand CAD$2,512.39 to be sent along with another large donation we expect to receive soon.

The Cubans have known how to multiply the funds they have received to produce billions of dollars worth of service to Haiti. Their steadfast commitment is to produce many billions of dollars more of life-giving and life-preserving service to the Haitian population. On meeting people such as Dr. Jorge Balseiro, we further our understanding of the fact that for revolutionary Cubans service such as that given by the Henry Reeve Brigades is an act of celebration of their achieved independence and sovereignty that has given them the freedom to do good. This heightens the special respect we have for Cubans and makes gratifying for all that are involved in the "To Cuba for Haiti" fundraising effort throughout Canada the continuing task of supporting Cuba's contribution to Haiti.

References

About Educational (n.d.). *Felix Varela y Morales, his educational ideas and the need for their presence in the Cuban Education Now.* http://abouteducational.blogspot.ca/2013/01/felix-varela-y-morales-his-educational.html. Retrieved April 10, 2014.

ArrowMight (n.d.). ArrowMight Canada Literacy/Numeracy Program Background. http://www.arrowmight.ca/docs/AM-FACT-History.pdf. Retrieved April 10, 2014.

Davys, Humphrey (1826). *Elementos de química aplicada a la agricultura en un Curso de Lecciones en el Instituto de Agricultura.* New York: Gray.

Ellis, Keith (2010). *First Poet of the Américas: José María Heredia and "Niagara Falls".*La Habana: Editorial José Martí.

_____ (1995). *The Role of Science in Cuban Culture.* Toronto: York Medical.

Guillén, Nicolás (2002). *Obra poética II.* La Habana: Letras Cubanas.

Kirk, John (1983). *José Martí: Mentor of the Cuban Nation.* Gainesville: University of Florida Press.

Martí, José (1963). *Obras completas.* La Habana: Editorial Nacional de Cuba.

_____ (1985). *Poesía completa.* La Habana: Editorial Letras Cubanas.

Torres-Cuevas, Eduardo (2002). *Félix Varela: los orígenes de la ciencia y conciencia cubanas.* La Habana: Editorial de Ciencias Sociales.

Chapter 12

Ernest Hemingway: One Canadian's Doorway into Cuba

BRIAN GORDON SINCLAIR

◇◇◇

I must confess: I have taken a lover. Her name is Cuba and I am deeply and irrevocably in love with her. I did not choose to love her. When I arrived on her doorstep ten years ago, I was looking only for information and inspiration to help me write a single theatrical play about the life of Nobel Prize winning author, Ernest Hemingway. Little did I know that the beautiful, compassionate people of Cuba would open a doorway leading to a marriage of hearts and minds and souls. The offspring of that marriage would be an epic seven theatrical plays called *Hemingway On Stage: The Road to Freedom* and, even more epic, a lifetime of friendships. Because I am an actor as well as a playwright, it was through the actual performance of my plays in Cuba that I was able to initiate those friendships. My experience, to now, has been limited to three major areas: Havana, Holguín, Santiago, and their surrounding towns and villages. In each place, the people of Cuba warmed my heart and lifted my spirits.

From Havana, I went to the fishing village of Cojímar for the 50th Anniversary of the meeting of Fidel Castro and Ernest Hemingway. Cojímar, a short drive east of Havana, is the location that inspired Hemingway's novella, *The Old Man and the Sea*. The celebration was held in *Pesca Deportiva Ernest Hemingway* and was attended by members of the family of Gregorio Fuentes (First Mate of Hemingway's boat, *Pilar*) – daughter, granddaughter, and grandson. My visit also included an interview by the press who wanted to know if I really believed that Fidel had caught the most fish in the 1960 Ernest Hemingway International Fishing Tournament. I told them that Hemingway had watched closely and that he had "an automatic built-in bullshit detector and a damn fine pair of binoculars." He would never award the silver trophy to anyone who had cheated.

I also met several elderly fishermen who, as boys, had actually known Hemingway. One presented me with a small hand crafted mask of Ernest's face and told me about a fishing song that Ernest wrote. He is going to get me a copy. Afterwards, we travelled to the Hemingway monument near the Castillo where a wreath was laid to commemorate the anniversary. This monument, a bust of Ernest, was crafted from the bronze propellers donated by the fishermen of Cojímar. It was a gesture of love and respect. Finally, we went to *La Terraza* restaurant where special pictures of Hemingway and Castro had been newly hung. The management graciously served *mojitos* and *daiquiris* to everyone. I then returned to Havana, taking with me the grandson of Gregorio Fuentes, on his way to teach English to a class of waiting students and more than willing to give me a lesson or two on Cuba.

The next day was a magic day. I spoke as Ernest to the gathered crowd on the front balcony of *Finca Vigía*, now *Museo Hemingway*, directly in front of Ernest's writing room. For the first time in this humble actor's life, I was able to describe Ernest's home, *Finca Vigía* while, at the same time, pointing to the real building, the real saltwater swimming pool and the many mango trees as I described the creation of a children's baseball team named after Hemingway's son and called the Gigi All-stars. A gentleman named Jorge still operates that team and "Hemingway On Stage," and was very pleased to help arrange safety helmets for all the players.

At the end of the speech, which was offered in English with simultaneous translation by the fabulous Susana, I was able to present some computer accessories to the Director of Museo Hemingway as well as a modest donation raised for the ongoing work of the museum. In return, the Director of Havana Club distilleries presented me with a special edition rum: *Ron Vigía Reserva 18 Años Producción Limitada*. It bears the Hemingway *Finca Vigía* crest. You know, I'd always wanted to try an eighteen-year-old rum but now that I've got it, it seems too precious. I don't want to break the seal.

I then made one more speech about dedicating the Nobel Prize Medal to the people of Cuba and the fishermen of Cojímar while depositing the medal at the *El Cobre* Sanctuary. As Ernest I said a small, sincere prayer of gratitude, which can be read in full in the Santiago section of this chapter. In the midst of the prayer, I swear, someone inside me said, "It's good to be home." Strange the things we sense but I do know that my voice cracked and I truly felt a presence. I concluded the prayer by crossing myself and saying "Amen." At that moment, every person in the audience, including the old fishermen and their wives, echoed me in a gentle but soul stirring "Amen." It was a true and holy moment. Just then, for one brief, glorious instant in time, Ernest Hemingway had come home. Later, the museum director, Ada, looked in my eyes and said, "Ernest is very happy today." The next day, because the appearance had been filmed, several million Cubans watched "Ernest Hemingway" pray for the people of Cuba on the cultural segment of the national news.

It is of tender, personal moments that I wish to write, and Holguín, Cuba provided many of these moments. When I performed at the *Unión de Escritores y Artistas de Cuba* (UNEAC), the headquarters for the Union of Artists and Writers of Cuba, my audience consisted primarily of a wonderful group of Cuban students who were studying English. Also in the audience, uninvited, was a very large cockroach that chose the middle of one of my speeches to scuttle noisily across the floor. Since admission was complimentary, I couldn't very well throw him out; so I continued. When I spoke of the Cuban flag and the love of Cuba, the students rose to their feet in applause. This old actor's heart was very proud at that moment. I hope the cockroach enjoyed it too.

I also remember, with great fondness, the night a dear friend, Elizabeth, joined me in an attempt to see a play celebrating the Cuban

Revolution and written by a Portuguese playwright, Leandro. Because of a technical problem, the performance was cancelled. Elizabeth, Leandro and I, along with a Colombian-born Bostonian, headed for the cafés of Holguín's entertainment district. The conversation flowed and so did the time as we all entered into a lifetime of friendship but the hour was late and no traditional taxis were available, only bicycle taxis. With great revolutionary fervour, we leaped into three different bicycles. Each of us was transformed into an instant general. The race was on! I shouted the command "Beat those bikes to the Hotel Pernik!" The drivers huffed and puffed and strained their muscles and finally one pulled ahead by a few lengths and stopped in front of the hotel. Out stepped the winner. It was … Ah, I am sorry, but you know a gentleman never tells. I will tell you, however, that with the amount of laughter exuding from all the worthy combatants; no one was disappointed, least of all the Cuban drivers.

On the last day of this visit, I travelled with a group to the attractive town of Baguanos. Here, the whole town came to greet us. Cheering people with flags and signs were at the intersections approaching the town and when we finally stepped off the bus, the town square was full. The band was there, military cadets were there and then six little drum majorettes marched forth and performed their tiny-perfect, precision routine. When they finished, the anthem played and they all stood very still at attention, radiant in their youth. It was then that it must have rained. How else could you explain the moisture rolling down my cheek?

Later, after visiting a street market, an art display and a cooking school (with lots of samples), we entered the town hall where we were entertained with music, song and poetry. There, I spoke as Ernest Hemingway. I told them that I had been out of Cuba at the moment of the revolution but that when I returned, I kissed the Cuban flag and stated that I believed in the absolute necessity of the Cuban revolution. I said that the photographers, at the time, did not manage to get a photo but today because of the *milagro*, the miracle, of theatre I would be able to pose, kissing the flag, for photos. I then said that this day was different. I said, "Today, I kiss the

Cuban flag because I believe in the absolute necessity of the freedom of the Cuban Five." I kissed the flag in honour of the Cubans imprisoned in America, held the pose briefly for photos and concluded by saluting and exclaiming, "*Viva Hemingway, Viva Cuba, Viva los Cinco Heroes!*" Would it be a surprise to say that the reaction was exceedingly positive?

Every arrival in Cuba feels like a spiritual return to a home where that special part of me has been too long away. My next visit to Holguín was a lot like that. I was there, ostensibly to perform for the 20th *Che* Guevara Brigade, a band of adventurous Canadians of all ages determined to experience the real Cuba. After the show, there was a deluge of questions: "What Hemingway books can I read? How do I start writing? How do I learn to speak in front of an audience?" Each question meant that a curiosity had been aroused. They also told me that, in my play, *Hemingway's HOT Havana*, I had demonstrated a very special love for Cuba, a love that they too hoped to share. If you have ever wondered about the mandate of Hemingway On Stage, the reaction of the Brigade demonstrates that mandate precisely.

A second show was for *Las Romerías de Mayo* (the pilgrimages of May). This cultural festival celebrates the founding of Holguín and, over the years, has become both national and international. It all started with a parade. God, I love a parade!

They marched into the city square, heads held high, through hundreds if not thousands of spectators, cheering, mesmerized by the pageantry. In the presentation area, a choir of white shirted singers stopped to sing. Beethoven's Ode to Joy rose, not from their throats, but from their hearts. Silver paper rained from a balcony and we felt the joy enter our hearts in that special, shivering kind of way. We were transported.

Next, a horde of Harleys roared in, beautifully restored with flags flying in the morning air. Then the band, red shirts stepping out, brass instruments shining, gleaming in the sun, followed by beautiful elegant girls, child and teen, draped in the flamenco finery of passionately graceful dance. Then came the vintage cars, trucks loaded with workers, revellers, all celebrating this day of joy, and bringing joy to those, like me, who watched, spellbound.

The audience for my second performance also consisted of many Spanish students of English. They were an exceptional audience, responsive and attentive. I knew their English was good because I could actually see the comprehension in their eyes. They smiled, they listened and some cried. You see, when you mix love and death, love of Cuba and the death of Ernest Hemingway, some people will be moved to tears. Later, in conversation, these students displayed a knowledge and an awareness of Hemingway that I can only wish existed in North America. They were warm, they were loving and they were smart. They said I touched their hearts. Truth is, they touched mine.

Santiago de Cuba is hot in every way, temperature, music, art and emotion. Like no other city, it arouses passion. It is also home to Roberto and Juan.

Roberto is a brilliant barber who cuts my hair in the old-fashioned way and with great passion. He massages my scalp, cleans and tightens the pores of my face, and carefully trims the hair of both beard and head. Like any proud artist, he surveys the result of his work and pronounces me acceptable to walk on stage and perform. Roberto likes to cut the hair of "Ernest Hemingway". He is just as happy to cut my hair. He is proud; he is a master of his craft and he knows that true artists have great respect for each other.

Juan is a special man. He knows everyone in Santiago and he likes to make things happen. Sometimes, however, things happen to him, like hurricane Sandy. When Sandy hit Santiago, Juan and his family were at home. Outside, the winds of destruction roared and pounded. Have you ever heard the thunder of tanks in the midst of war, rumbling, shaking the very firmament? This was Santiago. This was Sandy. All Juan could do was to lie in bed, desperately grasping the sides, staring at the ceiling and praying that it would not collapse. His wife was curled up, locked in a ball, shaking and unable to talk. His daughter, elsewhere, listened fearfully to the sound of other roofs being blown away and watched, a strange smile frozen on her face, as her own roof lifted ominously in the violent air. She could not speak, only smile because, as she said later, she was "scared to death." In another room was Juan's son. Like all eleven-year-old boys he had his own reaction to the storm. He slept through it all, totally oblivious to the raging outside world. Juan and his family survived. Others did not.

It was Juan who first took me to *El Cobre*. We climbed the hill outside the city past the rugged, symbol-laden sites of local ceremonies and rose to a view of an exquisite picture-perfect lake glowing blue and gold from the copper content, sparkling like a jewel in the heavens. Below was the church containing the *El Cobre* Sanctuary, beautifully restored for the visit of Pope Benedict. This was the church where Ernest Hemingway's Nobel Prize Medal was to reside, a gift to the people of Cuba.

Ernest Hemingway's Nobel Prize Medal was stolen from the *El Cobre* Sanctuary, located approximately twenty miles outside Santiago de Cuba, sometime in the 1980s. One version of the theft suggests that the thieves were not unknown to the local residents. When word reached Raúl Castro, he reputedly issued an ultimatum, "Return the medal within seventy-two hours or face the consequences. I know who you are." Although the medal was returned, it was never again put on public display and remained, in hiding, under the care of the Archbishop of Santiago. Rarely has it been seen. The last person I know to have seen the medal was Ernest's granddaughter, Mariel Hemingway. Through a combination of successful performances and my contributions to the Hemingway legacy at Finca Vigía, I had become the modern embodiment of Ernest Hemingway and on December 6, 2011, I was granted the rare privilege of viewing, holding and performing with the medal. A film crew from *Mundo Latino* captured the event for use, eventually, in a multi-part documentary about Hemingway in Cuba.

There is no proof that Hemingway ever accompanied the medal to Santiago; nevertheless, I created a scene that depicts the arrival of the medal at the *El Cobre* Sanctuary. In discussing this scene with the staff of the Archbishop of Santiago, I explained that it was in the spirit of Hemingway but based on poetic or dramatic license. Soon a message arrived from the Archbishop's secretary, "We approve your 'license.'" This is the text from the scene in the original play *Hemingway on Stage:*

Hemingway:

After the war, I finally completed *The Old Man and the Sea* and I was almost killed in a plane crash in Africa. In 1954, for one or both of those things, I was awarded the Nobel Prize for Literature. This is a part of what I said:

(He picks up the speech and reads.)

"Writing at its best is a lonely life…A true writer should always try for something that has never been done before…Then sometimes, with great luck, he will succeed…It is because we have had such great writers in the past that a writer is driven far out, past where he can go, out to where no one can help him."

(He returns the speech.)

I dedicated my Nobel Prize Medal to the fishermen of Cojímar. Although I had told this story of an old man and his fish to the whole world, it is their story and they should share this medal.

A medal is worn close to the heart and my heart is in Cuba. The good people of Cuba have taken me into their hearts and caused me to live here longer than I have lived anywhere else. This is my true home.

Later, after a ceremony at the Modelo Brewery, I travelled with the medal to Santiago de Cuba and entered the church. There, in the *El Cobre* sanctuary, I knelt at the feet of the Patron Saint of Cuba and deposited the medal.

(He closes his eyes and prays)

Silently, I prayed for the protection, the peace and the prosperity of the warm, friendly, generous people of Cuba.

(He opens his eyes)

In Cuba, the people accepted me unconditionally. I could breathe and be happy. It is my clean, well-lighted place.

(He crosses himself)

Amen.

The preceding stories represent but a few of the special moments I have enjoyed in Cuba. How I wish there were time to tell you of all the others…of the ghosts of the Sierra Maestra, the ghosts that are still there. I know this. I have been there. I have felt them, sensed them, still there on guard for freedom and change…of Rosalba who cared for the dogs of the Hemingway estate and who died of cancer because she cared more for others…of Adi who travelled to China to learn a new language to help her people…of all the people who work at the Cuban Institute of Friendship with the Peoples, people like Kenia and Esperanza and Sandra and Amaury and Miriam, people who help because they love to help… and of the young teacher fresh with a Master's Degree who speaks of art and souls and rising spirits and I know that she is the future of Cuba, young and vibrant and in the process of being reborn in her search for truth. These are the people of Cuba and they are all special.

Now, as I sit in the cold winter snows of Canada, I feel a soft, lonely ache in my heart. I need my love; I need my Cuba. Soon, Cuba, I will walk once more through the doors of your love and embrace you, for you are in my heart, a part of me, forever. Thank you, Ernest Hemingway and thank you, Cuba.

Conclusion

NINO PAGLICCIA

◇◇◇

The search for solidarity, its meaning, implementation, and practice can be qualified as an on-going historical struggle where "the many different radicalisms of the past generation are linked together… and continued unabated into Latin America, extending to Cuba… The root impulse of this journey has been a search… for existential fellowship, for authenticity, for personal meaning, and community – for solidarity."

(Gosse 1993: 8-9)

The solidarity movement for Cuba, for the Cuban Revolution, is the most precious treasure we have. Because they are with us despite governments, they are with us anytime. And you know, to have friends like that also fuels us to keep fighting for the faith and for the good of humankind.

His Excellency Ernesto Sentí
Former Cuban Ambassador to Canada
At the Breaking the Silence Conference
Toronto, November 2007

In his book, *Cuba: A Revolution in Motion*, author Isaac Saney frames the Cuban Revolution as an evolving, transforming, and renewing process (Saney 2004). So we should not be surprised at recent reports of new economic policies in Cuba that aim to modernize the economy. Observers from all sides of the political spectrum speculate whether these changes are signs of Cuba embracing pro-market reforms and slowly abandoning the socialist path, or whether the country is transitioning into a new socio-economic model as it claims. After all, Cuba has demonstrated over time its willingness, openness, and astonishing agility at developing new unique ways of doing things and re-inventing itself with an earnest sense of vision, perfectionism and endurance. One outstanding example is the opening of a modern tourist sector as a trigger for the much-needed economic recovery following the collapse of the Soviet Union and the socialist block in the early 1990s. Canada is not new to transition either, and we are also observing economic and social changes under a majority Conservative Government - with its own brand of economic and political survival - that are no less intriguing in terms of their unexpected and uncertain outcomes. These changes in Canada may well impact negatively the traditional "policy of constructive engagement" with Cuba at a political level. Cooling off of Ottawa-Havana relations were already observed in the first Harper minority government (McKenna and Kirk, 2012: 154-156).

As we entertain important questions about the role of solidarity under these changing scenarios, and whether or not the new conceptual and empirical solidarity is adapting to the changing realities of Canada and Cuba, it is precisely at this conjuncture of changes that becomes important to take stock of the Cuba solidarity movement in Canada and share the work done so far, including achievements, failures, and expectations.

Kirk and McKenna (1997: 178, 182), in their book *Canada-Cuba relations, the Other Good Neighbor Policy,* conclude their analysis with a suggestion that Washington should consider adopting the Canadian approach towards Cuba: that is, "pragmatic" and "normal" relations. That would be quite a welcome step forward in terms of a state-to-state relation from the current U.S.-Cuba affairs, especially at a time when the

American people seem to be more open to normal relations[1]. However, state-to-state relations tend to focus solely on such pragmatic topics as trade advantages, competing interests, ideological hegemony, domestic electoral postures, and controlling geo-political positions. This is the prevalent model of foreign relations for countries with market-based economies. On establishing the connection between Canadian foreign policy (by the state) and public diplomacy (by Canadian citizens) through international development programs, Rebecca Tiessen observes, "Canadian citizens have the potential to shape foreign policy" (Tiessen 2010: 142). However, in the presence of decreasing international development assistance on the part of the Canadian government, we must consider a fresh start of public diplomacy where non-state agents, social movements, and civil society fill in the gap in international relations that is left unattended by the state[2]. I have explored elsewhere (Pagliccia 2010) the revival of the concept of solidarity in a socialist context as a tool of foreign policy, noting that solidarity is not an end goal but a process, and its practice can be dynamic and compelling. I will add, it is necessary.

However, we cannot ignore the difficulty of, and opposition to, any shift to a people-to-people foreign policy that involves the notion of solidarity within the dominant political thinking. The concept itself, perceived to embody a certain ideology, as it did in its origins, may be seen as an obstacle to its implementation. Reluctance to the use of the concept of

---

1   Over 98,000 U.S. citizens visited Cuba in 2012, up from 73,500 in 2011 and twice the number compared with five years ago, according to an online report by the National Statistics Office (www.one.cu). The numbers do not include more than 350,000 Cuban Americans estimated by travel agents and U.S. diplomats to have visited the island last year. Because Cuba considers them nationals, they are not listed in its tourism statistics. (http://www.reuters.com/article/2013/10/18/us-cuba-usa-tourism-idUSBRE99H0J320131018). In contrast, at the UN vote in 2013, only the U.S. and Israel voted against a resolution condemning the U.S. embargo of Cuba.

2   In a piece published in the Huffington Post, Kenneth Wollack, the president of the National [U.S.] Democratic Institute, makes a similar appeal for "people-to-people-based foreign policy" in the American context. (http://www.huffingtonpost.com/kenneth-wollack/the-importance-of-people_b_188974.html

solidarity is exemplified by the recent announcement by the Permanent Council of the Organization of American States (OAS). In March 2014, at its special meeting, the OAS approved a declaration whose title is, "Solidarity and support for democratic institutions, dialogue, and peace in the Bolivarian Republic of Venezuela." The meeting was convened on Panama's request in order to consider the situation in the protests by the opposition in Venezuela. Panama, the United States and Canada raised objections to the document. Panama formally recorded its reservation to the declaration for the reason that "it [did] not agree with the inclusion of the word "solidarity" in the title of the Declaration, because the point is to lend support to dialogue, peace, and democracy." (OAS 2014). I believe Panama missed the real point, as if "support to dialogue, peace, and democracy" could happen without solidarity for democratic institutions. How can support take place without solidarity? How can peace flourish without the nurturing of solidarity? How can democracy exist in the absence solidarity?

Indeed at present, foreign relations towards Cuba based on solidarity encounter similar reluctance by the U.S. and Canada in the Americas. In contrast, the principle of solidarity is written in Article 12 of the Cuban Constitution as "the notion of the moral (and instrumental) duty and the readiness of all members of society (both in Cuba and the world) to ensure the well being of the collectivity and to share more equitably in the product of collective enterprise." (Veltmeyer and Rushton 2013: 240). This notion has been associated with true democracy and the broader human development and it is precisely the tenet by which several countries in Latin America (Antigua and Barbuda, Bolivia, Cuba, Dominica, Ecuador, Nicaragua, Saint Vincent and the Grenadines, Venezuela, and Saint Lucia) have formed the *Alianza Bolivariana para los Pueblos de Nuestra América,* or ALBA (Bolivarian Alliance for the Peoples of Our Americas) in their attempt to establish a new paradigm of international relations that is based on equality, cooperation and solidarity.

The official Canadian government foreign policy towards Cuba is a frequent topic of scrutiny and analysis. What is less examined is the kind of international relations driven by people, which I call "solidarity-based people-to-people foreign relations." This kind of international relations directly engages Canadians with the people of Cuba spontaneously, collectively and systematically, in order to build connections and advocate links, cooperation, and support that are based on the fundamental principle of solidarity. Solidarity is essential in foreign relations; in fact, as shown in this volume, it has been at the centre of people's foreign policy that for over fifty years has connected a large section of Canadians and Cubans regardless – and at times in spite - of the formal government policies.

As anticipated in the Introduction, I highlight in these concluding remarks some common aspects of the different contributions in this volume as a means to observe the evolution and the many ways that Cuba solidarity can be, and has been, viewed and expressed as a unifying concept between Canadians and Cubans.

In her Chapter 1, Lisa Makarchuk gives us a Canadian's eyewitness experience of the Cuban Revolution and the early transformation in Cuba that triggered a widespread "exhilaration, hope and inspiration." She fittingly conveys the mood at the time with her question "Who would not feel solidarity with a people so intent on building their country in the face of such overwhelming challenges?" Effectively the Cuban Revolution inspired a whole movement in North America with the creation of the Fair Play for Cuba Committees (FPCC) in the U.S. (Gosse 1993) and Canada (Wright 2009). "The Canadian FPCCs enjoyed the support of several members of the Co-operative Commonwealth Federation (CCF) and its successor organization, the New Democratic Party (NDP), some of whom were elected politicians, as well as liberals, revolutionary socialists, independent leftists, university professors, students, housewives, church people, writers and others" (Wright 2009: 98). Peace groups that were quite active at the time of the Cold War were also quite supportive

Nino Pagliccia

and in fact they "strongly believed in organizing delegations of individuals to engage directly with the so-called 'enemy' and to try and solve global problems outside government frameworks" (Wright 2009: 108).

In Chapter 2, Elizabeth Hill reports about the "beginning of a movement" when Canadian-Cuban Friendship groups sprung up across Canada as offshoots of the FPCCs. The movement has not only been limited to English-speaking Canada. Among others, an organization in Québec, called *Carrefour Culturel de l'Amitié Québec-Cuba* (Cultural Crossroads of Québec-Cuba Friendship) was formed in 1979 that issued a regular newsletter called *Québec-Cuba Sí!* Today, more than a dozen organizations operate under the umbrella *Table de concertation de solidarité Québec-Cuba* (Coordination Board of Québec-Cuba Solidarity) founded in 2002[3].

While Diane Zack in Chapter 3 gives us a sample – and yet wide-ranging list - of solidarity actions undertaken in Canada, myself, and Tamara Hansen and Ali Yerevani in our respective chapters focus on two specific projects that have a tremendous impact for their significance as expressions of solidarity. In Chapter 4 I describe the *Che* Guevara Volunteer Brigade that has brought to Cuba hundreds of Canadians of all ages to make a symbolic, yet meaningful, contribution to establishing people-to-people ties. Further, I provide direct testimonials from former *brigadistas* and conclude, "any people-to-people link is a process rather than an immediate short-term goal. In fact, over the twenty years of being in operation, the *Che* Guevara Volunteer Work Brigade clearly has focused on the process. In this sense, there is no final single outcome from the coming together of two peoples representing two different social systems and political views. Rather, we can only expect the establishment of a sustained process of sharing ideas, solidarity and friendship based on mutual respect."

---

3   http://www.solidaritequebeccuba.qc.ca/index.php?option=com_content&task=blo
     gsection&id=5&Itemid=13

The second project, presented by Hansen and Yerevani in Chapter 5, addresses the case of the Cuban Five and may be perceived to be more political in nature as it takes on the seemingly questionable U.S. judicial system. The case of the Cuban Five imprisoned in the U.S. is possibly, together with the anachronistic U.S. blockade of Cuba, the most pressing issue of Cuba as a nation and most Cubans as individuals. The Cuban government considers this case a top priority and has made it a foreign policy issue by appealing to all friends in the world who in turn have developed campaigns in support of the Cuban Five. The response has been outstanding to include well-known international supporters such as Noam Chomsky, Ramsey Clark, Günter Grass, Mairead Maguire, Emma Thompson, Alice Walker, and Lord Rowan Williams, among others. The importance and urgency of the case of the Cuban Five for Cuba is affirmed in Stephen Kimber's book *What Lies Across the Water – The Real Story of the Cuban Five:* "Nothing will change between Cuba and the United States until they resolve the issue of the Five." (Kimber 2013: 258).

The affinity of Canadian and Cuban unions is made evident by Heide Trampus in Chapter 6 with a detailed account of Canadian labour support actions for Cuba over the years through the Canada-Cuba Labour Solidarity Network. The Cuban National Workers' Central Union (*Central de Trabajadores de Cuba*, CTC) has a unique role in Cuban society as an active decision maker in economic matters based on a model of co-operation; quite the opposite is true in Canada where labour must assert its rights in an adversarial model. Yet, worker-to-worker links can be, and are indeed, established in the spirit of solidarity.

Wendy Holm's Chapter 7 on Cuban cooperatives appears to take a detour from our focus on Canadian solidarity. However, her chapter is a welcome detour for two main reasons. First, even the less informed about Cuba would have heard about the major gains of the Cuban Revolution: free education and healthcare for all Cubans. That has remained true at the worst of times in Cuba. What may be less well known are the advances in the development of cooperatives and the more fair management of land. Holm tells us, "by the late 1980s, Cuba's farm sector had become one of the most highly industrialized in the world. Within a decade, it all collapsed [due to the Special Period] and had to be re-invented. Only one decade later, Cuba was recognized as a world leader in sustainable, organic farming methods and in urban agriculture." In this chapter we learn about the unique Cuban *organopónicos* and what made this transformation possible while pursuing the road to food self-sufficiency.

The second reason for the relevance of Holm's chapter in this volume is the affirmation that solidarity has many different ways to show bonds, not least important of which is the farmer-to-farmer relationship. Through this relationship "four Cubans were brought to Québec City to attend IMAGINE 2012/ Québec International Summit of Cooperatives" offering an international audience to Cuba's farming advances. Domestically, the relationship also helps in "making it very successful in disseminating teachings from scientific and technical institutions through its national structure, allowing information to reach farmers even in the most remote areas."

Isaac Saney in Chapter 8 gives a touch of hard reality in Canada where "the Harper regime has adopted a profoundly ideological approach to foreign relations" with its persistence in ending "Cuba's socialist project." The Canada-Cuba solidarity movement has strived to work towards keeping Ottawa in check and work with Parliamentarians in maintaining a fair relationship with Cuba. Ottawa has largely ignored the Canada-Cuba solidarity movement appeals, in spite of the existence of an "Inter-Parliamentary Group on Cuba (IPGC)." Saney writes that, "The IPGC has been in existence for more than fifty years [and] while the IPGC has taken...progressive steps, they engage in their work without any reference to or interaction with the Canada-Cuba solidarity movement. Indeed, for the most part the IPGC is generally unaware of the breadth and scope of the activities of the movement across the country. Thus, in practice the IPGC and the Canada-Cuba solidarity movement have worked in isolation from each other." This is a situation that we advocate needs to change in order to reflect a wider Canadian voice and benefit from a well informed movement about Cuba that has been consistent for over fifty years.

Writer and activist Arnold August in Chapter 9 also gives us a first-hand view of a very effective type of solidarity in the form of scholarly publications and public speaking that highlight Cuba's unique distinctiveness. In reference to his recent book on democracy in Cuba (August 2013), he says, "Writing and speaking about democracy in Cuba is a specific type of solidarity that differs from much of the conventional collective solidarity actions that I have participated in since the early 1990s." August also highlights the significance of penetrating the established media and how the "effort in taking up the challenge of opposing the media war against Cuba by striving to analyze the Cuban reality is not a sole endeavour, as some may believe. On the contrary, it is a collective undertaking, just as it is with solidarity groups."

In much more details in Chapter 10, Claude Morin stresses the importance of combating disinformation and to inform honestly about Cuba as a solidarity action. Morin affirms that it is necessary to have an intimate and direct knowledge of Cuba in order to counter disinformation, "The quest for honest information must feed our solidarity." Much work has been done in Québec with the media in order to provide a balanced and truthful image of Cuba. The dissemination of documentaries, coverage of news, letters to newspapers editors and supply of communication pieces are essential tools of solidarity for the movement across Canada in order to guide public opinion.

We concur with Morin, "the inclusion of this chapter in this book is likely to bring us closer to our common tasks." He pointedly directs us to the need to enhance our internal (Canadian) solidarity as a pre-condition for international solidarity.

The last two chapters by Keith Ellis and Brian Gordon Sinclair are inspirational and throw some light on the authentic deeper motivation

Nino Pagliccia

that compels to Cuba solidarity. The drive that moves us to act, to become activists, to be in solidarity against all odds is often intangible, inexplicable, and indescribable, but both Ellis and Sinclair bring us very close to a palpable comprehension of that sentiment where Cuba is seen as luring us to embrace pride, respect and dignity for human kind.

Ellis in Chapter 11 describes successful humanitarian hurricane relief campaigns for the people of Cuba that have raised larger amounts than the Canadian government's pledge. Often the state-to-state relation is mired not only in ideology but also in mistrust, whereas "the zeal with which we [Canadian people] responded...was due in fact to our knowledge of Cuba's generosity to the peoples of countries that are ravished by natural disasters, by the spontaneity with which they see the affected people simply as human beings and with no regard to their ideological tenets or political allegiance."

The important contribution of Ellis' chapter is the reflection around generosity as another aspect of solidarity and a glimpse to its origins as a practice. Observing the spirit of Cubans' internationalism vis-à-vis Canadians' internationalism, Ellis takes us back on a short trip through Cuban history showing that a resolve to independence, sovereignty and moral values preceded the Cuban Revolution with historical figures like Félix Varela, José María Heredia, and José Martí. This long tradition of patriotism turned into a mission for internationalism and solidarity literally by exporting healthcare and education missions to other poor countries. One of those recipient countries has been earthquake-stricken Haiti motivating "The governments of Norway and Namibia, recognizing the capabilities of the Cubans..., to give their help to Haiti through Cuba." Similarly, and in contrast to the poor response of the Canadian government towards Cuba, the Canadian people – as if replicating the altruism of Cubans - also responded generously with large donations to Haiti through the government of Cuba. This Cuba-Canada-Cuba-Haiti solidarity pathway represents an outstanding example of the multiplier effect that solidarity can generate through people-to-people ties.

Sinclair in the final Chapter 12 gives us a more personal experience of his "discovery" of Cuba and its people. Sinclair's imagery of unexpectedly "falling in love" with Cuba as he embarked in retracing the steps of Ernest Hemingway in Cuba is stirring. Likely, that is the same sentiment that made Hemingway donate his Nobel Prize medal to the people of Cuba. This reminds me of a quote attributed to *Che* Guevara, "The true revolutionary is guided by great feelings of love." If *Che's* revolutionary love is that intimate feeling that compels us to act and to want "to be with," that sentiment is not too far away from solidarity. I value the importance of people-to-people relations when people are the inspiration, rather than selfish interests.

In conclusion, this volume has intended to weave the thread of Cuba solidarity that has tied together the fabric of the Canadian movement for more than five decades. I have argued in the introduction that these accounts are not isolated stories, but are part of a larger framework that I call "solidarity-based people-to-people foreign relations." I hope that reading through the pages of this volume the reader is able to recognize more than fifty years – that is, two generations – of unconditional people-to-people Canadian solidarity with Cuba. In this long-term interwoven relationship, the keywords to remember are "unconditional" and "solidarity." There is nothing unconditional about the traditional state-to-state relations, and certainly there is no solidarity. Government foreign policy is driven by monolithic and often personal or party ideology and politics - hence the contradictions and diplomatic confrontations on issues. People-to-people foreign relations, conversely, are driven by citizens' issues and by human concerns, by and large removed from politics and ideology[4]. It is as diverse in representation as the people involved.

---

4   There are examples of shifts at the municipal level in Europe where "Rome's central strategy shifted from a more "economic" (pro growth) to a more "political" one (aimed at improving the city's position in the global and European order) and later to a more "social" orientation (centered on solidarity, peace and human rights concerns)" (d'Albergo 2006: 1).

Nino Pagliccia

The Canadian government could enrich its foreign policy by applying its philosophy of constructive engagement with Canadians, particularly on issues where citizens, rather than corporate entities, have an interest.

There are many good contributions to foreign policy with deep analyses by political scientists, scholars, and journalists. Those are welcome in the spirit of a democratic society and may well have an impact on decision makers. However, the undemocratic approach to foreign policy increases when powerful and wealthy lobby groups, representing self-interests rather than constituencies, gain the attention of officials in power and exert undue influence on legislation and policies that shape our foreign policy. A truly democratic balance can only be restored when people and civil society are given equal opportunity and space in decision-making. Canadians are willing and ready. Reflections on five decades of people-to-people relations between Canadians and Cubans based on solidarity show that a paradigm shift in the current foreign relation is not only desirable but also possible. What are still needed are the political will and the recognition that solidarity may well be the missing link in human interactions leading to peace and justice among nations in the twenty-first century. All governments should be encouraged to tap into this powerful human resource.

References

August, Arnold (2013). *Cuba and its Neighbours – Democracy in Motion*. Halifax, Winnipeg: Fernwood Publishing, and London New York: Zed Books.

d'Albergo, Ernesto (2006). The Global Mayor. The Politics of Rome's International and Transnational Agency. *Cuaderno di Ricerca* n. 7. Aracne Editrice, Rome, Italy.

Gosse, Van (1993). *Where the Boys are: Cuba, Cold War America and the Making of a New Left*. London: Verso.

Kimber, Stephen (2013). *What Lies Across the Water – The Real Story of the Cuban Five*. Halifax and Winnipeg: Fernwood Publishing.

Kirk, John M. and Peter McKenna (1997). *Canada-Cuba Relations: The other good neighbor policy*. Gainesville: University Press of Florida.

McKenna, Peter and John Kirk (2012). Through Sun and Ice: Canada, Cuba and Fifty Years of 'Normal' Relations. In Peter McKenna (Ed.), *Canada Looks South – In Search of an Americas Policy*. Toronto: University of Toronto Press.

OAS (2014, March 7). Solidarity and support for democratic institutions, dialogue, and peace in the Bolivarian Republic of Venezuela. Permanent Council resolution CP/DEC. 51 (1957/14). http://www.oas.org/consejo/resolutions/dec51.asp. Retrieved April 30, 2014.

Pagliccia, Nino (2010). Solidarietà: la rinascita di un vecchio concetto socialista. In Luciano Vasapollo and Ivonne Farah (Eds.), *Panchamama. L'educazione universale al Vivir Bien*. Roma: Natura Avventura Edizioni.

Saney, Isaac (2004). *Cuba: A Revolution in Motion*. London New York: Zed Books.

Tiessen, Rebecca (2010). Youth Ambassadors Abroad? Canadian Foreign Policy and Public Diplomacy in the Developing World. In J. Marshall Beier and Lana Wylie (Eds.), *Canadian Foreign Policy in Critical Perspective*. Oxford: Oxford University Press.

Veltmeyer, Henry and Mark Rushton (2013). *The Cuban Revolution as Socialist Human Development*. Studies in Critical Social Sciences Book Series. Chicago: Haymarket Books.

Wright, Cynthia (2009). "Between nation and Empire: The Fair Play for Cuba Committees and the Making of Canada-Cuba Solidarity in the early 1960s". In Robert Wright, and Lana Wylie (Eds.), *Our Place in the Sun – Canada and Cuba in the Castro Era*. Toronto: University of Toronto Press.

Contributors

Arnold August

Arnold August has an MA in political science from McGill University. The Montreal-based writer, journalist and lecturer is the author of *Democracy in Cuba and the 1997–98 Elections* (Editorial José Martí, 1999). He has also contributed a chapter entitled "Socialism and Elections" to the edited collection *Cuban Socialism in a New Century* (University Press of Florida, 2004, Contemporary Cuba series edited by John Kirk). In 2013, he was presented with the Distinción Félix Elmuza, Cuba's highest journalism award, by the association of Cuban journalists (UPEC) for outstanding work carried out by journalists. Between 1999 and 2012, he wrote more than 40 articles for alternative websites on Cuba, the Cuban Five and Latin America, many of them also in Spanish and French. His latest book is *Cuba and Its Neighbours: Democracy in Motion* (Fernwood Publishing/Zed Books, 2013). It is also published in Spanish and Korean. www.democracycuba.com

Keith Ellis

Keith Ellis (Jamaica, 1935) is Professor Emeritus, Department of Spanish and Portuguese, University of Toronto and Professor of Merit, University of Havana. He is a Fellow of the Royal Society of Canada and has been honoured with Cuba's Distinction for National Culture and was made an honorary member of the Union of Writers and Artists of Cuba. He was granted the title Doctor Honoris Causa by the University of Havana and was the first awardee of the Dulce María Loynaz International Prize. He was also awarded the Andrés Bello medal by the Ministry of Culture of Venezuela and the medal of the city of Poitiers. He taught Latin American Poetry until his retirement, publishing many books and articles in this area and in others. His poetry has appeared in several books and journals and in several languages. He has been involved in Cuban solidarity work since 1959.

Tamara Hansen

Tamara Hansen was born in Burnaby, British Columbia, Canada, and became politically active in high school. From 2006-2010, she served as an executive member of the Canadian Network on Cuba (CNC) and from 2008-2010 was also co-chair of the network and the national coordinator of the Ernesto *Che* Guevara Volunteer Work Brigade. She was a founding member of Vancouver Communities in Solidarity with Cuba (VCSC) and the Vancouver International *Che* Guevara Conference. Tamara has been the coordinator of VCSC since 2005 and has travelled to Cuba 13 times. Tamara has written extensively on Cuban politics since 2003, including the book *Five Decades of the Cuban Revolution: The Challenges of an Unwavering Leadership* (Battle of Ideas Press, 2010). Tamara is a high school teacher of French with a B.A. in French & First Nations Studies and a B.Ed. in Environmental Education. She lives in Vancouver, Canada.

Elizabeth Hill

Elizabeth Hill is a founding member of the Canadian-Cuban Friendship Association Toronto established in 1977; she is currently its President. She helped organize CCFA activities, such as Film festivals, tours for Cuban musicians, demonstrations and meetings calling for the release of the Cuban Five, and the annual Toronto-Cuba Friendship Day at Toronto City Hall Square. In 1988 Elizabeth was elected a public school trustee on the Toronto Board of Education and served for 6 terms until 2006. She is currently a co-chair of the Canadian Network on Cuba. She received the Friendship Medal from the Council of State of the Republic of Cuba in March 2011 in recognition of her solidarity work.

Wendy Holm

Wendy Holm is an award-winning Canadian Agrologist, columnist, author and professional speaker. Her outspoken columns in defence of Canada's farmers and sustainable public policy for our farm sector have won her seven national journalism awards since 2002. Wendy holds an honours B.Sc. in Business Administration (Long Island University, 1970), a M.Sc. in Agricultural Economics (UBC, 1974) and is currently a Graduate Student in the Master of Management, Cooperatives and Credit Unions program, Sobey School of Business, Saint Mary's University, Halifax (2nd year). Editor and contributing author of the book *Water and Free Trade* (1988), Wendy was named a Distinguished Alumni of UBC in 2008, has received two Queen's Medals for her "contribution to community" and was named Agrologist of the Year 2000. In 2008, Wendy was the Western Canada recipient of Farm Credit Canada's Rosemary Davis Award for passion and commitment to farming.

John M. Kirk

John M. Kirk is professor of Latin American Studies at Dalhousie University. He is the author/co-editor of 13 books on Cuba, ranging from the political thought of José Martí to the role of the Catholic Church in Cuba. In recent years his work has focused on Cuban medical internationalism, and he is the co-author of *Cuban Medical Internationalism: Origins, Evolution and Goals* (Palgrave Macmillan, 2009). He is a member of the editorial board of *Cuban Studies and The International Journal of Cuban Studies*, and is the editor of the *Contemporary Cuba* series of the University of Florida Press.

Contributors

Lisa Makarchuk

Lisa Makarchuk arrived in Cuba in June 1961, the Year of Literacy. She worked as a newscaster, writer and translator at a long wave English-speaking radio station, and later at Radio Havana Cuba, the shortwave station broadcasting out of Cuba. She was part of the team that produced the first issues of the Cuban newspaper Granma in languages other than Spanish for the benefit of delegates attending the *First Tricontinental Conference of Solidarity with the Peoples of Asia, Africa and Latin America*, which took place in Havana in 1966. Involved in solidarity work in favour of freedom for political prisoners in Spain and in Portugal at the time of their dictatorships, she also took part in campaigns for nuclear disarmament, ending the war in Viet Nam and, later, freeing the Cuban Five. She is one of four Canadians to be awarded the Medal of Friendship by the Cuban Council of State through the Cuban Institute of Friendship with the Peoples (ICAP).

Claude Morin

Claude Morin (Ph.D., Université de Paris-X and École Pratique des Hautes Études, Paris) taught Latin American history at Université de Montréal from 1973 to 2006. He was editor and co-editor of the Canadian Journal of Latin American and Caribbean Studies (1980-88). He authored or edited six books, wrote close to 30 articles and chapters for journals and collective works. Most of his research has dealt with colonial Mexico and Peru, contemporary Cuba, Central America, international relations and revolutionary politics in the Caribbean Basin. He was and still is a regular commentator in francophone media about events and processes in the area. He has been travelling extensively all over Latin America for more than forty years, with many sojourns in Cuba. He is now leading cultural tours in the region.

Nino Pagliccia

Nino Pagliccia received his political formation and university degree in Economics in Venezuela where he lived for 24 years. After his postgraduate work at Stanford University he moved to Canada where he has been a Research Statistician at the University of British Columbia (UBC) since 1986. He has managed *Cuba Research Projects* in collaboration with Cuban partners with a particular focus in *Social Organization and Global Health*.

Nino has been the vice-president of the Canadian-Cuban Friendship Association in Vancouver and founding co-chair of the Canadian Network on Cuba. He has lead groups to do volunteer work in Cuba for over 12 years. He has travelled often to Cuba and within Cuba where he has participated extensively in fieldwork both as a researcher and as a volunteer. He has authored or co-authored many peer-reviewed journal articles and has contributed chapters to edited books mainly related to Cuba.

Isaac Saney

Isaac Saney is on faculty, College of Continuing Education, Dalhousie University, and an adjunct professor, Department of History, Saint Mary's University, both in Halifax, Canada. His work has been published in several highly respected journals and magazines. He is the author of the acclaimed book, *Cuba: A Revolution In Motion* (Zed, 2004), and has lectured on Cuba across Canada, the United States, the United Kingdom, the Caribbean and in Africa. Saney is currently co-chair and national spokesperson for the Canadian Network On Cuba, the national umbrella organization for the Canada-Cuba solidarity and friendship movement.

Brian Gordon Sinclair

Brian Gordon Sinclair is considered to be the foremost dramatic interpreter of Ernest Hemingway in the world. He is the author of a seven-play epic detailing and illuminating the life and literature of Ernest Hemingway. The plays are written under the overall title of Hemingway On Stage: The Road to Freedom and each play provides an intimate insight into the circumstances which shaped the famed author's life and inspired him in his writing. Performed internationally and in support of the Cuban Five, they are must see productions for anyone intrigued by the life and death of Ernest Hemingway. Brian is also the Patron of the *Estrellas de Gigi*, the children's baseball team at Museo Hemingway. He is currently editing and revising a collection of stories about the original 1940's team. The book is to be called, The Homerun Kid: The True Story of Ernest Hemingway's Baseball Team.

Heide Trampus

Heide Trampus is an Early Childhood Educator by profession. As a Labour and Peace activist she participated in a "Fact Finding Mission" to El Salvador and Nicaragua in 1986. Her involvement with Cuba Solidarity goes back to the late 1970's and she is the present coordinator of the "Worker to Worker, Canada-Cuba Labour Solidarity Network". She has received the "Enrique Hart" distinction from the National Union of Public Administration Workers (SNTAP) in Cuba and the "Lázaro Peña" medal from the Cuban Workers Central (CTC). Heide has attended eight out of the nine "International Colloquiums Against Terrorism and for Justice and Freedom for the Cuban Five" in the city of Holguin, Cuba and attended the "Five days for the Five" activities in Washington, DC. She was instrumental in forming the "Friends of the Five Committee" and organizing the conference "Breaking the Silence, Justice for the Five, Peoples Tribunal and Assembly" in Toronto in September 2012.

Ali Yerevani

Ali Yerevani (Izadi-Kharrazi), was born to a Tatar-Turk family in Gorgan, Iran. In high school he joined the underground movement against the U.S. puppet monarch. He moved to the U.S. in 1975 and became active in the Iranian students' movement. He returned to Iran in 1979 to join the Iranian revolution as a revolutionary socialist organizer. He left Iran in late 1984 and since then has been a social justice organizer in Europe, the U.S. and Canada. He has been involved in organizing, leading, initiating and a founding member of dozens of social justice organizations such as the Free the Cuban 5 Committee –Vancouver, Vancouver Communities in Solidarity with Cuba, Battle of Ideas Press, Fire This Time Movement for Social Justice and the Vancouver International *Che* Guevara Conference. Ali is the political editor of Fire This Time Newspaper and Battle of Ideas Press. He lives in Vancouver, Canada.

Diane Zack

Diane Zack has been active in the Canadian solidarity movement with Cuba since the mid-1990s. She has served as president of Manitoba-Cuba Solidarity Committee since 2001. Diane also served on the executive of the Canadian Network on Cuba from 2004 – 2008 as both co-chair and co-chair of projects and campaigns. She was co-chair for the CNC for the Breaking the Silence conference on the Cuban Five held in November 2007 in Toronto. She is a semi-retired teacher, currently teaching English to newcomer adults in Winnipeg, including an occasional Cuban.

List of Cuba Solidarity Organizations in Canada

Organizations Members of the Canadian Network on Cuba (CNC)

Alberta
Canadian-Cuban Friendship Association (CCFA-Calgary)
www.ccfacalgary.ca

Cuba Edmonton Solidarity Committee
www.cubaedmontonsc.wordpress.com

British Columbia
Canadian-Cuban Friendship Association (CCFA-Vancouver)
http://www.ccfavancouver.ca

Cuba Education Tours
www.cubaexplorer.com

Free the Cuban Five Committee-Vancouver
http://www.freethe5vancouver.ca

Vancouver Communities in Solidarity with Cuba (VCSC)
www.vancubasolidarity.com

Manitoba
Manitoba-Cuba Solidarity Committee
dlzack@shaw.ca

Nova Scotia

The Nova Scotia-Cuba Association (NSCUBA)
www.nscuba.org

Ontario

Asociación de Cubanos Residentes en Toronto
cubanosjgg.blogspot.ca/

Canadian-Cuban Friendship Association (CCFA-Kingston)
www.kingstonccfa.com/

Canadian-Cuban Friendship Association (CCFA-Niagara)
dr@drlinksinternational.com

Canadian-Cuban Friendship Association (CCFA-Toronto)
www.ccfatoronto.ca

Canadian-Cuban Friendship Association (CCFA-Windsor)
ccfawindsor@gmail.com

Friends of the Cuban Five-Toronto
www.freethe5peoplestribunal.org

Hamilton Friendship Association with Cuba
info@cubacanada.org

Hemingway on Stage
www.briangordonsinclair.com

Ottawa-Cuba Connections
www.ottawacuba.org

CNC Member Groups with a Cross-Canada Presence

Communist League
cllc_can@bellnet.ca

Communist Party of Canada
www.communist-party.ca

Communist Party of Canada (Marxist-Leninist)
www.cpcml.ca

Canadian Union of Postal Workers
www.cupw.ca

Young Communist League – Ligue de la jeunesse communiste
www.ycl-ljc.ca/

Organizations not Members of the CNC

British Columbia
Victoria Friends of Cuba
http://victoriafriendsofcuba.wordpress.com

Ontario
Toronto Forum on Cuba
http://www.torontoforumoncuba.com

Worker to Worker
w2wcclsn@hotmail.com

Nova Scotia
Los Primos
http://losprimos.ca

Québec
Table de concertation de solidarité Québec-Cuba
www.solidaritequebeccuba.qc.ca

Index